T0418368

Faith and Community

In the series *Religious Engagement in Democratic Politics,*
edited by Paul A. Djupe

Rebecca A. Glazier

Faith and Community

How Engagement Strengthens Members,
Places of Worship, and Society

TEMPLE UNIVERSITY PRESS
Philadelphia • *Rome* • *Tokyo*

TEMPLE UNIVERSITY PRESS
Philadelphia, Pennsylvania 19122
tupress.temple.edu

Library of Congress Cataloging-in-Publication Data

Names: Glazier, Rebecca A., 1982– author.
Title: Faith and community : how engagement strengthens members, places of
worship, and society / Rebecca A. Glazier.
Other titles: Religious engagement in democratic politics.
Description: Philadelphia : Temple University Press, 2024. | Series:
Religious engagement in democratic politics | Includes bibliographical
references and index. | Summary: "Examines the impact of congregational
community engagement efforts for places of worship, their members, and
democracy"— Provided by publisher.
Identifiers: LCCN 2023049495 (print) | LCCN 2023049496 (ebook) | ISBN
9781439925294 (cloth) | ISBN 9781439925300 (paperback) | ISBN
9781439925317 (pdf)
Subjects: LCSH: Little Rock Congregations Study. | Faith-based community
organizing—Arkansas—Little Rock—Case studies. | Community
development—Arkansas—Little Rock—Religious aspects. | Religious
communities—Arkansas—Little Rock. | Little Rock (Ark.)—Religious life
and customs.
Classification: LCC BV625 .G55 2024 (print) | LCC BV625 (ebook) | DDC
277.67/73—dc23/eng/20240220
LC record available at https://lccn.loc.gov/2023049495
LC ebook record available at https://lccn.loc.gov/2023049496

Printed in the United States of America

9 8 7 6 5 4 3 2 1

Contents

List of Tables and Figures

Tables

Figures

Acknowledgments

This book became a reality because of the people and communities of faith in Little Rock, Arkansas. It has been my joy to get to work with them since I founded the Little Rock Congregations Study in 2012. They have welcomed me into their worship services, shared sacred moments with me, and trusted me and my research team with the things that matter most, for which I will be forever honored and grateful. I am especially thankful to those congregations that were willing to be featured as case studies in this book. Getting to know the members and leaders of these places of worship was a privilege and a joy. I have done my best to treat their stories with the care and respect they deserve.

I owe an enormous debt of gratitude to our Clergy Advisory Board, a thoughtful group of diverse clergy who provide our team with feedback and advice on everything from the wording of survey questions to event speakers. The research in this book was conducted over more than a decade, with the collaboration of other faculty, including Warigia Bowman, Kirk Leach, and my dear friend and research partner Gerald Driskill. I appreciate Gerald's ability to see the big picture in our work and to always put people ahead of research.

Over the years, the work of the Little Rock Congregations Study has been funded by a variety of sources, including a Centennial Center Grant from the American Political Science Association, a Jack Shand Research Grant from the Society for the Scientific Study of Religion, multiple grants from the Methodist Foundation of Arkansas, and a Global Witness Offering from Second

Presbyterian Church, as well as summer research grants and graduate research assistantship funding from the University of Arkansas at Little Rock. Every single one of these funding sources has gone to support student researchers, who have always been the heart of the Little Rock Congregations Study. This research would not have been possible without them. All 202 students who have worked on the project since 2012 are listed in the appendix— I am so grateful to each and every one of them!

I wrote the bulk of this book while on sabbatical in the fall of 2022. I was able to get the writing done with the help and support of a great community of colleagues, friends, and family. Chantelle Davidson spoiled me with an amazing writing retreat in Corona del Mar, Sean Theriault set me up with a wonderful writing retreat at his condo, and Amber Boydstun was the best writing accountability partner (and best friend!) I could ever ask for. Tracking poms and earning silly emojis on the Google Sheet she made kept me going through the worst writer's block. I have the best, most supportive family. My parents are my biggest cheerleaders, my brothers tease because they love, and my son, Wilk, is the light of my life. I am also grateful for my Glazier family, who have shown me how beautiful it is to keep loving the family you choose. I consider myself a person of faith, and I am thankful for my own community of faith and the divine support I have received in doing this work.

I am blessed to be part of a great academic community in the American Political Science Association and the Society for the Scientific Study of Religion. I am thrilled to be publishing this book with Temple University Press, in a series edited by Paul Djupe. Since my early days as an assistant professor, Paul has been a kind and thoughtful mentor. He is a giant in the field and was the editor of the journal *Politics and Religion* when I published my first solo-authored article there, using data from the Little Rock Congregations Study. Just as he has pushed, guided, and asked probing questions to help make this book better, he helped get that first manuscript to publication. I am so grateful for his mentorship then and now.

In 2023, the American Political Science Association honored me with the Distinguished Award for Civic and Community Engagement, based in large part on my work with the Little Rock Congregations Study. This award acknowledges civic and community engagement work by a political scientist that merges knowledge and practice and has an impact outside of the profession. I am so honored by this recognition and hope that this book furthers the impact of this work beyond academia.

Faith and Community

1

Congregations in Crisis

On an overcast and humid summer morning in Little Rock, Arkansas, volunteers from Saint Mark Baptist Church are handing out backpacks filled with school supplies to administrators from local schools who pull up in SUVs, sedans, and even one school bus. "We will hand out seven hundred backpacks to six schools and to the Little Rock Police Department," says Ingrid Green, one of the staff members for the outreach ministry at Saint Mark and the person organizing the volunteers this busy morning. "Y'all have a good school year!" a volunteer calls as school administrators drive away with every spare inch of their cars crammed with backpacks. One answers back through their open window, "We love Saint Mark!"

Not only are school representatives coming by for backpacks this morning, but the near-daily food distribution for those in need is also underway. The outreach building on the Saint Mark campus is bustling with nearly a dozen volunteers. Pastor Glenn Hersey prints out a time sheet recording the hundreds of volunteer hours donated by church members each month. "It's amazing," he says. "They give of their time; they give of their service."

This morning, the volunteers are all wearing green "Saint Mark Outreach" T-shirts—they even gave me one for the day as I joined in the effort of handing out backpacks and meals. As they work, the volunteers talk and joke with one another, building on friendships that have grown as they have worked together four days a week for years organizing and planning the backpack distribution and distributing food to unhoused people. "You develop a camaraderie because you are working toward the same goal; you meet people;

you become like family," Ingrid explains. "He becomes like my dad, working alongside me. She becomes like my sister, passing out clothes. He becomes like my brother, bringing supplies in. So, that develops a bond that can't be broken."

Many congregations in the Little Rock area support local schools—donating supplies, assisting the teachers, and tutoring the kids. Saint Mark has one of the largest programs, with their building full of volunteers this morning distributing supplies. The schools that show up include some that teach students in a great deal of need—nearly all of their students qualify for free or reduced lunch. Saint Mark and other congregations step up at the start of every school year with support and supplies.

But the schools aren't the only ones to benefit; the members that give also say that they, in turn, receive. One of the regular volunteers at Saint Mark, who has been working in outreach there for over fourteen years, is a retired schoolteacher. She told me that, once she started serving, "I found out I was having more fun doing it than the people that were being helped. It's a good feeling to know that you can help someone."

Looking beyond the efforts of Saint Mark Baptist Church and other congregations in Little Rock, it is clear that they are part of broader community-engagement efforts all across the United States. Through things like back-to-school events and food distributions, places of worship across the country are engaging to serve their communities. In fact, data from the 2018–2019 National Congregations Study, a major national study of U.S. congregations, indicate that 79.6 percent of congregations, representing 88.5 percent of all members, participate in at least one social service program (Chaves et al. 2021). These social programs can take many different forms—the most popular tend to be food programs (48.1 percent), programs for youth and children (32 percent), or programs that address individuals' physical health needs (18 percent) (Chaves et al. 2021, 122).

Yet congregations are facing challenges on many fronts—there are plenty of reasons why community engagement may not be at the top of their priority lists. With their primary goal being the spiritual well-being of their members, congregations must carefully prioritize their activities (Wielhouwer 2004); community engagement is not a given (Cnaan and Curtis 2013). From the outside, it is understandable why places of worship might not choose community engagement as their top priority.

For one thing, many congregations are struggling with decreasing membership. In 2020, 47 percent of Americans said they belonged to a church, mosque, synagogue, or other place of worship, down from 70 percent in 1999 and below the 50 percent majority for the first time (Jones 2021). Some places of worship might feel like they are doing triage on their own membership—they don't have the resources for community engagement.

Additionally, the COVID-19 pandemic has changed the way many places of worship are engaging with their own members. Figuring out that new normal is difficult enough without putting resources toward engaging with the community beyond their own congregation. The pandemic precipitated declining attendance for some congregations, especially smaller and older congregations, some of whom simply didn't or won't recover (Wang 2022).

And, at this particular moment in history, some community engagement might be perceived as political, even divisive. For instance, some research finds that people want places of worship to stay out of politics—a Pew Research Center survey in 2019 found that 63 percent of respondents agreed with that statement and 76 percent said places of worship should not come out in favor of one candidate over another (Smith et al. 2019). Views on religious involvement in politics may be more nuanced than they first appear, though. Other research on Protestants shows that only 35 percent want congregations to keep out of political matters, with another 27 percent on the fence (Djupe 2019). As negative partisanship becomes more common in the United States (Abramowitz and McCoy 2019; Abramowitz and Webster 2016), clergy and members alike may be eager to keep even the appearance of politics out of their congregations. While some community efforts may be perceived as more political than others, any efforts at community engagement could be seen as distracting from the vital, spiritual missions of religious institutions.

Thus, community programs may end up being a low priority for most congregations, who assign few resources to them (Chaves 2004) and focus instead on the spiritual well-being of their members (Ammerman 1997a; Davidson 1986). As Mark Chaves characterizes it in his foundational research on the topic, "The vast majority of congregations are involved in social services in only a peripheral way" (2004, 50). Even in urban areas, where the needs are more directly on congregations' doorsteps, community services are only a fraction of what they do with their time and resources (Livezey 2000). There are many reasons why a congregation might get involved in the community—from theological imperatives to a desire to meet the needs of their neighbors to motivated and connected members. Yet community engagement often ends up a low priority for places of worship. The evidence in this book shows that when congregations put resources behind engagement, significant benefits follow.

As my morning distributing backpacks and food with the volunteers from Saint Mark Baptist Church demonstrated, community engagement has many positive outcomes—it benefits members, strengthens places of worship, and helps society as a whole. The people who are serving feel happy and uplifted; they feel a greater sense of connection to their congregation, which is strengthened in turn, and community members receive needed service. Simply put, community engagement is an all-around good thing. The congregations who do community work know the truth of this simple statement—*community engagement is a good thing*—because they live it. In the following pages, both qualitative and quantitative data show how the more people and places of faith reach beyond their own walls and into their communities, the greater the benefits will be.

The Challenges Facing Congregations Today

For many congregations in a world that seems to be increasingly secularizing, their very survival is on the line. A study of nearly three dozen Protestant denominations found that 4,500 churches closed in 2019, while about 3,000 opened (Shimron 2021). The Presbyterian Church (USA) alone dissolved 104 congregations in 2021 (Scanlon 2022). The challenges facing places of worship are daunting, and clergy are doing all they can to help their members grow and flourish. Foundational research by Nancy Ammerman (2001, 2005) shows that, for the vast majority of congregations, caring for members is the top priority. Looking beyond membership—to evangelism or community engagement—is almost always a secondary priority. When one takes stock of the challenges facing congregations today, it is clear why religious leaders might be singularly focused on their members. Why should community engagement even enter the conversation? Congregations don't have the time or resources for what has traditionally been considered a peripheral activity (Chaves 2004), especially during a time of crisis.

The following pages flip this reasoning around completely. By using data from the Little Rock Congregations Study—a long-term, multimethod, community-based research project that I direct in Little Rock—I demonstrate how, for each of the major challenges facing congregations today, community engagement is not a distraction, but a potential solution. More detail on the methods of the Little Rock Congregations Study, a project that has included multiple faculty collaborators and over two hundred student researchers since its inception in 2012, is provided in Chapter 2. Here, a few highlighted findings show how the challenges of declining attendance, disengaged members, and polarization can all be addressed through community engagement.

The Challenge: Declining Attendance

One challenge that many congregations are facing is declining worship service attendance. The National Congregations Study periodically asks if the number of regularly participating adults has increased, declined, or stayed about the same over the past two years. In 2007, 17.2 percent of congregations said they saw a decline in regularly participating adults. In 2019, that number was 39.1 percent (Chaves et al. 2021, 70). The Faith Communities Today survey has been studying congregations nationally for twenty years and found that between 2000 and 2020, the median attendance size decreased by over 50 percent—from 137 to just 65 attendees in weekly worship services (Thumma 2021, 11). It can be hard for congregations to launch or staff major community engagement initiatives with such steeply declining numbers.

This decline is especially marked for younger generations. Religious affiliation for twenty-to-twenty-nine-year-olds has fallen off a cliff in recent decades. According to the General Social Survey in the United States, in 1986 only 10 percent of those in their twenties said they were not affiliated with any religion. By 2016, that number was up to 36 percent (Pearce and Gilliland 2020). By 2022, it was 46 percent (Davern et al. 2021). And it is not just because they are young. That is, they aren't growing up and deciding to become more religious. While there is an overall trend toward secularization among all generational cohorts, each subsequent generation—from the Silent Generation, to Baby Boomers, to Gen X, to Millennials, to Gen Z—is less religious than the last (Cox 2022). The "religious nones," as they are known, are on the rise (Burge 2021).

This means that American society as a whole is generally becoming less religious through replacement but also as less religious cohorts raise less religious children (Brauer 2018), a demographic process that has been documented by scholars in Europe (Voas 2009). So, at a broad, societal level, cohort shifts in religiosity are underway, but at a local level, individual congregations feel this process as their membership ages and fewer young people attend. In 2020, young adults made up 23 percent of the population but only 14 percent of the churchgoers (Thumma 2021). Frankly speaking, this demographic shift toward aging congregations can mean the end of a small congregation (Burdick 2018).

In the face of declining attendance, one impulse may be to put all the attention on current congregation members and not spend resources on community engagement. But community engagement may be exactly what is needed to revitalize a faith community.

A Solution: Community Engagement

Many young people who are not religious say that they are looking for more meaning than the worship services they encounter can provide (Drescher 2016; Jaradat 2020; Liang and Ketcham 2017). Others may be disillusioned by what they see as hypocrisy, greed, and bad behavior by leaders or members in organized religion (Pew Forum on Religion & Public Life 2009). For Gen Z, social action, community service, and even protest participation can help meet their spiritual needs (Jaradat 2020; Packard 2016). Young people want more than just worship; they want to see their leaders and fellow members actively doing good; they are searching for identity and purpose (Meyer 2019).

Of the nine community issues our research team asked about in a major survey of 2,293 congregation members in Little Rock in October 2020, the priorities of younger members were not much different than the rest of the congregation—they thought foster care and children were more important and health care and crime were less important, but otherwise there were no differences we could identify statistically. However, when we asked a follow-up question about whether they would be willing to volunteer to help their congregation get engaged in addressing each community issue, in six of the nine issues, younger members were significantly more likely to say they would volunteer than older members. This pattern held even for some issues that they thought were less important, like health care. This finding of eager youth volunteerism is particularly noteworthy because in our data, and in national data and academic research, older adults are more likely to volunteer, both inside and outside their congregations (Verba, Schlozman, and Brady 1995; Wilson 2000). They just tend to have more time and be in a season of life that lends itself more easily to service. But these data show that young people are eager to get engaged with community issues at their place of worship—they just need a project. Thus, resources spent on community engagement are not likely to be wasted. On the contrary, they can draw in and excite younger members. Chapter 4 talks more about how community engagement is associated with increasing attendance.

The Challenge: Post-COVID Disengagement

Another challenge facing congregations is a lack of engagement from members, especially in the wake of the COVID-19 pandemic, which introduced a massive external shock to congregations and the way they conceptualize worship and community (Cooper et al. 2021; Giles, Dyas, and Payne 2021). Many are still getting their bearings, and community engagement may be far from top of mind. Although more and more places of worship are returning to holding services the same way they did before the pandemic, there are a significant number of attendees, about one in five, who are opting to substitute virtual worship for in-person services (Nortey 2022). And, sadly, some congregations simply won't recover from the impact of the pandemic (Wang 2022).

Congregations have long been places of social connection and fellowship (Giles, Dyas, and Payne 2021). Research conducted on Christian denominations shows that one in three practicing Christians stopped attending during the pandemic, either virtually or in person; even more important, those people who stopped attending were more likely to report feeling insecure and anxious, compared to those who didn't stop attending (Barna Group 2020). This disconnection—as people fail to return to worship services as the pandemic wanes or as they opt to stay online—has important consequences for members and congregations.

For those who come back to in-person worship services, the new normal may feel different than what they are used to. There may be fewer people in the pews, fewer events, and fewer opportunities for fellowship and service. Congregations that weren't able to maintain connection with their members during the pandemic lost not only attendance but also social capital (Hollar 2020), the important relationships of trust and belonging that come from being together and connecting week after week. So how can those be rebuilt?

A Solution: Community Engagement

Perhaps surprisingly, when we asked over two thousand congregation members in October 2020 about the priorities they would like their places of worship to set during the pandemic, they didn't say they wanted more opportunities to socialize and fellowship. Their two highest priorities—statistically indistinguishable from one another—were spiritual growth and helping those in need. Our interviews with clergy reveal that they often see these two as connected. As one leader put it, "Faith isn't just thoughts you think or beliefs you give assent to, but faith is what you do. And so, if we are going to be a community of faith, there needs to be things that we are doing that embody and illuminate the faith we profess." Another said, "Caring about our poor and needy neighbors is one of the most important principles in our faith. We have a statement made by Prophet Muhammad, peace be upon him. He says, 'He is not a believer, the one who goes to bed with his stomach full and his neighbor hungry.'"

By prioritizing community engagement, congregations can reengage their members, bring spiritual vitality to their places of worship, and do good in their communities (Thumma 2021, 27). Chapter 6 discusses in more depth our data on the priorities of congregants and clergy, but one interesting finding is that younger members are more likely to say their priorities are spiritual growth and helping those in need—they rank those priorities significantly higher than the older members of the congregation do. The motivations for community engagement are surely diverse and vary by organization and individual, but for some, it is part of a spiritual practice. Congregations literally create community, both through their religious commitment to seeing the shared humanity of all people and through their practical activities of bringing people together (Bane, Coffin, and Thiemann 2001). Once again, community engagement might be a way to not only bring people back but to engage younger generations as well.

The Challenge: A Divided Society

Yet, even if congregations do decide to get involved in the community, some clergy may worry about the consequences. Engagement on some issues and not others may be seen as taking political sides in an environment where every decision is fraught and it is easier to just stick to religion. About two-thirds of U.S. adults say that places of worship "should keep out of political matters" (Smith et al. 2019). For clergy, who risk alienating their congregants or losing their legitimacy if they are seen as inappropriately political (Olson 2009, 372), community engagement that may be perceived as political can be risky (Glazier 2018). They may even see a drop in offerings if their efforts are not well received or are seen as too overtly political (Calfano 2010; Calfano, Oldmixon, and Gray 2014). Clergy who spoke out during the civil rights movement, who got crosswise with their congregations on labor issues, or who were active in anti-war protests know too well the negative consequences of engagement when divisions run high (Friedland 1998; Gill 2011; Hadden 1969; Pope 1942; Quinley 1974; Wuthnow 1988).

Partisan hostility in the United States continues to rise, with double-digit increases in 2022 in the percentages of both parties who say that members of the other party are dishonest, immoral, unintelligent, and closed-minded, compared to 2016 (Pew Research Center 2022a). Leading a congregation under such circumstances can be a very demanding job. And it has been getting more difficult. In 2022, 42 percent of Protestant pastors said that they had given "real, serious thought to quitting the full-time ministry," an increase of 13 percent from the previous year (Barna Group 2022). And 38 percent of those pastors said that "current political divisions" were one reason they were considering stepping away from the ministry. Even among those who haven't considered leaving the ministry, 32 percent said that current political divisions negatively impacted their ability to lead at their church (Barna Group 2022).

A Solution: Community Engagement

As people sort themselves into more homogeneous neighborhoods and social groups (Bishop 2009), places of worship are one location where people can have positive interactions with those who hold different political views than they do (Djupe, Neiheisel, and Sokhey 2018). And one great way to build congregational warmth and fellowship is to do service together (Patterson, Madsen, and Alleman 2022; Shi et al. 2019). More than any trust fall or ropes course, bringing members of a congregation together to serve and give back to the community will unite them with a sense of purpose in doing good (D. Campbell 2013), which is likely right in line with the teachings of most religious traditions.

There are many benefits to diverse congregations (Dougherty and Huyser 2008), including congregations that are ideologically diverse (Zhang et al. 2018). Data presented in Chapter 3 shows that congregations with more ideological diversity—that is, congregations that have both liberals and conservatives at worship services—tend to have members that feel more politically efficacious. As opposed to the jaded and disengaged feelings that many people experience in modern society, the people in these congregations believe that their voices matter and that they can make a difference. In Chapter 4, we also learn that ideological diversity in a congregation is a strong predictor of service to the congregation. Serving in the community can bring people together (Wojcieszak and Warner 2020). When members serve together, both inside and outside a congregation, it can help counter division and discord in society. When members feel like their voices matter, previous divisions may feel a little less significant. Service or friendship groups in a congregation may provide a place for people who would otherwise feel like political outsiders or deviants to connect and build community (Finifter 2014).

The Role of Congregations in Communities

Community engagement may be the solution to what ails religion in America today, but what exactly do we mean by community engagement? Places of worship do many things. They support the spiritual development of their members, they provide a place for friendship and fellowship, and they provide opportunities for higher purpose and meaning (Djupe and Gilbert 2009; C. Harris 2020; Inzlicht, Tullett, and Good 2011; Park 2005; Park, Edmondson, and Hale-Smith 2013; Schwadel et al. 2016; Taylor et al. 2016). But they are also often important anchor institutions in communities and, as such, provide critical social services and fill key community needs (Clopton and Finch 2011; Cnaan et al. 2002; Cnaan, Sinha, and McGrew 2004b). Religious institutions are often at the heart of communities, where "much of the philanthropic, public social support, mental health, and spiritual and moral well-being" of the community is centered (Thumma 2021, 3). This is part of what it means to be engaged in the community.

But community engagement by congregations can take a variety of forms. In the 1800s, for instance, places of worship were a key means of support for the elderly, before the government implemented Social Security (Chaves 2004, 85). In modern times, research suggests that congregations are stepping in to "patch the social safety net" as government services change and crises like the Great Recession impact communities (Warren, Waring, and Meyer 2019). With changing roles for government and congregations, and sometimes greater needs, communities have asked for more from both government and places of worship (Bane, Coffin, and Thiemann 2001).

Thus, today we see diverse forms of engagement, like congregations hosting small groups that talk about local concerns, adopting a neighborhood elementary school in need, or opening their doors to share meals with the hungry. Generally speaking, congregational community engagement means reaching beyond the membership to serve or connect with the broader community. The congregations that we work with in Little Rock support medical ministries, do regular neighborhood cleanups, distribute food to those who are elderly or homebound, care for refugee families, mentor children, and easily run a dozen other short- and long-term community programs. Chapters 3–5 each feature a vignette of a Little Rock congregation and their community efforts. Chapter 6 features four in-depth case studies of congregations, each telling the stories of different ways of engaging. As the following sections demonstrate, this community engagement is both theologically and socially important.

Theologies of Community Engagement

From a theological perspective, many religious traditions have teachings related to community service and social engagement. The simple pronouncement known as the "Golden Rule"—to treat others as you would like to be treated—is found in virtually every religious tradition (Tanenbaum Center for Interreligious Understanding, n.d.) and could be seen as a foundation for doing good in one's community. As many religious traditions uphold an ethic of community and of treating one's neighbors well (Ammerman 2005; Cnaan et al. 2002; Wattles 1996), community engagement in the name of religion may be seen as appropriate and even required.

For instance, many Christian denominations have missions related to community service and engagement (Cronshaw 2020; Sapp 2011; Satyavrata 2016), and caring for one's neighbors (and neighborhoods) is seen by many as a Christian imperative (Janzen et al. 2016; Outka 1972). From the liberation theology that leads some African American clergy to greater civic engagement (Lincoln and Mamiya 1990; Love 2017; Wood 2002) to the Catholic Church's welcoming attitude regarding migrants and refugees (Hollenbach 2020; McKinney, Hill, and Hania 2015), the directive to care for one another often leads churches and their members to look beyond themselves and into their wider communities (Dirksen 2020; Sapp 2011).

Beyond Christianity, we see a similar impetus to engage for the greater good in many other religious traditions. In Islam, religious scholars often turn to historical stories and statements by the Prophet to argue in favor of engagement and community cooperation, including across religious lines, "as long as the goal is something that Islam upholds as good and beneficial" (Altheimer 2022). Since 9/11, in particular, many Muslims living in the West have come to see community engagement as an opportunity to build bridges and dispel stereotypes (Vergani et al. 2017). As one Muslim put it, "We're the first ones to hold hands when things like that [September 11, Boston bombings] happen 'cause we know that obviously there's going to be an after-effect on many of the community. . . . That's really what shapes us, having that consciousness, knowing that there must be action taken" (quoted in Vergani et al. 2017).

As with many faith traditions, there is a great deal of diversity in Judaism, including in levels of religious activity and orthodoxy (Aronson et al. 2019). There is a rich tradition of community engagement and social activism in Judaism. This is often referred to as the process of *tikkun olam*, or "repairing the world," and it provides one theological imperative for community and social action (Krasner 2013; Winer 2008, 433). For some Jewish people, it is not just the theology of the Torah—the creation of all humanity in God's image, the command to love your neighbor as yourself, the Exodus from Egypt—that informs community service and engagement. Indeed, the modern Jewish experience of the Holocaust can be a central touchstone that both illustrates human brutality and calls the Jewish people to a moral responsibility for all humankind (Fackenheim 1970).

Similar religious calls for community action and service in other faith traditions abound. In Buddhism there is a tradition of "engaged Buddhism," which links inner spiritual transformation to the need for social transformation (Rothberg 1998; Yukich 2017). In the Sikh tradition, the concept of *seva*, or "selfless service," motivates community engagement and is especially meaningful to younger adherents (Kaur Luthra 2021). In the Baha'i faith, there is a strong belief in the oneness of all humanity and in being citizens of the world, both of which naturally lead to community engagement (Warburg 2018).

Whereas most of the focus on community engagement and service across faith traditions tends to be on personal action for spiritual growth or religious obligation, among minority religious traditions, in particular, there is also a focus on community engagement to benefit the faith. For instance, Sikhs and Hindus, like Muslims and other minority faith traditions in the United States, sometimes see a religious imperative in interfaith engagement to educate the community about their faith and reduce negative perceptions (Kaur Luthra 2021; Yukich 2017).

Engaging with the community outside one's particular circle of believers should not be seen as beyond religion. Indeed, a close theological read of many faith traditions shows that such engagement is actually central to religion. Although this book is written from the perspective of social science, the data show that there is something to this consistent thread of loving and serving outside yourself. All these faith traditions seem to be on to something. There are consistent religious imperatives for engagement across faith traditions. And, as the data show, there are also real, tangible religious benefits to community engagement.

The Social Benefits of Community Engagement

Beyond the theological reasons motivating community engagement, there is a vast social science literature on the benefits of community service. Research suggests that people who serve their communities live longer, more fulfilling lives (Aknin and Whillans 2021; Corporation for National Community Service 2007). Among older people, volunteering helps them stay healthier longer, generating social capital and improving many health indicators—from blood pressure to depression indexes (Onyx and Warburton 2003). Younger people see many of the same advantages of volunteering—they have happier, healthier lives, and are also more likely to stay out of trouble (Wilson 2000). When service is part of their education, they improve academically, are more engaged civically, and have a stronger lifelong commitment to volunteerism (Sax 1997).

Social science research also suggests that there are positive outcomes associated with being active in one's congregation. For instance, people who are active in their congregations are happier and more civically engaged (Pew Research Center 2019b; Putnam and Campbell 2012). They are less likely to suffer from depression, commit suicide, or get divorced (Amato and Rogers 1997; Idler 2014; Li et al. 2016; VanderWeele et al. 2016). They are more likely to have a stronger social support network, give charitably, and engage in their local communities (Lim and Putnam 2010; Putnam and Campbell 2012; Strawbridge et al. 2001).

It's reasonable to expect that being part of a community-engaged congregation will amplify these benefits as members enjoy the advantages of both church membership and community service. Indeed, research indicates that it is community involvement in social institutions, which fosters psychological well-being, that may be one of the greatest drivers linking happiness and generous behaviors (Konow and Earley 2008). At a time when loneliness and social isolation are increasingly concerning public health issues, with health consequences as detrimental as smoking or obesity (Holt-Lunstad et al. 2015), places of connection, like congregations, are a literal lifeline for people.

Congregations are key community institutions—and there are strong theological and social reasons for them to be engaged in their communities. But with so many pressures on clergy and so many challenges facing congregations, it can be difficult to prioritize community work. This book argues that doing so is critically important—for individuals, for congregations, and for democracy. The next section introduces the unique project that makes such an argument possible.

The Little Rock Congregations Study and Community-Engaged Research

The data used in this book are drawn from more than ten years of community-based research in one southern city: Little Rock, Arkansas. Through surveys and interviews with both members and leaders in diverse congregations all across the city, we can better understand the impact of community engagement—how it benefits members, congregations, and society as a whole. Because we have been doing this research and building relationships with congregations in a single community for a long time, the data are unique and rich, providing valuable insights into the relationships between faith and community engagement.

I started the Little Rock Congregations Study (LRCS) in 2012, partly out of an interest in better understanding the impact of religion in that particular presidential election between Mitt Romney and Barak Obama, and partly as a way to get my students out of the classroom and into the community to participate in research and learn in ways they never could by listening to me lecture. Ever since, student researchers have been critical to the success of the LRCS. Our interdisciplinary research team has successfully grown the LRCS over the years—with no institutional budget and sporadic grant funding—because we have dedicated researchers and students who love our community and have developed trusting relationships with our community partners (Glazier, Driskill, and Leach 2020). Since 2012, 202 graduate and undergraduate students have been a part of our research team (they are listed by first name in Appendix B under "List of All Student Researchers Who Have Contributed to the Little Rock Congregations Study").

Not only have the students contributed as key research partners, but participating in the LRCS has given many students an opportunity to develop valuable research skills, gain experience for graduate school or employment, connect with their community, and even change their worldviews as they engage with new people (Glazier and Bowman 2021). In 2016, we partnered with the University of Arkansas Clinton School of Public Service, bringing forty graduate students onto the project; these students helped expand the number of interviews we could conduct and also served as mentors for the undergraduate students (Glazier and Bowman 2021).

At its heart, the LRCS is a project about faith-based community engagement—the impact that community engagement has on people of faith, how their congregations and clergy encourage engagement, how places of worship themselves benefit from engagement, and how it affects the broader community. Most of our data are collected at the individual level. We are asking members and leaders of congregations about their personal experiences as opposed to doing a community impact assessment of their efforts. Thus, the findings our research team are most confident in concern how people are affected by serving their communities, attending community-minding congregations, and hearing community-oriented sermons.

But people are much more than statistics. Throughout the book, you will find case studies of real congregations in Little Rock illustrating how they are *doing* community engagement. Sometimes these cases will be used to further illuminate causal relationships, and sometimes they will be helpful examples of the diversity of ways that congregations are serving the community.

A Preview of the Results

The main argument of this book is that community engagement has many benefits to recommend it to congregations. The following chapters use both qualitative and quantitative data to illustrate those benefits. Chapter 2 describes the LRCS in more depth, including how we have collected data over the years, what our methods are, and what our congregations are like. Chapter 3 presents the first substantive evidence about the benefits of community engagement specifically to individual members. This chapter demonstrates how community engagement is associated with greater spiritual health, higher life satisfaction, and a stronger sense of political efficacy.

Chapter 4 looks at the benefits of community engagement from the perspective of the congregation itself. In Chapter 4, we find that congregations that are more engaged in the community also have higher levels of congregational warmth, higher attendance numbers, and members who are thriving spiritually. Chapter 5 takes an even broader perspective: how community engagement benefits society. Beyond the direct provision of social services by congregations, which are significant in many communities, community engagement is also associated with a stronger sense of political efficacy, or feeling like one's voice matters. Community-engaged congregations are also more likely to be ideologically diverse, making them one of the last places in America where people haven't completely self-sorted into ideological silos but can have positive interactions with people from other political backgrounds. Improving efficacy and encouraging ideological diversity are added side benefits of congregational community engagement that are good for democracy.

Chapters 3, 4, and 5 each contain a case study of a congregation that represents the process described in that chapter: benefits to members, congregations, or the community. In Chapter 6, we look at four additional case studies as examples of how congregations might do community engagement. Because congregations differ in size, resources, and theology, engagement looks different across congregations. These examples show how all kinds of congregations can see benefits from engagement, but there is no "one size fits all" model.

Chapter 7 looks closely at two community issues that congregation members and leaders identified as particularly important in Little Rock: education and race relations. In this chapter, I describe why congregations might prioritize these issues, what is being done on them in Little Rock, and how engaging on issues like these can help members, congregations, and society. Chapter 8 concludes the book with a vision for a democracy where congregations—led by trusted clergy—are more engaged in their communities, helping members improve their political efficacy, making a difference on important community problems, and strengthening social capital. It is also up front about the drawbacks congregations might face when choosing community engagement and how they might address those. Places of worship are often at the heart of their communities. The more they invest in connecting there, the better off their members, their institutions, and we all will be.

Conclusion

Although some may fear that community engagement pulls focus away from congregations' top priority (their members), takes up resources that are in short supply, and comes with potential risks, it also provides solutions to many of the challenges facing congregations today. My research team and I have been studying faith-based community engagement through the LRCS—a long-term, community-based research project in Little Rock, Arkansas—for over a decade. We have found that when congregations are engaged in the community, it benefits individuals, places of worship, and society as a whole. This book advances the argument that community engagement is a good thing and that places of worship should do it more often. Not only will it make congregants happier, healthier, and more spiritually content people, it will make congregations more vibrant, close-knit places, as well, and even improve democracy along the way. Community engagement should not be shunted down the list of priorities as congregations address the many challenges facing them—it should be elevated.

2

The Little Rock Congregations Study

Little Rock is a great city for a study of religious congregations. Deep in the Bible Belt, there are plenty of congregations to work with inside the city limits. Although the numbers fluctuate over the years, as congregations are planted or fail, are renamed or whither in a pandemic, our research team has consistently identified between 350 and 400 active religious congregations in the city of Little Rock. Little Rock has multiple Jewish and Islamic congregations, Buddhists and Baha'is, and diverse Christian denominations.[1]

Little Rock is also a racially divided city with about 50 percent of the population ethnically non-Hispanic white and about 42 percent of the city Black or African American (U.S. Census Bureau 2017). The city contains affluent suburbs, rural areas, and poor urban areas where religion tends to thrive (McRoberts 2005). All of this religious, ethnic, and economic diversity is packed into about 120 square miles, with the University of Arkansas at Little Rock and around eight thousand graduate and undergraduate students right in the middle. This diverse profile makes Little Rock a great place to study religion and community engagement.

---

1. According to our dataset, Little Rock's congregations are dominated numerically by three religious traditions: Black Protestant (about 31 percent), evangelical Protestant (about 43 percent), and mainline Protestant (about 18 percent). According to 2010 census data available from the Association of Religious Data Archives (ARDA), the Little Rock/North Little Rock metropolitan area (which includes the outlying city of Conway) has about 9 percent Black Protestant, 70 percent evangelical Protestant, and 9 percent mainline Protestant, demonstrating just how diverse the city of Little Rock itself is when it comes to religious traditions.

And that's exactly what we've been doing since I founded the Little Rock Congregations Study in 2012. The LRCS is a community-based research project, which means two things to our research team: first, that we involve community members in the research, and second, that we use the results of the research to benefit the community (Israel et al. 1998). For our research team, community-based work "is not just a methodological approach to doing research, but a mutually-beneficial way of engaging with our community" (Glazier, Driskill, and Leach 2020, 28). From this important grounding, we established three main goals for the LRCS: (1) to better understand the impacts of faith-based community engagement, (2) to get students out of the classroom and into the community to have meaningful learning experiences, and (3) to return helpful findings to the congregations we work with.

The following sections detail how we have worked to meet these goals, after first describing the data collection efforts of the first decade of the LRCS and the analytic approach followed in the book.

Collecting Data about Religion and Community Engagement

Since the beginning of the LRCS in 2012, we have surveyed 326 clergy (across four iterations) and 4,220 congregants from forty-three different congregations (across three iterations) and talked with 339 leaders and members through interview or focus group conversations. The various data collection efforts of the LRCS are summarized in Table 2.1. Through all our data collection efforts, we have been trying to answer an overarching question: what are the impacts of faith-based community engagement? The data that we have, detailed here, make it possible to examine how an individual member's participation in their congregation's service projects, a religious leader's sermons on community engagement, or a congregational culture of outreach can each have an impact—on members, on places of worship, and on the broader community.

When we first began working with congregations in 2012, our project was pretty small. We had just one class of students and the idea that we wanted to know more about what was going on in congregations during the presidential election between Mitt Romney and Barak Obama that seemed imbued with religion. We set our sample area as the city of Little Rock and got to work identifying and contacting every place of worship in the city limits (2012 $n = 396$). We reached out to clergy with mail surveys in the spring and summer. From those responses, we chose a purposive sample of five Christian congregations in the fall of 2012—one Black Protestant, one mainline Protestant, one evangelical Protestant, one Catholic, and one from the Church

		Participating congregations	Clergy surveys	Clergy interviews	Congregant surveys	Focus group participants
Year	Focus					
2012	Politics	5	64	5	452	22
2016	Community engagement	17	84	68	1,475	102
2018	Nonprofit partnerships	—	112	27	—	—
2020	Community engagement	35	66	37	2,293	36
2021–2022	Racial justice	—	—	22	—	20

TABLE 2.1 LITTLE ROCK CONGREGATIONS STUDY DATA COLLECTION EFFORTS, 2012–2022

of Jesus Christ of Latter-day Saints, colloquially known as Mormon. We handed out paper surveys on the Sunday before election day and entered survey responses by hand into spreadsheets. We conducted short focus groups with small numbers of congregants on site after worship services to ask them about how religion influenced their political decision-making.

In 2016, we established a partnership with the Clinton School of Public Service, another institution in the University of Arkansas system, and forty of their graduate students participated in the research project as part of their field research methods course.[2] We kept updating our list of Little Rock congregations and again sent mail surveys to all clergy in the city limits (2016 n = 392). We also conducted interviews with as many of the responding clergy as we could and sought to increase participation in the congregation member surveys. As detailed in the following section, we were able to increase trust with the congregations in our community and, with the increase in student researchers, worked with seventeen congregations in 2016. These congregations were selected through a mix of purposive sampling (including extensive outreach to underrepresented congregations) and gladly welcoming congregations who were willing to work with us.

Feedback from our community partners indicated that many of the congregations were providing important social services in the community and sought opportunities for collaboration. In 2018, we conducted a special data collection effort with clergy to learn more about partnerships with nonprofits and services provided. Our survey effort in 2018 was the first time we used mixed survey methods, using email, mail, and telephone surveys to reach 112 clergy members (2018 congregation n = 370). We also surveyed nonprofits in 2019 to get their perspectives on collaboration with congregations.

---

2. For more details on how both graduate and undergraduate students learned from their research participation in 2016, see Glazier and Bowman (2021).

The third major iteration of the LRCS was in 2020 (n = 365). We moved the survey online for this data collection effort, which ended up being good timing due to the COVID-19 pandemic. Because we did not have email addresses for all clergy, we also used Web contact forms and Facebook messages to reach them. From these responses, we sent out invitations to be interviewed, during which we told clergy about the full study and invited them to participate, ultimately working with thirty-five congregations. Once again, we purposefully reached out to underrepresented congregations to help balance our sample, although the challenges of the pandemic made this difficult, as I discuss in more depth later in this chapter. Electronic surveys for congregation members proved very useful, though, because the pandemic made it impossible to physically visit congregations and distribute surveys by hand. Some of the congregations we worked with did have older members, and we provided paper surveys and addressed, postage-paid envelopes for these congregations.

Finally, using feedback from our community partners, and considering current events, like the murder of George Floyd and the Black Lives Matter protests, our research team focused on race and faith for our 2021–2022 data collection. We interviewed congregation leaders in Little Rock and national leaders on faith-based racial justice, and we created resources that congregations who were interested in racial justice work could use to get started. These resources are publicly available on our project website and include three different models of faith-based engagement in racial justice, suggested reading lists, questions for self-reflection, and commitments. We gathered community feedback on these resources through congregation focus groups (Glazier, Driskill, and Hanson 2022).

Our approach to doing community-based and multimethod research builds on the excellent work of many scholars who have been researching in this field for years. Studies like the Chicago Latino Congregations Study survey both members and leaders (Burwell et al. 2010). The National Congregations Study does in-depth interviews with clergy across the country (Chaves et al. 1999). We aimed to learn from these scholars and—with our limited resources—execute a rich and accurate study of faith-based community engagement in Little Rock. The result of the first eleven years of community-based research on congregations and engagement by the LRCS in Little Rock is a vast and deep collection of both qualitative and quantitative data. The academic publications that have resulted from this work are listed in Appendix B.1, and the community reports that have been created for public distribution are listed in Appendix B.2. All the data that do not contain identifiable information are available for download through the Association of Religious Data Archive (ARDA).

Community-Based Research with the Little Rock Congregations Study

The identity of the LRCS as a community-based research project is central to the work we do. Doing community-based research means collaborating with the community to do work that is mutually beneficial—it has to matter to the community as well as align with the research goals of our academic team (Hotze 2011). Congregations don't have to participate in our research. Community-based research relies on voluntary community participation (Riffin et al. 2016). Our work through the LRCS wouldn't be possible without clergy and congregations that are willing to work with us. We have to build and respect those relationships as part of the research process to make sure that community members feel heard and research results inform community problems that they care about (Teufel-Shone et al. 2019). For our research team, finding the right balance here has meant making adjustments over time.

For example, when we first began working with congregations, at the time of the 2012 U.S. presidential election, our surveys contained a number of political questions, including questions about vote choice and vote confidence. This led to some interesting findings. For instance, in 2012, Mitt Romney, a member of the Church of Jesus Christ of Latter-day Saints, was running against Barack Obama, who attended a majority-Black church in Chicago led by a politically outspoken pastor (Abdullah 2012; Gonzalez 2012). Because we included the political questions we did, we could compare the vote choice, and confidence in vote choice, of respondents from the Mormon congregation that participated in our study to respondents from the Black Protestant congregation that participated in our study. Those results are presented in Figure 2.1.

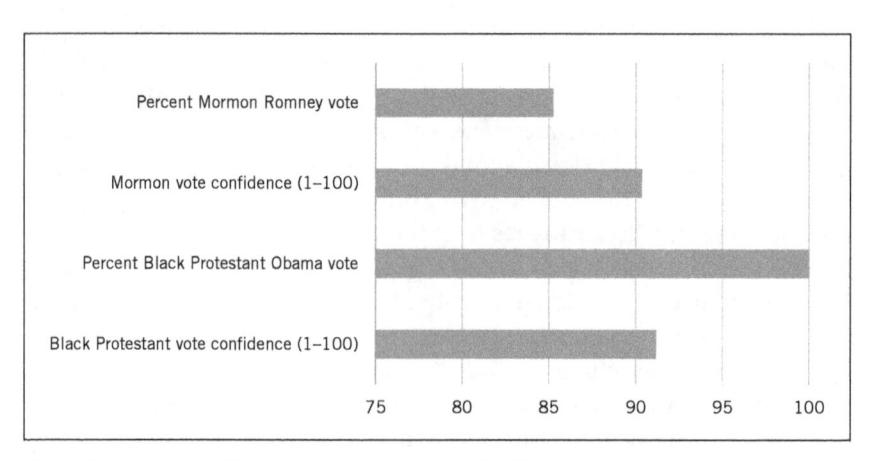

Figure 2.1 Average 2012 Vote Choice and Vote Confidence, by Religious Tradition

It turns out that both religious groups voted strongly for the candidate affiliated with their faith tradition and were very confident in their choice, with the Black Protestants in our sample being uniform in their support for Obama, while about 15 percent of the Mormons in our sample broke with their coreligionist and reported that they wouldn't vote for Romney.

But the leadership and the members of the congregations we worked with in 2012 were somewhat uncomfortable with the political nature of the questions on our surveys. As the director of the project, I fielded a few concerned phone calls, some respondents used the margins or the open space provided on the survey to let us know that they found the subject matter inappropriate for church, and we weren't sure we were meeting a need in the community.

As our research team prepared to field our surveys again in 2016, we changed the nature of the questions to focus less on overt politics and more on the consequences of political participation that we were most interested in. Instead of vote choice, we asked a battery of participation questions that included donating to a campaign and persuading someone to vote. Instead of party affiliation, we opted for a question that allowed respondents to place themselves along a liberal to conservative ideological spectrum. We also included a battery of questions about community engagement that included questions measuring political efficacy (Glazier, Driskill, and Leach 2020). Information about all of our survey questions is available in Appendix A.

With these revised questions, we could still learn information we were interested in from an academic perspective, but we could also return findings that were more valuable to the community participants. We became more interested in the impact of faith-based engagement—what were the consequences for individuals, congregations, and communities when places of worship talked about community issues and provided service in the community?

Our research team believes these are deeply political issues. That is, they have consequences for whose voices are heard and how resources are distributed. As later chapters detail, when people and their congregations get engaged in the community, it can change people's sense of efficacy, influencing whether they believe their voice matters and whether they can make a difference—beliefs that matter deeply for democracy. Engagement can also make congregations warmer and more spiritually thriving places—characteristics that most clergy are eager to have at a time when attendance is dropping for many places of worship. And engagement can mean help for critical community problems that might otherwise go unaddressed.

Our community-collaborative approach to research through the LRCS was refined further with the establishment of our Clergy Advisory Board in 2019. This board, made up of a diverse group of religious leaders from across the city, provides input on survey questions, advises on research topics more broadly, and advocates for the LRCS in the community.

By responding to the community we work with, we shifted our research to be more about the aspects of faith-based community engagement that mattered to them. Developing responsive and reciprocal relationships helped us build trust with our community partners in a virtuous spiral that improved future collaborations (Goldberg-Freeman et al., 2010). In the end, we didn't mind dropping the questions about partisan politics, because what we learned by focusing on faith and community was so interesting and yet still politically relevant.

Sharing Our Findings with the Community

A critical part of doing long-term community-based research is building trust with the communities you study. For our research team, one of the ways we have done that is by sharing our findings with our congregation partners and the broader Little Rock community. When findings are readily shared with communities and they can learn about potential solutions, they are much more likely to see the benefits of research (Bracic 2018; Damon et al. 2017).

We share our findings through publishing reports, holding events to share what we have learned, and publicizing our results on social media (Glazier and Topping 2021). As noted previously, the research reports we have generated for the community are listed in Appendix B.2 and are all publicly available on our project website. With a long-term project like the LRCS, it is especially important that community participants see results coming back to them (Goldberg-Freeman et al. 2010; Kennedy et al. 2009). These deliverables create a positive feedback loop by building trust and reinforcing study legitimacy (Goldberg-Freeman et al. 2010).

Because getting our results out to many community members can be challenging, social media is one way to provide a public record of relevant information from the project and disseminate deliverables to a large number of people (Glazier and Topping 2021). More than a static web page on a university domain, which the public will rarely encounter, a social media presence engages the community where they are. Of course, as academic researchers, we have to be careful to stay professional as well as accessible, so we make sure our project Facebook page links directly back to the more academic university website.

Sharing our findings with the community is closely related to the research questions our team decides to ask. We want to ask questions that matter to the community, and then we want to share the answers with them. We want our congregation participants to be partners in the project and benefit from the research—not just be subjects in a study that only academics will read.

When we moved to an almost entirely electronic data collection effort with congregations in 2020, instead of having students hand out physical paper surveys at worship services as we did in 2012 and 2016, it not only kept our research team safe during a pandemic, it also saved us opportunity costs. The move to electronic surveys enabled us to spend more of our time on data analysis, and less time on data entry, and allowed us to quickly return specific results to each participating congregation. This innovation meant that each congregation we worked with in 2020 received a sixteen-page report with the survey results from their responding congregants. Producing these reports—before the end of the fall semester—was resource intensive, but it meant a timely, meaningful, and tangible deliverable to our congregation partners. This is just one of the ways we have built trust with our congregation partners over time.

What Community-Based Research Means for the Data Used in this Book

The LRCS data were collected through a community-based research project, in multiple iterations, over the course of more than ten years, and the resulting data have both benefits and drawbacks. Because trust and relationships are so important to community-based research, they influence the kind of data we have had access to over the years. In this section, I describe what it has looked like to build trust with the Little Rock faith community and why the data in this book are so unique.

Simply put, community members will not participate if they do not trust researchers (Lucero et al. 2020). One way that researchers can build trust is by listening to community members and bringing them into the research process (Rickenbacker, Brown, and Bilec 2019). We have found that holding meetings to both share and listen can be important steps in building partnerships (Goldberg-Freeman et al. 2010), and we have consistently increased the amount of time we give to meeting with clergy groups and individual congregations and leaders to talk about the research results of the LRCS.

Although returning meaningful results to the community is one of the foundational goals of the LRCS, it did take some time for our research team to learn how valuable it can be to involve community participants in the research process itself. One event that helped bring this lesson home for us was the Religious Leaders Summit we held in 2019. This event brought together over fifty clergy from diverse religious traditions around the city of Little Rock. At this summit, our research team facilitated discussions among the religious leaders about the major problems facing Little Rock, presented the results of our research findings, and brainstormed ways that we as researchers could do work that would inform and support their efforts to improve our city. The summit also featured Democratic and Republican elected officials as speakers. As a result of the summit, we added additional questions on race to our 2020 survey of congregations, as well as questions about physical, mental, and spiritual health. Adjusting our survey in response to clergy input built trust.

The mayor of Little Rock, himself an associate pastor at a large Black Protestant church in the city, spoke at the event and told the crowd, "We, as members of the clergy, have to get outside our sanctuary walls. It's great to take care of those within the sanctuary, but we have to get beyond. In these new times, it's about education justice, economic justice, interpersonal justice. It warms my heart to be before you today and see so many faith leaders. At the end of the day, we're all about people, about love—Muslim brother or sister, Jewish brother or sister, or Christian brother or sister. At the end of the day, we all love this city and each other and want to do good." Just hosting this kind of event built goodwill and trust within the religious community in Little Rock and signaled to religious leaders that the researchers were serious about listening to them.

Another way that we brought clergy into the research process and sought to build trust throughout the community was by getting endorsements for our work from people in trusted positions—both religious and community leaders. Before our 2020 data collection effort, we had a number of people endorse the project with statements of support, including prominent clergy from major faith traditions, the university chancellor, and the city's mayor. We also reached out to the leadership of religious organizations—for example, the Presbytery of Arkansas—to ask them to encourage their congregations to participate. We released a blog post on our website that brought together statements of support from fourteen different religious, nonprofit, and community leaders. We also worked with university and local media to promote the upcoming study and help recruit congregational participation. These and other key stories from the LRCS website are listed in Appendix B.3.

The strong upside of collecting data from participants in a community-based research study is that they trust you enough to be part of it. Community-based research has been gaining prominence, led mostly by scholars in the fields of sociology and medicine, who have found that data collected within communities are more representative and provide greater context for interpretation (Bracic 2018; Damon et al. 2017; De Las Nueces et al. 2012). We see these benefits directly in our own research. For instance, our response rates are much higher than for most telephone surveys, which have declined in recent years to around 6 percent (Kennedy and Hartig 2019). Our congregation survey response rates are around 27 to 44 percent, depending on the congregation.[3]

---

3. These numbers are from our 2016 data collection, when paper surveys were distributed in person at worship services, providing us with an accurate denominator to calculate response

Because of the trust we have built over the years, through hundreds of clergy interviews, religious leaders have shared their very valuable time to talk with us about personal and meaningful aspects of their faith and congregational life. Our community-based data thus have added value, compared to projects that are based in a lab or that try to reach the same populations without these trusting relationships. We can get better data and interpret it more accurately when we talk with people in trusting, context-filled conversations (Riffin et al. 2016).

But the question we always ask ourselves as researchers is: who is not here? Who are the congregations that aren't participating? For instance, although we regularly have a number of evangelical churches participate in our research, their participation numbers do not reflect a representative sample of Little Rock evangelicals. Why don't more evangelical churches participate in our research? Part of the reason may be due to many evangelical churches' decision to focus more on spiritual matters, relative to community engagement (Iannaccone 1988; Leege and Kellstedt 1993). Research indicates that evangelical churches tend to do less community service, although this certainly varies by congregation, because there is more of a theological emphasis on individual salvation (Chaves 2004). Given this difference in priorities, evangelical churches may be less likely to participate in a research project that they know focuses on community engagement. Interestingly, this orientation toward community engagement may be shifting, with recent research showing white evangelicals "coalescing around the significance of local engagement" (Mulder and Jonason 2017, 106).

Evangelical churches have also historically been associated with the suburbs. Mark Mulder's (2015) insightful case studies of seven white congregations that relocated from Chicago neighborhoods to nearby suburbs in the 1960s and 1970s illustrate this historical relationship and the power that congregations can have to make and remake communities. This physical distance from the poverty and social problems that often occur in urban centers may make it easier for suburban congregations to neglect community engagement. In his classic study, Gibson (1961) argued that the mostly white Protestant churches who had fled the cities for the suburbs were in captivity there; Davidson (1986) expands this argument to say that they aren't the only ones. Congregations who cut themselves off from the social needs of their communities are limiting the potential of their organizations and their members. Indeed, most of the case studies in this book are of urban congregations—they tend

---

rates. In 2020, when surveys were distributed by congregation leaders to their members electronically using a survey link specific to each congregation, we were not provided with an email list for each congregation for privacy reasons and so do not have the denominator necessary to calculate 2020 response rates.

TABLE 2.2 BLACK PROTESTANT PARTICIPATION IN THE LRCS OVER TIME					
Study year	Format	Number of congregations	Number of Black Protestant congregations	Number of respondents	Number of Black Protestant respondents
2012	In person	5	1	579	39
2016	In person	17	5	1,457	385
2020	Online	35	7	2,293	102

to be physically present in areas of greatest need and thus more likely to get involved.

Additionally, as we think carefully about the question of who is not present in our research, we note that the pandemic was particularly challenging to the relationships we had built with congregations. Especially in the early months of the pandemic, as we were preparing for our 2020 data collection and recruiting participating congregations, it effectively eliminated the possibility of meeting with religious leaders and congregations in person due to health and safety concerns. This had consequences for the congregations we were able to connect with and recruit for participation in our 2020 study.

In 2020, our participation was significantly lower from Black Protestant congregations, compared to previous years of the study—comparisons that are presented in Table 2.2. We believe that the disproportionately lower participation for Black Protestant churches is at least partially due to our inability to foster relationships and build trust face-to-face because those relationships are especially important in communities of color where institutional trust is understandably lower (Hsu, Hackett, and Hinkson 2014; Webb Hooper et al. 2019; Welch, Sikkink, and Loveland 2007). Additionally, it is possible that the importance of dealing with the trauma and pain of events like high-profile murders of Black men and women by police rightly took precedence over our research study.

In looking at the pooled sample of congregations that have participated in the three major waves of the LRCS, presented in Table 2.3 in the next section, we know that our study overrepresents mainline Protestant congregations and underrepresents Black Protestant congregations. Thus, we recognize that the results we present are not generalizable to the United States. They aren't even generalizable to Little Rock. What they are is a deep and valuable look into community engagement across a diverse subsection of congregations in a single U.S. city in the South.

The Value of Multimethod Research

What is really valuable about the research of the LRCS is that it provides insights into the impact of community engagement from multiple perspectives—

congregants and clergy—using both qualitative and quantitative data. How are individual members impacted by community engagement? How does greater community engagement change a place of worship? And how do these impacts aggregate up to societies? Being able to come at these questions from multiple angles and use multiple data sources with different strengths and weaknesses really helps us get a clearer picture of what is going on with religion and community in Little Rock.

Because of the rich data we have collected over more than a decade of the LRCS, the analytic strategy employed in the subsequent chapters draws on multiple data sources and types. In some cases, the key variables of interest are consistently measured across all three major waves of the LRCS (2012, 2016, and 2020). In those cases, we are able to present analyses of pooled data. In some cases, however, the questions of greatest interest when it comes to community engagement were not introduced until later survey iterations. The most recent congregational survey year, 2020, provides the largest sample and most robust set of variables, and so those results are often presented when more complex models are called for or more specific community-engagement variables are being examined. Details on the specifications of statistical models are provided at the appropriate place in each chapter, but for methods-minded academics, the deep statistical details can be found in the footnotes or in the appendix.[4] Appendix A, in particular, describes all the variables in the models we use, the specific question wording, and the summary statistics for each.

Throughout, qualitative data are used to help add depth to our understanding of the statistical results and provide additional insights. Through inter-

---

4. Here is one of those deep statistical footnotes. In terms of the modeling strategy, OLS regression, ordered logit regression, and Poisson models are used, as appropriate, given the nature of the dependent variable and are noted in each case. Clustered standard errors are used to account for the interdependence of responses clustered by congregation (Primo, Jacobsmeier, and Milyo 2007), a widely used strategy for correcting for violations of nonindependence (Huang 2016; Musca et al. 2011) and an additional way to account for unmeasured aspects of congregational culture. An alternative modeling strategy would have been to use a multilevel model (MLM), which is intended to account for dependence present in nested data (i.e., individuals nested in congregations) and result in more accurate standard errors (Snijders and Bosker 1999), but given the nature of the LRCS data, clustering standard errors is a more appropriate modeling strategy here for two reasons. First, because some congregations are quite small—some with only a dozen respondents, for instance—clustering is a better option (Coyne et al. 2010; Thomas and Heck 2001; Thomas, Heck, and Bauer 2005). Second, while MLM is a powerful modeling technique, clustering standard errors allows researchers to more simply address the heterogeneity between the observations in nested data (Huang 2016). Missing data is dealt with in most cases using multiple imputation in STATA. In some cases, individual-level measures are created based on congregation averages of theoretically important variables. Additionally, some clergy responses are included as individual-level congregation-wide variables. Descriptions of all variables are available in Appendix A and are usually provided as appropriate in the following chapters.

views with clergy and focus groups with congregation members, we can learn more about what motivates certain community-engaged behaviors and what their impacts are. These quotes are almost always anonymous in the chapters that follow, although some context about the positionality of the source may be provided—for instance, if they are a volunteer versus a religious leader, part of a large versus a small congregation, and so on.

Finally, each of the following three chapters contains a case study, and there are four congregational case studies in Chapter 6. These case studies are a deep dive into what engagement really looks like on the ground. They provide the stories of real places of worship in Little Rock, Arkansas, and illustrate how they are working in the community. These case studies sometimes show how statistical findings play out in reality and sometimes show how individual congregations might be exceptions to a statistical trend. In the following three chapters, the case studies are used to help validate the causal processes at work in the statistical models that are presented (Goertz 2016). In Chapter 6, the four case studies are presented as examples of how community engagement might be done—by congregations of different sizes, from different religious traditions, and with different resources. These case studies were purposefully selected to represent diverse congregations so that any readers might be able to see themselves or their congregation in some part of the story.

Our multimethod approach is able to provide insights that straight statistical analyses or a series of case studies alone could not. Our findings are bolstered by the fact that they are made through rich, multimethod data. The different perspectives complement one another: the quantitative data can provide a starting point that reveals new insights and trends that we otherwise may not expect (Hammond 2005). These findings can lead us to look for more information in our interview data or—because the LRCS is a long-term, community-engaged research project—ask new questions in the next iteration, creating a dialogue between research and theory (Goertz 2016). What may have been just a number in a data table becomes a real story we can understand more clearly with the context of qualitative data (Greene, Caracelli, and Graham 1989; Mark and Shotland 1987). When findings converge, it increases our confidence in their validity (Greene, Caracelli, and Graham 1989). When they don't, it can challenge us to reexamine how we are measuring concepts and who we are talking with. In the next section, we look closely at some data that illustrates how valuable our multimethod approach can be.

Little Rock's Congregations

There are forty-three different congregations that have participated in congregation-level survey data collection with the LRCS but fifty-eight congregation/year data points in our dataset because of repeat congregation participants

TABLE 2.3 LRCS PARTICIPATING CONGREGATIONS, BY RELIGIOUS TRADITION AND RESPONDENTS, 2012–2020		
	Congregations	Respondents
Mainline Protestant	16	1,238
Black Protestant	13	526
Evangelical Protestant	12	630
Catholic	5	1,211
Mormon	4	284
Jewish	4	72
Islamic	3	119
Other	1	41

over the years (and one Catholic congregation where we distributed English-language surveys at one service and Spanish-language surveys at a different service and treated the two as separate in the analyses). Although the number of congregations in Little Rock changes from year to year, this represents around 15 percent of the approximately 360 places of worship in the city limits. Table 2.3 shows the breakdown of the sample by religious tradition and respondent number.

The pooled data in Table 2.3 demonstrate numerically a few things that we learned about the congregations of Little Rock through our research. It can be easier to build trust with mainline Protestant congregations, who have significantly higher education levels (average of 4.3 on a scale where 1 = less than high school and 5 = postgraduate) than the rest of the sample (average of 3.9 on the same 1 to 5 scale, $p < 0.05$) and are more willing to let university researchers ask them a bunch of questions. Black Protestant congregations especially tend to be smaller, which is another reason why personal relationships can be so important. Whereas clergy may come and go with organizational assignments, in small congregations, the members are often closely involved with how things run, and maintaining relationships with them can be helpful for research participation. It took thirteen participating Black Protestant congregations to get 526 respondents but only five participating Catholic congregations to get 1,211 respondents. So, the size of the congregation makes a big difference for our respondent numbers, making Catholics overrepresented in our sample when the congregant is the unit of analysis, compared to the proportion of the population they make up in Little Rock.[5]

Despite these flaws in the data, we have a pretty diverse sample. In the Bible Belt of America, we asked questions about faith, community, and pol-

---

5. According to census data available from the ARDA, in the Little Rock/North Little Rock metropolitan area, Catholics make up about 8 percent of religious adherents (Association of Religion Data Archives 2010).

itics, and we had congregations from wards of the Church of Jesus Christ of Latter-day Saints, Jewish temples, and Islamic mosques—all religious minorities in our city—return to participate in multiple iterations of our study.

What can we learn from the pooled sample of all three congregation-level data collection years? Well, to be honest, in 2012, we were just getting started, only worked with five congregations, and asked a lot of questions about politics that we didn't carry through to later studies. But there are some neat data points that can help us learn more about the congregations at this early stage and also illustrate the importance of using caution in relying on numbers alone.

The first row in Table 2.4 shows a significant liberalization in the average ideology score over time, moving away from the upper, more conservative, margin on a normalized 0 to 1 scale and toward the middle. By 2020, it is nearly exactly at the center at 0.53. This seems to indicate that Little Rock's faith communities are moderating politically. But there may also be selection effects at work; as the study expanded to more congregations, those congregations could have been more politically moderate or liberal—we may see more mainline congregations participating, for instance—thus moving the mean toward the center.

At the same time, we see that political activity increased. This variable is a count of frequency of political activities like donating to a political campaign or attending a political rally and runs from 0 to 18, so the increases are small but significant compared to 2012 (information on how political activity and all of the variables are measured is available in Appendix A). This finding seems to indicate that the members of these congregations are becoming more engaged in politics, perhaps mobilized by increasingly contentious 2016 and 2020 presidential election campaigns.

TABLE 2.4 CHANGE OVER TIME IN THE MEAN VALUE OF VARIABLES COLLECTED THROUGH LRCS CONGREGATION-LEVEL SURVEYS

	Study year		
Variable	2012	2016	2020
Conservative ideology* (mean score, very liberal to very conservative, 0 to 1 scale)	0.62	0.55	0.53
Political activity* (mean score, count of political activities, 0 to 18 scale)	5.48	5.83	5.99
Worship service attendance* (mean score, never to more than once a week, 0 to 1 scale)	0.77	0.79	0.72
Respondent n	452	1,475	2,293

Note: Ideology scores in 2016 and 2020 are significantly lower than in 2012. Political activity scores are significantly higher in 2016 and 2020, compared to 2012. Worship service attendance is significantly lower in 2020, compared to either 2016 or 2012.
* $p < 0.05$

This is where it is particularly important to remember the makeup of the sample. While the LRCS is a long-term study, it is not a panel study. The participating congregations and responding members change from year to year. Only five congregations were part of the research in 2012. That sample was dominated by a large Catholic parish, which may have different political views than a more representative sample of places of worship in Little Rock, which would include more evangelical and Black Protestant congregations, as our sample did in later iterations. Thus, while the data in Table 2.4 do provide some insights regarding Little Rock congregations, they may not be insights that statistics alone can fully capture.

That is why, in the analyses in the following chapters, we don't just present summary statistics without context. We tell the story of community engagement in Little Rock through more sophisticated statistical models that account for multiple variables at once. We augment those results with insights from real clergy and congregants to help us understand the context in which they take place. And we use the relationships we have built over a decade to tell the stories of what community engagement is like in practice.

And so, to understand what the numbers in a table like Table 2.4 mean, we have to go deeper. Take, for instance, the second-to-last line in Table 2.4, which shows a significant decrease in worship service attendance in 2020. This question asked respondents how often they attended worship services, with response options ranging from never to multiple times a week, which were then normalized on a 0 to 1 scale. Seeing the worship service attendance decline in Table 2.4, one response might be that this is in line with research on declining attendance across the United States (Cox, Clemence, and O'Neil 2019; Inglehart 2021; Pew Research Center 2019a). Another response might be to recall that the survey was conducted in 2020, before COVID-19 vaccines were available and when many congregations had stopped meeting in person. This move to virtual worship could have contributed to a decline in worship service attendance (Sharp 2021; Wang 2022).

Our research design makes it possible to look more closely at this question, using a variety of data sources—first through a 2020 question on whether the respondent is attending more or less and then followed up by an open-ended question on why their attendance changed. Of the 2,293 respondents to the survey we distributed in October 2020, 74 percent ($n = 1,697$) said that they were attending about the same as they were a year ago (before the pandemic). Around 18 percent ($n = 413$) said that they were attending less, and around 8 percent ($n = 183$) said that they were attending worship services more often. Thus, for the vast majority of our respondents, their attendance remained unchanged in 2020. For those who did change, most decreased their attendance. We can find out more by asking why.

Each of the 596 respondents who said they were attending less or more than they had been a year ago were asked a follow-up question about why their attendance had changed and were provided with an open-ended text box to respond. A team of undergraduate research students enrolled in a research practicum course helped develop a codebook using inductive and deductive methods and then coded the 479 responses that we received into six main categories, represented in Figure 2.2. Intercoder reliability was evaluated against the coding standard set by the professor of the course (and director of the LRCS) until reliability reached a minimum of 92 percent agreement and Cohen's kappa of 0.88 when tested on a coding sample of seventy-five random responses. The codebook used to code these open-ended responses is available in Appendix D under "Open-Ended Worship Service Attendance Codebook, 2020 LRCS Survey of Congregation Members."

As Figure 2.2 illustrates, far and away the most popular response was the category "COVID in general," which was assigned to generic answers like "COVID" and "the pandemic." When combined with the category "Specific COVID reasons," which included more detailed responses like "Got out of the habit during COVID pandemic" and "COVID—not sure how clean the church and chapel are," reasons associated with COVID-19 accounted for 76 percent of all responses given for why attendance had declined in the previous year.

Thus, the open-ended survey data show that the greatest impact in 2020 came from COVID-19. But it is still important to remember that the impact of the COVID-19 pandemic varied greatly by congregation. Some congrega-

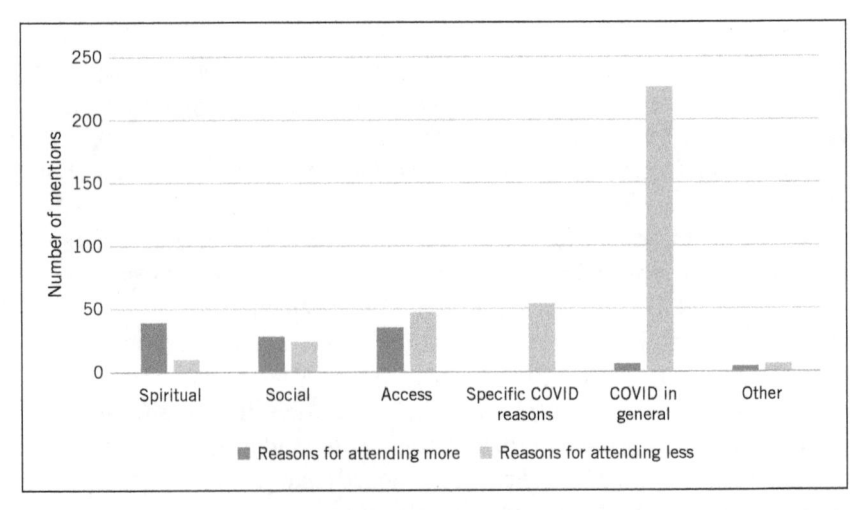

Figure 2.2 Open-Ended Responses for Why Attendance Changed, Compared to a Year Ago

tions were ready to pivot and be online, and some weren't. I distinctly remember driving down the road one day in 2021 and seeing one of the smaller evangelical churches that was part of our 2020 study literally being demolished. I knew it was struggling at the time of the survey. They had just hired a new pastor to try to help an aging and shrinking church, but then the pandemic hit and it was more than the church could withstand. For many smaller churches, especially, COVID-19 was the last straw (Sharp 2021). Others were scrambling to stay afloat. As one clergy member told us in an interview, "COVID is changing a lot of things. So, we have had to pivot to online because there has not been an online presence, which I have found frustrating at this point."

Some of the larger congregations that already had online giving set up and online worship services streaming were in a better position to stay connected to their members, as we learned through our interviews with clergy. One pastor of congregational care at a large Black Protestant church saw the pandemic as "a blessing in disguise" because the grief ministry at that church moved online during the pandemic and, as a result, they are now able to support many more people in the church and even across the country. People were inviting their "cousins and their cousin's cousins to join these Zoom meetings," and they were getting the support they needed to walk through some of the most difficult times of their lives. Other large congregations even told us that they saw increases in virtual attendance and online giving during 2020 as new people joined in to view services remotely and give to the congregations' efforts to support those in need during the pandemic. According to our data (carefully gleaned by student researchers scouring the Internet and making numerous phone calls), in Little Rock between 2020 and 2022, five congregations merged, six permanently closed, thirty-three ceased all discernible activity, and nine were founded.

What this brief look at attendance data shows is the value added from a multimethod approach to understanding congregations and communities. Clearly, the numbers in Table 2.4 tell only a small part of the story of what has happened with attendance at worship services over the years of the LRCS. In Chapter 4, we get even deeper into the story with a model using 2020 data that includes many community-engagement variables and illustrates the ways community engagement is related to increased attendance. But first, let's take a closer look at the congregations in our dataset and see what community-engaged congregations look like.

What Do Community-Engaged Congregations Look Like?

Because we didn't start asking questions about community engagement until the 2016 iteration of the LRCS, the following analysis only includes congregations from 2016 and 2020, resulting in fifty-three congregation/year observations in the dataset. For each congregation, we calculated a mean congregation-level community engagement score by averaging the community engagement scores of all respondents for that congregation. The community engagement scale includes six questions and a range of twenty-five possible data points, rescaled to run from 0 to 1 here for ease of interpretation. The congregational average is narrower, running from a low of 0.58 to a high of 0.81. In order to compare the differences between the least and the most community-engaged congregations, we looked for natural cut points in the data and separated out the highest and lowest. Thus, we created variables to compare the least engaged congregations (those falling below 0.70, congregation $n = 8$, respondent $n = 599$) to the most engaged congregations (those above 0.78, congregation $n = 12$, respondent $n = 629$). Each category represents around 15 percent of the respondent population. How are these congregations different from each other?

Table 2.5 presents the mean scores for the most and least engaged congregations on a number of demographic, political, and religious variables of interest and indicates that the two types of congregations are quite different indeed. In more community-engaged congregations, members are much more likely to be Black, more educated, younger, less well-off financially, and more liberal. While there is no difference in average political activity between the two categories of congregations, the most engaged congregations are more likely to have members who report hearing sermons about politics and community topics. The most engaged congregations are more likely to serve out-

TABLE 2.5 MEAN VALUES FOR THE LEAST ENGAGED AND MOST ENGAGED CONGREGATIONS, 2016 AND 2020 POOLED LRCS DATA			
	Least engaged congregations	Most engaged congregations	Significant
Black or African American identity	0.07	0.42	Yes
Education	3.87	4.14	Yes
Year born	1957	1962	Yes
Income	5.28	4.83	Yes
Conservative ideology	0.67	0.35	Yes
Political activity	6.08	6.25	No
Political sermons	1.06	1.79	Yes
Community sermons	1.01	1.39	Yes
Service to congregation	2.46	2.14	Yes
Service outside congregation	1.91	2.27	Yes
Worship service attendance frequency	0.77	0.72	Yes
Congregation size	273	111	Yes
Prayer	2.49	3.20	Yes
Scripture	3.41	3.79	Yes
Providentiality	7.69	7.66	No

side their place of worship, while the least engaged are more likely to serve at their place of worship. Worship service attendance is higher among the least community-engaged congregations, but prayer and scripture reading are higher among the most community-engaged congregations. Interestingly, the religious measure for providentiality—people believing that God has a plan that they can help bring about—is the same for both categories of congregations. Both kinds of congregations are filled with members who believe they are doing God's will. The least community-engaged congregations also tend to be larger, indicating that personal connections and relationships in smaller congregation may help further community-engagement projects.

In 2018, the LRCS did a survey just of congregation leaders, and we asked specifically about community programs and services congregations provide to the community. Eight of the twelve most engaged congregations in the merged 2016/2020 dataset used to generate Table 2.5 participated in that survey. These eight clergy represent four Black Protestant, three mainline Protestant, and one Catholic congregation. They range in size from fewer than fifty members attending each week to over four hundred. Although there were seventy-two evangelical congregations in this merged sample, only one of the twelve most engaged congregations was evangelical, and that one did not participate in the 2018 survey on collaboration with nonprofits. This may be due to evangelical congregations' historical focus on spiritual matters, as opposed to community engagement (Chaves 2004; Iannaccone 1988; Mulder and Jonason 2017). Focusing on the most engaged congregations that responded to the 2018 nonprofit collaboration survey, their responses give us some additional insights into how these most engaged congregations view community engagement.

For instance, the clergy from those congregations—the 8 who responded to the survey—were significantly less likely than the other 104 clergy in the sample to believe that faith alone could take care of social ills (as measured by agreement with two statements: "If enough people were involved in the church, social ills would take care of themselves" and "Churches should put less emphasis on transforming the social order and more on individual salvation"). Interestingly, the leaders of these most engaged congregations weren't offering more services to the community. These congregations—as with congregations all across the United States and beyond—were involved in the community in a variety of ways. They provide social services as diverse as food pantries, drug and alcohol addiction recovery, educational support, prison ministries, and so on (e.g., Ley 2008, Greenberg, Greenberg, and Mazza 2010, Kerley et al. 2010, Unruh and Sider 2005, Twombly 2002). But when we compared the work they were doing to the work of the least engaged congregations, we found no difference in the number of social service programs they hosted. Instead, we saw two key differences in the data.

First, the leaders of the most engaged congregations were significantly more likely to say that "political activism is an important part of my church's historical legacy and tradition." This is noteworthy because it indicates that, at least at the level of the leadership of the congregations, they see a connection between their community work and political activism. Second, all of these leaders said they had plans to partner with other organizations in the community to provide services in the coming year (compared to 67 percent of the rest of the sample). In an interview, one of these leaders said of their congregation, "We definitely have an outreach focus," and went on to list a number of other partners they collaborate with on a neighborhood food pantry, as well as a nonprofit medical ministry they support and an annual interfaith event they host. For these most engaged congregations, community engagement means working together to solve problems, not just coming to the community with a solution.

Conclusion

In later chapters, we use the methodological richness of the LRCS to dig deeper into these findings to learn more about how service and engagement are connected—and how they both benefit individual members. We show how attendance—the congregational connection and warmth that come from serving together, even more than just people in pews—can make a big difference for places of worship, especially during challenging times. And we look more closely at how political activity and community-related sermons might be relevant for larger questions of efficacy and democracy in societies where trust is waning. In Chapter 6 we also see how different congregations set different priorities. Community engagement is not the top concern for every place of worship, and engagement looks different for different congregations.

These are complex issues to parse, but the data of the LRCS provides an in-depth, community-based, multimethod look at important questions facing congregations and communities. Congregations and leaders have many priorities competing for their time and resources, but community engagement can yield significant benefits: for members, for congregations, and for communities.

How Engagement Helps Members

The image of congregational community engagement many of us have in our minds might look something like the Saturday Adopt-a-Block events that Little Rock's Central Church of Christ hosts. At the events, enthusiastic twentysomethings set out a picnic lunch, play catch with neighborhood kids, and clean up trash in the park. The church members are helping beautify public space, connecting with members of the community, and supporting those in need as they distribute food and change burned-out light bulbs for the elderly.

But many religious people might remind us, upon seeing such a scene, that it is not just the community and the people being served who are benefiting. "It is more blessed to give than to receive," they might even tell us. Who benefits from a community service event like the one described here? In this chapter, we look closely at both qualitative and quantitative data from the LRCS to evaluate whether and how the members of a congregation benefit from engagement in the community.

But first, we take a look at what might lead an individual to get engaged in community service in the first place and how we can measure those influences.

What Predicts Individual Community Engagement?

The LRCS is unique in the multimethod approach it takes to understanding the nature of community engagement. Because of this approach, we can measure community engagement in multiple ways and at multiple levels of analysis. When we think about individual people attending places of worship, we can imagine their potential community engagement being influenced through at least five different paths. This is illustrated through the simplified model in Figure 3.1.

First, individuals are going to bring their own personal characteristics to a given situation, including the decision to get engaged in the community. The academic literature on political and community engagement suggests a multitude of factors that may contribute to greater participation—from personal religious beliefs about the importance of service (Einolf 2011) to having more free time or resources to dedicate to it (Verba, Schlozman, and Brady 1995). Thus, an individual, denoted with the number 1 in Figure 3.1, might show up to any given worship service ready to receive, dismiss, or just not have time for messages they might encounter about community engagement, depending in part on their personal characteristics.

Second, as individuals sit in their place of worship listening to their clergy, they are receiving both implicit and explicit cues about community engagement. Perhaps there is a sermon about volunteering for a citywide day of service. Maybe the clergy urges members to vote in an upcoming election. Implicit messages abound in fellowship halls that may be "festooned with posters" about community events and service opportunities (Wald, Owen, and Hill 1988). Whatever the message, clergy are usually highly respected by their members, especially when it comes to issues of morality and truth

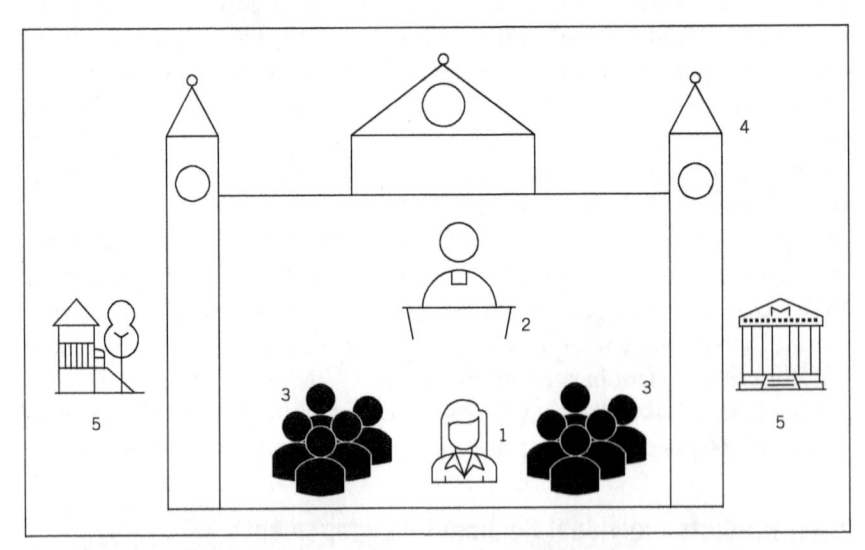

Figure 3.1 Types of Influence on the Community Engagement of an Individual Congregation Member
Note: (1) Personal characteristics, (2) Clergy, (3) Fellow congregants, (4) Congregational culture, (5) Community connections.

(Djupe and Calfano 2009; Olson 2009). While most individuals' experiences of religion are quite local and personal, historically, there are examples of clergy urging social engagement on a broad scale, from the civil rights movement (Hadden 1969; Williams 2002) to nuclear weapons (Goldzwig and Cheney 1984; Russett 2015), environmental issues (Lieberman 2004; Baugh 2016), and the 2020 racial justice protests following the murder of George Floyd (Religion News Service 2021).

While the leader in Figure 3.1 (denoted with a number 2) is shown at a pulpit, clergy messages aren't always delivered in formal sermons. Congregations are places that maintain and transmit social norms (Wald, Owen, and Hill 1988). On a subtler level, clergy themselves might be active in the civic and political life of the city and, while they may not preach about it, the individual members may see their clergy's posts on social media, hear hallway conversations after services, and notice them out and about at community events. They may follow these subtle cues and align their views and behaviors accordingly (Mangum 2008; Stroope 2011).

Third, individual members attending worship services are also surrounded by other members attending worship services, denoted with the number 3 in Figure 3.1. These fellow members are often their friends (Schwadel et al. 2016), and if they are engaged in the community, they may invite their fellow members along to service projects, ask them to sign petitions, or tell them about an upcoming rezoning hearing. Even if they don't receive a direct invitation, individual members may know about and admire a lay leader who also serves on the board of a local charity or may hear other members in the hallway talking about an issue with the school board. Just attending worship services more often tends to be associated with higher levels of community involvement (Driskell, Embry, and Lyon 2008; Driskell, Lyon, and Embry 2008; McClure 2017).

Fourth, the congregation itself may have an influence on individual members. Here, we are not talking about the other members, but about the programs, the structure, and even the theology. This influence may come through the opportunities the congregation provides for community engagement—for instance, through hosting a small group dedicated to community issues or through regular service projects (McClure 2017). Places of worship can be social and community centers (Ellison and George 1994; Greenberg 2000; Jamal 2005; Lincoln and Mamiya 1990; Min 1992). Or it may come through the nature of the religious tradition itself. For some religious traditions, social engagement is more central to their understanding of living their faith (Barnes 2011; McClure 2014; Polson 2016). The broader congregational culture is represented by the structure of the building in Figure 3.1 and is denoted with the number 4. Research shows that congregational culture can play a significant role in encouraging community engagement (Glazier 2019a).

Finally, the context of the community outside the congregation can influence engagement (Cavendish 2000; Glazier and Street 2020; Polson 2016). For instance, foundational work by Mark Chaves (2004) finds that congregations in poor neighborhoods provide more social services—likely because they see community needs and want to do something to help. But resources matter as well; if the congregation itself is quite poor, as opposed to a middle-class congregation that commutes into a downtown location, it may struggle to provide the services the community needs (Chaves 2004, 53). Congregations with fewer members may not have the resources to do community engagement in the same ways that larger congregations do. Religious values—at both the individual level and at the level of the faith tradition—can influence the extent and type of engagement (Johnson, Cohen, and Okun 2013; McClure 2017; Polson 2016). Personal connections to specific nonprofits or community groups are often the way that community-engagement projects at congregations get started or persist (Bakker 2013; Gazley et al. 2022). Sometimes, the success of a project may come down to the enthusiasm and personal commitment of just one or two supporters (M. Harris 1998, 193).

There is a complex interplay of forces among clergy, congregation, and community in Figure 3.1, and they are likely mutually reinforcing, as well. For instance, Djupe and Gilbert (2003) find that a longer amount of time serving in the ministry and also being at a single congregation for a longer amount of time can help clergy become more familiar with the kinds of political activities that are seen as appropriate by their congregations and also determine how much time and resources they have to devote to community engagement. Going one step further, they also find that clergy "take up political activity when their congregations are not well represented in their communities" (65).

Thus, the context of both congregational and community need may contribute to the extent of individual engagement, perhaps mediated through clergy messaging or congregational culture.

Figure 3.1 distinguishes five different types of influence on the community engagement of an individual congregation member, but it is important to recognize that the elements represented in Figure 3.1 often come into contact with and even influence one another. Thus, there are many potential religious influences with regards to community engagement that an individual might experience as part of a faith community. But when we consider all these factors together, which ones lead to greater community engagement by individuals?

Measuring Community Engagement

What leads an individual person to be more community engaged? The first decision to make in trying to answer this question is to determine the appro-

TABLE 3.1 SURVEY QUESTIONS USED TO MEASURE COMMUNITY ENGAGEMENT	
Engagement variables	Question wording
Community action	Summary measure of agreement (1 = Strongly disagree to 5 = Strongly agree) with the following three statements: 1. I do things to make the community a better place. 2. I am aware of the important needs in the community. 3. I rarely talk with my friends and/or family about community problems (reversed).
Political efficacy	Summary measure of agreement (1 = Strongly disagree to 5 = Strongly agree) with the following three statements: 1. Becoming involved in political or social issues is a good way to improve the community. 2. Government is too complicated for me to understand (reversed). 3. I believe that I can personally make a difference in my community.
Community engagement scale	Combination of the community action and political efficacy measures
Service outside the congregation	In the past month, how many hours of unpaid service have you given outside your place of worship? 1 = Zero, 2 = One to five, 3 = Six to ten, 4 = Eleven to fourteen, 5 = Fifteen or more
Participate in a community group at their place of worship	Thinking about your activity during "normal" times, that is, not during a pandemic, do you regularly take part in any activities of this congregation that reach out to the wider community (for instance, visitation, evangelism, outreach, community service, advocacy)? Please check all that apply. Respondent was then presented with a variety of options. This variable represents those who checked the box corresponding to the option: "Yes, in community service or advocacy activities of this congregation."

priate dependent variable—that is, how we want to measure individual community engagement. Here, we take a few different approaches. First, we measure individual community engagement through six survey questions, added together to create a single scale. We can also separate out these survey questions into three that mostly focus on community action—how much is this person *doing* things to help their community? And three that mostly focus on political efficacy—how do they *feel* about their ability to make a difference? All the community-engagement questions we use are listed in Table 3.1.

We can also measure community engagement through the number of hours the person reports serving the community (these are hours served outside their place of worship) each month. At the individual level, one final way to measure community engagement is through membership in a group that is focused on community issues, meeting at their place of worship. Now, not every congregation will have such groups, but belonging to one is an additional signal that an individual is engaged in the community.

So, what leads to greater community engagement at the individual level? Here is where the heavy statistics come into play. Looking at the more than 2,200 individual members from thirty-five diverse congregations who participated in the LRCS in 2020, we used that six-question battery of community engagement as the dependent variable and found that a few key things predicted individual community engagement (the full results from the statistical model are available in Table C.1 in the appendix). The following factors were associated with respondents who were more engaged in the community:

- They were more likely to report hearing sermons about community engagement from their clergy.
- They were more likely to say that they were a member of a community-oriented group at their place of worship.
- They were more likely to volunteer outside their congregation.

There were a number of other interesting findings in this statistical model, as well. For instance, when it comes to politics, political activity and a more liberal political ideology were both associated with more community engagement. Because political activity and community engagement can sometimes look similar—attending meetings, talking about issues of public interest, and so on—it is likely that the two positively influence one another.

There are also religious variables that significantly influence individual community engagement. For instance, although people who attend worship services more often were not more likely to be engaged in the community, those who engage in devotional practices like prayer and scripture study more often were more likely to be involved in the community. Holding providential religious beliefs, or believing that one can help bring about God's will, also leads to more community engagement ($p = 0.07$).

A Hypothetical Congregation Member

In order to better understand how these different factors might affect an actual person—the kind of person depicted in Figure 3.1 and experiencing influences from clergy, other members, their congregation, and the community itself—we can use a statistical method called predicted probabilities to create a hypothetical individual and see how they might respond to different situations. Statistically, we make this person as average as possible, giving them the mean value on all the variables in the model—average education, middle-of-the-road ideology, attends worship services a couple of times a month, and so on. Our hypothetical person is a white female attending a mainline Protestant congregation, since those are the modal categories for these variables for which a mean value is nonsensical. She is the average age of sixty years old, as many of the congregations in our sample are "greying" along with others in America (Chaves et al. 2021; Earls 2021). The LRCS survey was conducted in 2020, so that means she was born in 1960, when the most popular baby name for girls was Mary (Social Security Administration, n.d.), and, since we are in the South, we will be properly deferential and call our hypothetical person Ms. Mary.

Now that she is named, the next step is varying just one key thing at a time in the statistical model to see how much of an impact it might have on Ms. Mary's predicted community engagement. Recall from Chapter 2 that the data we are using for these analyses is not representative of all congregations in the United States or even Little Rock. It is a diverse, but not representative, sample of thirty-five congregations and 2,293 respondents. The diversity of the sample helps us know exactly which variables are significant when we run statistical models. But we have to interpret the results with caution, knowing they don't apply generally.

We begin by imagining that Ms. Mary attends a congregation where the clergy never gives sermons on community topics (the lowest possible value). How might that impact her probability of community engagement, as measured by the community engagement scale described previously? We have rescaled this variable to range from 0 to 1 here, for ease of interpretation. In the case of Ms. Mary, when she hears no sermons on community topics, her community engagement score is predicted to be 0.67. Keeping everything else the same, but just changing the frequency with which she hears sermons on community topics from never to always (the highest possible value), Ms. Mary's predicted community engagement score increases to 0.78.

This increase means about 16 percent more community engagement for Ms. Mary—a change that is statistically significant; we can confidently say it is distinct. Thus, sermons on community topics—like serving in the community and helping those less fortunate in one's area—can have a pretty powerful impact on community engagement. A summary of this change, and of all the significant variables in the model, is presented in Table 3.2. The table presents the variables in the order of the strongest positive impact on community engagement, with community sermons being in the top third, but not the most powerful variable.

As the final column in Table 3.2 illustrates, the largest marginal shift in the model is for political activity. The most politically active person—the kind of person who often attends rallies, signs petitions, donates to political candidates, and tries to persuade others to vote—is predicted to have a community engagement score that is about 14 percent higher than the least politically engaged person, who never does any of those things. This finding makes sense because, in some cases, political activity and community engagement can look pretty similar (Glazier 2019a). Attending a community meeting isn't that different from attending a political rally. In both cases, people are willing to give

TABLE 3.2 PREDICTED PROBABILITIES OF COMMUNITY ENGAGEMENT
FOR A HYPOTHETICAL AVERAGE INDIVIDUAL (MS. MARY) AS SPECIFIC
VARIABLES ARE CHANGED FROM THEIR LOWEST TO HIGHEST VALUE,
ALL ELSE HELD AVERAGE

Variable	Ms. Mary's engagement at its lowest value	Ms. Mary's engagement at its highest value	Percent change in engagement from lowest to highest
Political activity	0.705	0.848	20.28%
Community sermons	0.673	0.781	16.04%
Service outside the congregation	0.700	0.802	14.57%
Education	0.702	0.754	7.40%
Providential religious beliefs	0.700	0.751	7.28%
Religiosity	0.719	0.756	5.14%
Attends a community group at congregation	0.736	0.752	2.17%
Female	0.770	0.744	−3.37%
Conservative ideology	0.782	0.710	−9.21%

their time and effort for the public good, and places of worship tend to build the kind of social capital that helps grease the wheels of both political and community engagement (Ammerman 1997b; Brown and Brown 2003; Cassel 1999; Putnam 2000; Putnam and Campbell 2012; Wuthnow 2002). Indeed, whether we are talking explicitly about politics or about community more broadly, "religion is one of the most important of the many ways in which Americans 'get involved' in the life of their community and society" (Bellah et al. 2007, 219).

Although congregations have some influence on the political activity of their members (which we account for statistically through the other variables we include in the model and by clustering standard errors by congregation), the effects we see here are really about how an individual person's political activity impacts their community engagement. The variables for hearing community sermons and belonging to a community group at the congregation—both significant predictors of community engagement—show the impact that the congregation itself can have on engagement. These variables are also measured at the individual level, but they tell us about things that individuals are experiencing and participating in at their places of worship. Without the congregation, we wouldn't see these effects, which contribute to significantly higher community engagement.

Tallying the Individual Benefits of Community Engagement

Thinking back to Figure 3.1, and to the statistical results of the previous section, there are a lot of factors that can influence how engaged an individual might be in the community. Now that we understand a bit more about what that might look like, we can turn to the big question of this chapter: does community engagement benefit individual members? Hearing sermons on engagement, being in a congregation with an engaged culture, even an ideologically diverse culture—these can all lead to engagement. But is that good for individual people? What impact might it have on their lives to be more engaged in their community?

We are going to look at three ways that individuals might benefit from community engagement. First are the spiritual benefits to community engagement that individuals may reap. Second are the benefits to individuals regarding overall life satisfaction, not in specifically religious terms. Third is the potential for political efficacy, or the sense that one's voice and perspective matter, that community engagement can engender.

The Religious Benefits of Community Engagement

Theologically speaking, the impetus to look beyond oneself to care for those less fortunate, contribute to the collective good, and try to build something more holy than the world we currently have is found across religious traditions (Ammerman 2005; Cnaan et al. 2002; Wattles 1996). From the Taoist admonition to "regard your neighbor's gain as your own gain and your neighbor's loss as your own loss" to the Islamic wisdom that "not one of you is a believer until he loves for his brother what he loves for himself" to the Christian command to "love thy neighbor as thyself," many faith traditions encourage action beyond oneself—following a "Golden Rule" to help serve and build a better community for others (Tanenbaum Center for Interreligious Understanding, n.d.). But from a social science perspective, do the data support the religious benefits of community mindedness?

Responding to feedback from our congregation partners who wanted to know more about the spiritual health of their members, we included a number of questions about spirituality on the 2020 LRCS surveys of congregants. And, statistical analyses of these survey data indicate that community engagement does have significant religious benefits. For this statistical model, we took a question about feeling God's love as the dependent variable. This question presented respondents with the statement "I feel God's love for me, directly, or through others" and then response options ranging from "Never or almost never" to "Many times a day." Do people who are engaged in the community feel God's love more often? The full results of the statistical model are available in Table C.2 in the appendix, but the short answer is yes. Community engagement is positively and significantly associated with more frequent feelings of God's love. Hearing community-oriented sermons also seems to help ($p = 0.07$).

Our 2020 survey contained a similar question about the respondent's spiritual well-being, this one asking about how close the respondent felt to God: "Compared to a year ago, do you feel closer to God or further from God today?" with response options from 1 ("I feel much further from God today than I did a year ago") to 5 ("I feel much closer to God today than I did a year ago"). In this statistical model, hearing community sermons predicted feeling closer to God. Additionally, serving outside of one's congregation was a significant predictor of feeling closer to God. The full model results are in Table C.3 in the appendix.

These findings fit with what our research team and I have heard as we have attended community events and service projects with congregations in our city since 2012. Many of the people who are out serving and engaging the community describe how they are motivated by their faith to do so. As one leader of a large Christian congregation said, "It's what reflects the heart and character of God; it's what we see Jesus doing." A volunteer from a different congregation told me almost the exact same thing at a community service project, saying, "This is something that Jesus would be doing."

But members also talk about how serving and giving are ways they draw closer to God. One great example of this is a volunteer I began chatting with at a neighborhood event one day. One of her goals was to share Jesus with members of the community through her service. But as she got out into the community and met people there, she connected with and learned from them. Speaking about one person in particular whom she developed a friendship with, she said, "She doesn't go to church. I don't think she's ever gone to church. I don't even think she really likes the idea of church . . . but the way that she serves people is without reserve. So just interacting with her and hearing what she's doing in the community and seeing her *be* Jesus even though she doesn't *know* Jesus like I know Jesus, is how she is really sharing Jesus with me." This relationship, built through community engagement and service, was both personally and spiritually meaningful to her. She went on to say, "I know Jesus, but I am not doing half as much as she is doing to serve people as Jesus would want us to serve. She just inspires me to do more and be a better neighbor."

Clergy who want their members to feel God's love more frequently and feel closer to God could do a lot worse than prioritizing congregational community engagement. Many religious people may say that this is true from a theological perspective. What the LRCS data are able to do is demonstrate, both quantitatively and qualitatively, that those who are engaged in the community, serving outside their congregation, and hearing community-oriented messages about volunteering and giving back are more likely to say that they feel God's love and closeness in their lives.

The Life Benefits of Community Engagement

While the spiritual benefits of engagement and service may be at the top of the minds and hearts of many clergy and congregants, what about other benefits that may come from community engagement? In our 2020 survey of congregants in Little Rock, we asked a question about life satisfaction: "All things considered, how satisfied are you with your life as a whole these days?" Respondents could then use a sliding scale to mark their satisfaction from "Dissatisfied" (0) to "Satisfied" (100). Average life satisfaction for our sample was 80.68.

We next developed a statistical model predicting life satisfaction, which finds that community engagement is significantly and positively associated with higher life satisfaction. The full model results are in Appendix C.4, but for our hypothetical Ms. Mary, what this looks like is a life satisfaction score of 71.8 at the lowest level of community engagement and 81.8 at the highest level of community engagement, a pretty nice increase in life satisfaction as a result of community engagement. This finding is another data point in a well-supported literature on "the paradox of generosity," which finds that people who voluntarily give their time and money to help others have higher levels of personal well-being (Smith and Davidson 2014).

Clergy may also be interested to know that, while traditional measures of religiosity, like worship service attendance, prayer, and scripture reading, were not significant predictors of life satisfaction, feeling warmly toward one's congregation was. The sense of community and belonging that come with being part of a congregation where one is really connected with the other members contributes strongly to life satisfaction.[1] This finding may also help us understand why ideological diversity is negatively associated with life satisfaction. People who belong to congregations where there are many people who hold ideological views different from theirs may feel isolated or even alienated at times from their fellow members. This experience could be contributing to the negative association with life satisfaction we see in the data.

Our 2020 survey also asked questions about both physical and mental health, both of which are influenced by many factors, some of which are surely beyond the scope of our statistical models. Although there are twenty-four control variables in each model, only about 5 percent of the variance is explained by them (the full models are available in the appendix as Table C.5 for physical health and Table C.6 for mental health). This means that we have

---

1. As an aside for the interested reader, income and age ($p = 0.08$) were also significantly associated with life satisfaction, indicating that wealthier and older respondents were more satisfied with their lives, a finding in line with previous research (Bomhoff and Siah 2019; McAdams, Lucas, and Donnellan 2012), although the relationship between age and life satisfaction tends to be curvilinear.

included a lot of demographic, attitudinal, and congregational information to try to understand what is contributing to mental and physical health, but there is still a lot that we don't know.

What we do know from these models is that serving outside of one's congregation is positively and significantly associated with better physical health and that being part of a congregation one feels warmly toward is associated with better mental health (and having a higher income is positively associated with *both* better mental and physical health), but that is about all we can say in terms of statistics.

One thing that is clear from the qualitative data is that people who engage in their communities really seem to find joy there. As one woman, who serves as a lay leader and often coordinates volunteers at her congregation, told me, "If you get people involved in the outreach projects, they have a good time." I spoke with another woman who had been volunteering with her congregation's homeless ministry for eight years. She said that she had always wanted to help by cooking for those in need, something that she learned from her mother: "When I see people less fortunate than I am, it makes me feel so blessed to be able to help them. My mom was like that." Many volunteers mentioned a tradition of service passed down through their families. Continuing to be engaged in the community is part of carrying on that tradition and adds meaning and richness to their lives.

The Political Efficacy Benefits of Community Engagement

In order for government "by the people" to work, the people have to believe that their voices matter in politics. This simple concept, which lies at the foundations of democracy, is what political scientists refer to as political efficacy. The classic definition of political efficacy was coined in 1954 as the "feeling that political and social change is possible and that the individual citizen can play a part in bringing about this change" (Campbell, Gurin, and Miller 1954, 187). We measure efficacy through a three-question battery, presented in Table 3.1 earlier in this chapter, which is part of the larger community engagement measure.

In this section, we separate out political efficacy and run analyses to examine how the other community-engagement measures we use in the research might influence it. The results of our statistical model show that community activities, the second half of the larger community engagement measure, are positively associated with political efficacy, as is serving outside of one's congregation. The full model is in Table C.7 in the appendix.

The political efficacy battery has also been rescaled to run from 0 to 1, so for our hypothetical Ms. Mary, moving from the lowest level of community activity to the highest would change her predicted level of political efficacy from 0.54 to 0.86—a pretty impressive gain of about 59 percent in terms of efficacy. These community activities are as simple as talking with one's friends and family about community problems and being aware of important needs in the community. But the higher one scores on this community activity battery, the higher one's sense of political efficacy. There are likely reciprocal effects at work here—as there are with political behaviors and efficacy (Finkel 1985). When people engage in the community, their efficacy increases, making them want to continue to engage in the community. This creates a kind of virtuous cycle that is good for individuals and democracy.

Efficacy is valuable for individual people because it helps them feel more connected to their community and like they can make a difference. Many social and community problems feel overwhelming, but when people of faith take concrete action, especially when they do so with their place of worship, it can help them feel like they are contributing in a meaningful way. A great example of this is how congregations across Little Rock, from diverse religious traditions, worked together after the U.S. withdrawal from Afghanistan in 2021 to sponsor twelve Afghan refugee families. Large congregations took in multiple families, while smaller congregations worked together to sponsor a family, and individuals gathered donations, organized carpools, built furniture, found used cars, and tapped into their networks to find jobs for the new arrivals.

Sponsoring a refugee family is a major undertaking that requires a long-term commitment and often help from dozens of congregation members. And congregations all across the city signed up to help because they saw the heart-breaking images coming out of Afghanistan, knew about the terrible struggles of these families, and wanted to contribute. As one volunteer told me, "It just happened because the need is there, and someone found it, so that's pretty special." Getting involved and seeing one's efforts make a difference is one way to build political efficacy, although it can take time. As one lay leader who helped coordinate the efforts to support the Afghan refugee families at her church put it, "The church has been lucky to have these relationships. It's one thing to do a [one-off, impersonal service event]. The Afghan families were different; they were our families."

TABLE 3.3 THE STATISTICALLY SIGNIFICANT BENEFITS TO INDIVIDUALS OF COMMUNITY ENGAGEMENT	
Community-oriented behavior	Individual benefit
Community engagement (six-question battery)	Feel God's love, higher life satisfaction
Community action (three questions from the six-question battery; only tested on efficacy)	Greater political efficacy
Hearing community sermons	Feel God's love, feel closer to God
Serving outside the congregation	Feel closer to God, better physical health

Not only does political efficacy benefit individual members, it is also incredibly important for societies and for democracy as a whole, a story told in more depth in Chapter 5 on how engagement helps communities. The statistically significant benefits individuals accrue through community engagement are summarized in Table 3.3.

How Engagement Helps Members: The Story of Canvas Community Church

The statistics make a compelling case that community engagement is a good thing for individual members. It improves their spiritual health and overall life satisfaction and contributes to their sense of being able to make a difference. But to really understand how people are impacted by congregational community engagement, it can be helpful to look closely at a single case. Not because it is representative or because we can generalize from it, but because it tells a story that illustrates findings in ways the numbers cannot. When it comes to connecting with people, Canvas Community Church has a great story to tell.

The first day I visited Canvas Community Church, they were having a commercial refrigerator delivered. Through a combination of grant funding, donations, and church funds, they managed to get together enough money for the fridge, which would help the church in its efforts to feed members of the unhoused population of Little Rock, whom the church calls "friends."

The delivery truck pulled up with the fridge right in the middle of the evening meal. The food was served by volunteers—most of them either presently or formerly unhoused themselves—to a line of Canvas Community friends that stretched down the block when doors opened at four in the afternoon. The delivery didn't disturb much, though. The shopping carts filled with to-go meals and supply bags were wheeled out of the way, the double doors were opened wide, and eager volunteers helped shift chairs and the trendy string lights that hang from the ceiling out of the way.

Canvas wasn't always so focused on serving their unhoused friends in Little Rock. The church began as a new plant in downtown Little Rock in 2009, but the homelessness problem literally showed up on their doorstep, most notably in the winter of 2011–2012 when an ice storm left many unhoused people freezing outside. Canvas decided to open its doors as an emergency warming center, and more than one hundred people slept for nearly a month in the relatively small space, sharing two bathrooms. That winter marked a turning point for Canvas, which had always sought to welcome those who felt like they didn't have a home in traditional church. Now, they make a more explicit effort to welcome those who find themselves, for whatever reason, literally homeless as well. In addition to having a focus on the unhoused community, Canvas also finds friends among the disabled and unemployed/underemployed communities, which invariably overlap with the unhoused community.

Pastor Paul, whom one of the formerly unhoused volunteers described to me as a "softie," says that Canvas is still trying to figure out how to balance their emphasis on love and relationships together with the nuts and bolts of providing for their friends' real physical needs. Another leader at Canvas, Pastor Kurt, put it this way: "As the early church was a community of people that cared for one another, so too is Canvas a praying, disciple-making community that reaches out to people on the edge of society. We, as Christians, must be our society's first responders." Pastor Kurt, who served multiple congregations, not just Canvas Community Church, passed away in July of 2022.

Canvas is not the kind of church where people walk around thumping Bibles, yet more than one person mentioned to me the scripture in Matthew 25 about feeding, helping, and serving those in need just as they would Jesus. It is clear that the people serving at Canvas are sincerely motivated by their faith and their love for those in need. One longtime volunteer spoke about a tradition of service in her family stretching back generations. And that deep, spiritual, and personal commitment is necessary because Canvas isn't for everyone.

Some churchgoers might be put off by pulling up to worship services and finding someone sleeping in the doorway of the church. Some might not want to sit next to someone who hasn't had access to a shower for a few days. Some might be a little apprehensive in a worship space with a person who was recently released from prison, is struggling with mental health issues, or just looks a little rough. But for many who come to worship at Canvas, that is exactly the point. As one volunteer put it, "Volunteering helps me be mindful of others' humanity."

Most people who serve and worship at Canvas actually have another church home where they worship Sunday mornings, but Canvas is where their hearts are. It is where they come to live out their faith, connect with one another, and build relationships. Pastor Kurt described the church as trying to do the "immediate work of listening and seeing." As they seek to be "agents of compassion" in their work with their unhoused friends in Little Rock, "it fulfills their lives in many ways as well."

One member I spoke with had been attending Canvas for more than seven years. Even though she had moved away from Little Rock to another city in Arkansas, she is still listed as a member at Canvas and considers it her church home. She was at Canvas volunteering at the "Dinner with a Purpose" meal and spiritual message one Monday night and told me about how Canvas had felt like a church with a bit of a split identity before the pandemic.

It was trying to be a family church focused on providing a full cadre of worship services but also being a church that explicitly helps those "friends on the street" in need. She said, "We needed to pick one thing and do it well. The pandemic was really a blessing in disguise because it helped us do that." And people like this worshipper keep coming back to Canvas—even when they move away—because of the spiritual commitment they have to serving there.

This is what is unique about Canvas—the connection between the inner, spiritual message of the church and the outer, service action that people take. When I asked the church leadership about why this link is so strong at Canvas, one thing they mentioned was the life experiences of their members. For many of them, life has been unpredictable or uncertain, which can lead them to feel a strong sense of urgency to act. The more theologically minded staff at Canvas also talk about the church's Wesleyan background and how inner transformation leads to outward works of love for one's neighbor. For both groups—whether it be life experience or theology—the result is a greater commitment to helping others and serving now. Pastor Kurt describes Canvas as "a place to grow discipleship. And for those who are disciples, it's a place to serve. It's a servant place."

The vision of Canvas Community Church is to "see lives transformed (our own and those of our friends experiencing homelessness) through relationships with one another and with Jesus Christ," and you could see that transformation in the formerly unhoused members of the leadership team, the committed volunteers, and the descriptions friends shared with me of how things had changed in the past ten years. One man described how, six or seven years ago, there were rough nights when people would be fighting on the street outside Canvas Community Church. Today, however, when those kinds of fights break out, instead of joining in, people break them up. When I pressed him to tell me more about what had changed, he said it was a feeling of community, of being welcomed and together.

When Canvas Community Church comes together for worship on Sunday nights, it tends to be a small and fairly informal service. The evening I attended, there were about twenty worshippers there, about half of whom were unhoused. Pastor Paul led the service, including the singing, along with his wife, and played an acoustic guitar to accompany the contemporary worship songs. The topic of the sermon was taken from Luke 13:10–17, about Jesus healing someone who was bent over with an infirmity and then being condemned for healing on the Sabbath. The discussion was participatory: what has us bent over? What do we need to be healed from? Do we ever condemn others for doing things or asking for things when we think the time isn't right?

On this last point, the discussion got particularly poignant. There are closets full of supplies for unhoused friends in Canvas Community Church. And Pastor Paul and others are happy to share with their friends in need. But if a meal is being served, a message is being delivered, or worship services are ongoing, they will ask them to wait. There are specific times for distributing supplies. If they open the cupboards, they know that people will crowd around and the meal, the message, or the worship will be lost. Pastor Paul very humbly posed the question: in asking people to wait, was he like the ruler of the synagogue who said there were six other days to be healed and Jesus should have waited for one of those?

This self-reflection and the powerful scripture discussion reveal the struggles inherent in running this kind of ministry. Pastor Paul invites the community to consider these important questions together and doesn't shy away from self-critique. But the love and protectiveness the community at Canvas feel for each other, and particularly for Pastor Paul, were clear through the discussion and later through prayer. As the leaders asked what things needed to be mentioned as points of gratitude in prayer, they were listed on a large whiteboard in the front of the room. Next, the leaders asked what things were challenges that needed to be lifted up in prayer as well.

When it came to gratitude, one unhoused friend called out, "Pastor Paul! He don't forget you." He proceeded to tell a story about how Pastor Paul came and found him in the park and brought a meal to him when he knew he needed it. Pastor Paul didn't forget him. With each point of gratitude, the leader called out "praise the Lord" and the congregation responded with "hallelujah!" With each specific challenge, the leader called out "Lord in thy mercy" and the congregation responded with "hear our prayer." This interactive, community prayer is symbolic of how Canvas functions—as a collective, hearing each other's concerns, bearing each other's burdens, and sharing each other's joys.

I saw this community again on a hot and humid Monday evening in July, when Pastor Paul welcomed around fifty unhoused friends into Canvas for a meal and a spiritual message. The meal was provided by volunteers from the nearby St. James United Methodist Church, and the message was part prayer, part meditation, and part self-care. Pastor Paul encouraged everyone to focus on their breathing, recall how God first breathed life into Adam, be grateful for their breath, and return to their breathing as a point of centering if ever they get mad or frustrated.

In the quiet of the open church hall, there was no anger, no short tempers. But as the friends finished their meals, prayed together, and took their plastic grocery bags filled with food for the next day away with them into the heat, one could imagine hungry bellies and flared tempers. Canvas Community Church is trying to give these friends not only food but a place to return and feel safe, along with strategies for building a better life. Community and government groups come to Canvas to reach the unhoused population and provide services. Unhoused individuals use the address at Canvas to receive mail. Social workers meet with people in transition there. And those who worship at Canvas act out their faith in tangible ways that change them for the better.

Conclusion

Places of worship have many ways to encourage community engagement: everything from sermons on volunteering and organized groups, to long-term community programs like the one at Canvas or simply fostering a culture of engagement. Members who are a part of these kinds of congregations are more engaged in their communities. And, as this chapter has demonstrated through a mix of statistical models, quotes from clergy and members, and the case study of Canvas Community Church, community engagement has a lot of benefits for individuals. When they are engaged in the community, they feel closer to God, have greater life satisfaction, and enjoy a stronger sense of political efficacy.

For leaders who are pondering the best route forward for their own congregations, this chapter has shown how much investing in community engagement can help their members. As previous academic research, and our data from the LRCS in later chapters, shows, caring for members is usually the top priority for congregations (Ammerman 2001, 2005). The findings in this chapter reinforce what the wisdom of many religious traditions has taught all along—the best way to care for members spiritually, emotionally, and even physically may be to encourage them to engage with and serve others.

But congregations still have limited resources. Creating and staffing groups dedicated to community topics, organizing service projects, and staying up to date on community issues takes time, effort, and money. The next chapter looks at the benefits congregations themselves receive when they get engaged in the community.

How Engagement Helps Places of Worship

During the early days of the COVID-19 pandemic in 2020, many places of worship struggled to stay engaged with their own members, much less the broader community. Yet, those difficult times also revealed the creativity and determination of many faith leaders and congregations. One example is City of Refuge Community Church, which faced the same challenge as many places of worship during the pandemic—how to bring people together for important religious rituals while also ensuring their safety. In order to maintain the tenets of their faith, they came up with an innovative solution: curbside Communion! Pastor A. Neal Scoggins says, "We married the sacred with safety. Using what the culture had shifted to in order to survive financially, our local church used the same principle to survive spiritually. It's the simple things that stand out. Driving a car to our church parking lot, while remaining physically distant, our masked and gloved servers were able to accomplish convenience, community, connection, and communion."

St. James United Methodist Church similarly adapted their core value to "engage and impact our city and the world with compassion." When the COVID-19 pandemic hit, they didn't stop serving; they adjusted their ongoing mission work and added additional service projects to meet new needs as they arose. They shifted meals with the unhoused from in person to to-go boxes, moved the on-site food pantry to a drive-through model, and safely distributed care bags to people and families in need all over Little Rock. Additionally, the members at St. James United Methodist Church brought meals to the medical staff at the University of Arkansas for Medical Sciences hospital and the VA hospital, and they sewed thousands of fabric face masks to donate. In speaking about the spirit of service that is so central to his congregation, Rev. Carness Vaughan says, "There's a hunger in people to find ways to make a practical difference with their faith. As our people are getting more deeply connected with Christ, they're searching for that outlet to exhibit their faith and to live out their faith."

For clergy like Reverend Vaughan and Pastor Scoggins, a stronger sense of congregational community and their members having a deeper faith are both goals worth striving for. Does congregational community engagement help them get there? This chapter looks closely at the benefits that congregations themselves might derive from community engagement, ultimately concluding that prioritizing community engagement is a worthwhile endeavor for most congregations.

Why Do Congregations Choose Community Engagement?

Although many congregations provide some kind of social service or are engaged in some community project, the extent varies across congregations. For instance, the data presented in Chapter 2 showed that the more community-engaged congregations in Little Rock tend to have more Black members, be more liberal in terms of ideology, and be smaller. But among both the most engaged and least engaged congregations, there is a great deal of ideological, geographical, racial, denominational, and size diversity. Both the lowest and highest categories of engagement contain Catholic parishes, Black Protestant congregations, small congregations with fifty or fewer members, and very large congregations with five hundred or more members. In both categories you will find congregations located in the heart of the city, as well as congregations located in wealthy suburbs. Engagement doesn't follow a single pattern. So, why might congregations choose to engage in the community?

From the perspective of the congregation, there are usually three, nonmutually exclusive, reasons behind the particular projects or services they get involved with. First, many congregations are seeking to meet community needs. Often, they are providing social services for their members and for people in neighborhoods near the physical location of their worship space (Ebaugh and Pipes 2001; Lewis and Trulear 2008). This is one reason why suburban churches may not be as engaged (Davidson 1986; Gibson 1961) and why congregations in poor neighborhoods tend to provide more social services (Chaves 2004). Religious congregations are often highly concerned with how the people in their neighborhoods and beyond are doing, and they provide social services that can serve as a kind of safety net for those in need (Cnaan, Boddie, and Yancey 2003; Cnaan, Sinha, and McGrew 2004a). As one religious leader told us, "We just believe that God loves people. We believe that churches need to help their community in a tangible way." In our conversations with clergy, we really saw them grappling with the best ways to serve people in need in the community. In speaking about how to get food to the hungry, one leader told us, "We're wondering if we need to move to a food truck type thing and actually go to neighborhoods, instead of asking people to come to our building. And so, we just keep wrestling. How do we serve our people?"

Another reason that congregations engage in the community is to meet the theological needs of their members, given their specific religious tradition. They may see serving the community as a religious imperative and so engagement helps them fulfill a religious obligation. Members may learn from their place of worship that "loving one's neighbor is not only functional, but pleasing to God" (Ammerman 1997b, 213). One of the clergy members we interviewed talked about community engagement as a calling from God, saying, "Our personal salvation calls us to the transformation of the world and a communal sense of salvation." Another linked it explicitly to the theology of their Christian tradition, saying, "I think theologically it's rooted in Christ's great commandment . . . to love God and love your neighbor."

Finally, congregations get involved in or especially committed to some projects because there are members of their congregations who are enthusiastic about that particular effort or have personal connections to that specific cause (Bakker 2013; Gazley et al. 2022; Reeves 2004). Sometimes all it takes is one dedicated leader to make a project happen. One pastor told us that sometimes a community project will get started because "a close friend will have their heart sort of break where God's heart breaks. And that's where you begin to find a place to reach out." Another clergy member put it this way: "Whenever they feel that their faith is calling them to do something, they're going to respond."

Here, I advance a fourth, more practical, reason why congregations might want to choose community engagement: it benefits them. The data we have collected through the LRCS builds on the literature outlined previously to demonstrate how congregations benefit from community engagement in at least three major ways: (1) increased attendance, (2) warmer congregational cultures, and (3) improved spiritual well-being of their members.

First, community-engaged congregations do better on key metrics that matter to religious administrators, namely worship service attendance and giving. Second, and related, community-engaged congregations have members who feel connected to and serve their congregations. Finally, because our research team is not entirely cynical, and also because we listened to our Clergy Advisory Board, which asked us to include more questions about the spiritual well-being of members, we know that the benefits of community engagement are more than just people in pews, volunteers for the fall festival, and larger donations for the annual giving drive. Community-engaged congregations also have members who are flourishing spiritually.

The Congregational Benefits of Community Engagement

In the following sections, we use surveys and interviews from the LRCS to demonstrate how congregations benefit from engaging in the community. We continue to measure community engagement in a variety of ways—through a six-question battery that combines community action and political efficacy, hours of service given to the community each month, membership in community groups at one's place of worship, and community messages from the clergy. These different measures of community engagement are discussed in depth in Chapter 3 and summarized in Table 3.1. As we see in the following statistical models, different kinds of community engagement benefit congregations in different ways. One of the messages of Chapter 3 is that "it's more blessed to give than to receive." Basically, in serving the community, individual members gain many benefits as well. That same lesson aggregates up for congregations. While members are serving together, they are also building relationships and connections with each other and with their congregation that make for a stronger, warmer congregational family. Thus, community engagement is not really something that happens "out there" distinct from the congregation itself. Often the service, its impetus, and its effects are closely tied to the congregation. Community engagement is good for congregations in at least three ways, described in the following sections.

Community Engagement Helps the Bottom Line

To put it in the bluntest terms possible, many congregations in the United States are struggling. Attendance is declining, the members that do attend are aging, and fewer people are reporting that they identify with organized religion (Burdick 2018; Pew Research Center 2019a). For congregations that rely on people in the pews, and contributions in the offering plate, to continue to function, this isn't just a problem; it is an existential crisis. In 2019, per-member giving as a percent of income was down 35 percent, compared to 1968 (Religious News Service 2022). Thousands of churches closed in 2019 (Shimron 2021), with the COVID-19 pandemic placing even greater pressures on congregations whose average size is shrinking (Thumma 2021; Wang 2022). At first glance, a congregation that is struggling might be hesitant to put their limited resources toward community engagement—how can they ask a small or aging congregation to give their time or money for a project that may not even benefit them directly?

In order to address this question, our research team modeled worship service attendance—the clearest sign of congregational health and a metric that many congregations watch closely—as a function of a number of variables, including community engagement. The full model results are available in Table C.8 in the appendix, but only four of the twenty-two variables in the model significantly predict attendance ($p < 0.05$). First, people who are more religious, as measured by the frequency of their prayers and reading of scripture, are more likely to attend worship services, a finding that makes intuitive sense. Second, hearing community sermons at one's place of worship is also linked to attendance. Of course, this relationship is likely to be reciprocal, as respondents have to be present in order to hear a community sermon. And third, people who serve inside their congregation are more likely to attend. Serving outside the congregation is not a significant predictor, so it is not the act of serving itself that leads to attendance, but rather, it is serving the congregation, and thereby forging a greater closeness with it, that increases the likelihood of attendance. Finally, people with higher incomes are less likely to attend worship services.

It is important to keep in mind that the statistical relationships in this model are not necessarily causal. But we can say that people who exhibit more private religious behaviors, hear more community sermons, and serve their congregations more are also the kinds of people who are more likely to attend worship service more frequently.

What does the magnitude of these effects look like in practice? Returning to our hypothetical church attender, Ms. Mary, first introduced in Chapter 3, we can set all the variables in the statistical model to the average and then just change one variable that we care about from its highest to its lowest value to see how powerful of an effect it has on attendance, calculations that are summarized in Table 4.1. Ms. Mary represents our average congregational member. If she is the least personally religious—that is, she never prays or reads scripture—her predicted probability of attending worship services once a week or more is about 49 percent. But if we move her personal religiosity value to the highest possible level, indicating that she prays mul-

TABLE 4.1 THE EFFECT OF RELIGIOUS AND COMMUNITY VARIABLES ON THE PROBABILITY THAT MS. MARY WILL ATTEND WORSHIP SERVICES ONCE A WEEK OR MORE

Variable	Lowest level (%)	Highest level (%)	Increase (%)
Religiosity (prayer and scripture reading)	49	91	85.7
Community sermons	63	89	41.2
Service to congregation	70	96	37.1

tiple times a day and reads scripture daily, her predicted probability of attending weekly or more increases to 91 percent. It's almost certain that Ms. Mary is going to show up for worship service each week.

We can do the same statistical calculations for the more community-minded variables that were significant in the model. The predicted probability that the average respondent who hears no community sermons will attend religious services once a week or more is about 70 percent. But if Ms. Mary hears many community sermons, her probability of attending at that level increases to about 89 percent. Again, Mary has to be present to hear community content in a sermon, so we expect a higher relationship on its face, but the content of the sermons may be doing some of the lifting in terms of encouraging attendance.

We take a closer look in Figure 4.1, which presents data on the average frequency of religious message content heard by those who attend worship services weekly or more. Figure 4.1 shows that the most popular messages are about spiritual growth (heard an average of 4.21 on a 1 to 5 scale, or a little above "often"), but messages encouraging members to help out in their community are not far behind at 3.88. Messages urging members to register to vote are the least common at 2.54, but they are also likely delivered only at specific times of year. This figure demonstrates that, for people who consistently show up for worship services, hearing messages about helping the community is pretty common.

The next variable we look at is service to the congregation. If Ms. Mary gives no service to her congregation, her predicted probability of attending

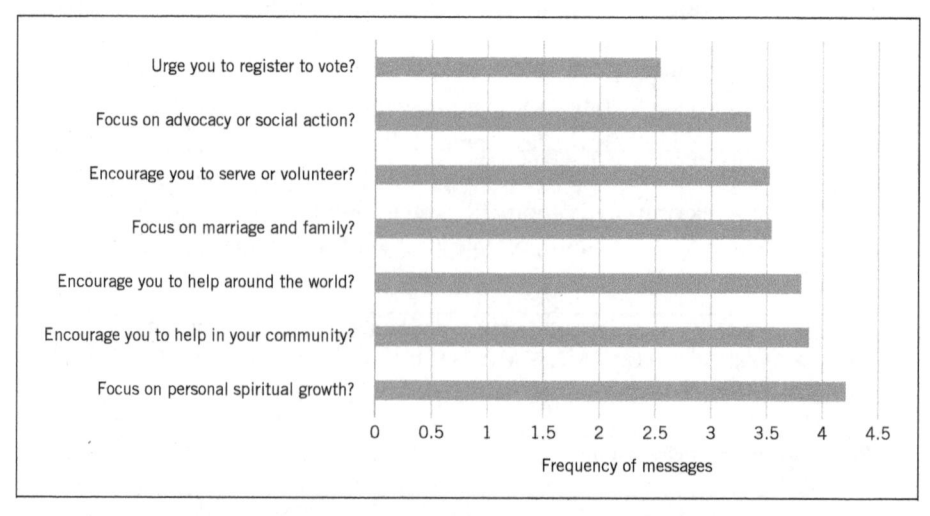

Figure 4.1 Among Those Who Attend Weekly or More, How Often Do the Worship Service Messages by the Religious Leader Address the Following?

Note: Frequency of messages: 1 = Never, 2 = Seldom, 3 = Sometimes, 4 = Often, 5 = Always.

once a week or more is 70 percent. But if she serves for fifteen or more hours a month at her place of worship, her predicted probability increases all the way to 96 percent.

One of the strengths of the LRCS research project is its multimethod approach. In addition to congregation member surveys, we can consult clergy surveys to understand more about what makes for a strong and growing congregation. In the summer of 2020, we asked the clergy whose congregations were part of our larger study, "Compared with two years ago—that is, this time in 2018—has the number of regularly participating adults increased, decreased, or remained about the same?" We also asked them about the social and community services that their congregations provided—things like food pantries, backpack drives for kids, health fairs, marriage counseling, and so on. The relationship between the two is clearly present in Figure 4.2. More community-engaged congregations, as measured by the number of distinct community programs they are providing, are also more likely to be growing congregations.

With only thirty-five clergy in this sample, statistical models can't control for many variables, but we were able to run a model that included variables for the congregation size and for how long the clergy member had been serving the congregation, as well as for two community-engagement vari-

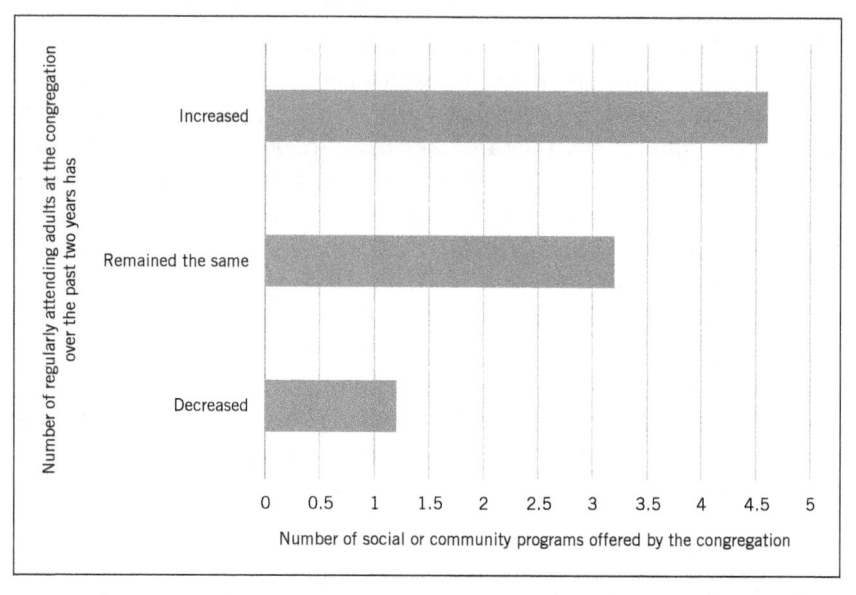

Figure 4.2 Positive Relationship between Community Engagement and Congregational Growth

Source: Data drawn from thirty-five clergy respondents whose congregations participated in the full 2020 LRCS.

ables: the number of services provided (the metric used in Figure 4.2) and whether or not the congregation had a group "to organize or encourage people to do volunteer work." The full model results are available in Table C.9 in the appendix. Only the two community-engagement variables predicted congregation growth, indicating once again the positive relationship between community engagement and increased membership.

Thus, the relationship here is not spurious—it's not that congregations that are already large are continuing to grow and are also able to provide these community services. The statistical model controls for both size and community programs, demonstrating that it is community engagement that contributes to growing membership. As a robustness check, a model using all sixty-three responding congregations from the 2020 clergy survey is available in Table C.10 in the appendix and shows the same substantive results—community engagement predicts increased membership. Thus, whether we are measuring it at the individual level (how often someone like Ms. Mary attends worship services) or at the congregation level (whether the total number of members attending a place of worship are increasing or decreasing), community engagement is associated with greater attendance.

If clergy want to increase attendance at their worship services, one way to do so is through a strictly spiritual path—getting members to focus on their spiritual growth. More time spent in prayer and studying sacred texts is strongly predictive of higher worship service attendance. But creating a community- and service-oriented culture at a congregation is also strongly predictive of higher worship service attendance. As clergy talk about community issues and the importance of service, and as members get engaged in serving their own congregations, they are more likely to return to worship services more frequently. And, as the next section demonstrates, creating a culture of service that extends *beyond* the congregation helps develop relationships and closeness *within* the congregation that can also lead to higher attendance and stronger members.

One great example of this is the Men of Faith program at Christ the King Catholic Church in Little Rock. The men in this program meet together at six on Friday mornings for presentations and small group discussions. As Father Erik describes it, "It gives men a chance to learn, but also to share with each other, which is something that doesn't happen automatically for men very often." When they first start attending the group, they may not have a clear sense about why they are there, but Father Erik sees great potential for growth from the experience for many of the men: "Maybe they'll volunteer for something at church. As they continue to grow, it broadens into who are the other people in the community that they can serve. The ones that really progress in that will begin serving at various levels, in house and out of house."

In fact, clergy often see community service and engagement as a path to spiritual growth for their members. As one leader said, "The service we do is more than just doing something nice. It's a chance to be relational with folks in a way in which God desires us to be relational with people. I think there's tremendous growth. I see people, particularly the ones that are making those sort of connections, those human connections, then being able to wrestle with scripture with greater understanding about what's being taught and the realities of the context in which we live."

Another metric that matters deeply to congregations, but may be slightly awkward to talk about, is giving. Donations from members are how congregations keep their lights on, their staff paid, and their community projects functioning. Does community engagement have any impact on this key metric? We asked respondents to our 2020 survey how much they give financially to their congregation. The full question wording and response options are available in Appendix A, but respondents could select anywhere from "I do not contribute financially here" to "I give a small amount whenever I am here" all the way up to "I give 10 percent or more of net income regularly," which was the highest response option. A statistical model, available in Table C.11 in the appendix, shows that giving is mostly predicted by personal and congregational variables. The community-engagement variables we have been using do not appear to have a direct impact on giving. Instead, community engagement is more likely to have an indirect impact through generating positive feelings toward the congregation.

The people who are more likely to give are those who are older, are wealthier, are more religious, attend more often, and belong to smaller congregations. In a smaller congregation, especially for those who are attending frequently, they are more likely to see their financial contribution making a difference and see the value in continuing to contribute or making a special donation if the need arises. Just like with the attendance model, giving service to one's place of worship is a significant predictor of giving. People who donate generously to their congregation feel a strong connection there. Community engagement could indirectly come into play here, since serving at one's congregation and out in the community tend to be mutually reinforcing behaviors. We can see how giving is strengthened through community-engaged behaviors directly related to the congregation by comparing some correlations in Table 4.2. Correlations are statistical measures of how often two variables occur together and range from –1 to 1. A correlation of 0 means there is no relationship between the two, while –1 means they never occur together and 1 means they always occur together.

In Table 4.2 we can see that there is almost no relationship between community engagement that is not directly connected to the congregation—as

TABLE 4.2 CORRELATIONS BETWEEN COMMUNITY-ENGAGED VARIABLES AND CONGREGATIONAL GIVING	
Variable	Correlation with congregational giving
Community engagement	0.02
Serving outside the congregation	0.03
Belonging to a community group at the congregation	0.23
Serving inside the congregation	0.27

measured by the six-item battery of community-engagement questions and hours of service given outside the congregation—and congregational monetary donations. But when we look at community-engagement measures that build connection to the congregation, like belonging to a community-engaged group at the congregation and hours of service given to the congregation, they both are more strongly correlated with congregational giving in monetary terms. Thus, community engagement that builds congregational connection is associated with higher levels of monetary giving.

The next section further develops the argument for how community engagement might indirectly improve congregational giving by strengthening congregational connections. All the statistical data point to people giving more when they feel more connected to their congregation. As the data in the next section show, serving the community together is a great way to build those connections and sense of congregational warmth.

Community Engagement Builds Congregational Connection

In addition to increasing attendance and giving, clergy want the members of their congregations to feel connected to each other and to their place of worship. They want people to feel, as we say in the South, like they have a "church home." One way we measure this sense of connection, or congregational warmth, is through agreement with a series of statements on our 2020 survey:

- My congregation feels like family to me.
- My congregation meets my spiritual needs.
- I feel like an outsider in my congregation (reversed).
- I would be prepared to invite friends or relatives to a worship service here.

We combined these four items into a single measure of congregational warmth, which serves as the dependent variable in the next statistical model and has been rescaled to run from 0 to 1. Full variable details are available in Appendix A, and full model results are in Table C.12, both in the appendix at the end of the book.

Why do some people feel closer to their congregation than others? Our statistical model shows that a number of community-related variables are significant predictors of congregational warmth. Hearing community sermons, belonging to a community group, and being part of a congregation with a higher average level of congregational warmth all lead respondents to report that they feel more warmly toward their own congregation. Interestingly, clergy political activity is also positively associated with congregational warmth, indicating that as members see their clergy actively involved in the community, they feel more warmly toward their congregation. A politically active religious leader may indicate the prominence of a congregation, making members feel more prestige or importance in being associated with it and thus higher levels of congregational warmth. For instance, Michael Owens (2008) finds that as government agencies have worked with Black churches to help them aid the poorest residents in their neighborhoods, those partnerships have empowered Black clergy, providing them with political authority and moral leadership in Black society. We also saw this prestige related to clergy community activity in open-ended survey responses from members in our own research. As one example, in response to an open-ended question about the best thing about their congregation on our 2016 LRCS survey of members, a respondent wrote, "Pastor strongly believes in community involvement." The strongest effect size in our model is belonging to a community group at the congregation, which is in line with the literature on the value of making connections through small groups at congregations (Djupe and Gilbert 2009; Hussey 2020).

Our model also shows a small but significant negative effect for hours of service given outside one's congregation. This finding indicates that the more one serves outside one's congregation, the less warmly one feels toward it. If we were to imagine our hypothetical Ms. Mary in this situation, if she were to give no service outside her congregation, her predicted feelings of warmth toward it would be 0.79 on a rescaled 0 to 1 scale of congregational warmth. If she were to dedicate fifteen or more hours a month to volunteering at, say, the local animal shelter caring for lost cats, Ms. Mary's feelings of warmth toward her congregation would decline by about 10 percent to 0.69. Why might this be? It is possible that Ms. Mary's hours of service outside her congregation are service done on her own. She isn't spending time with any members of her congregation when she is at the animal shelter. There are opportunity costs to volunteering, and Ms. Mary might be missing out on congregation events or Wednesday night Bible study because of her volunteering. This doesn't make her dislike her congregation; she is just missing opportunities to grow closer to them that other people, who are aren't spending as much time volunteering outside the congregation, are having.

When we encounter a statistical finding like this one that may be difficult to understand, bringing in qualitative data to provide context is a great way to improve our understanding—in this case, of how service affects congregational warmth. For instance, many clergy already seem to know the importance of engagement. At the "Time and Talents" fair at Second Presbyterian Church, each person receives a welcome message from the pastor, saying, in part, that "churches with high member involvement are places where people make friends and form community that is a gift to the church and to the member."

During the COVID-19 pandemic, building a sense of congregational connection became even more important for many places of worship. At a community service event one day, I began talking with a volunteer who had joined her congregation just a few weeks before things shut down in the spring of 2020. "I don't think I've ever felt so immediately a part of something," she said, in speaking about her congregation and the kinds of community service activities they continued to do throughout the pandemic. Her experience illustrates how having a community-engaged congregation helps create that congregational warmth, even in the most trying circumstances.

In talking with members, our research team heard so many great stories about building congregational community while serving. For instance, one member told us about how their church participated in a program with the Arkansas Food Bank to assist seniors by delivering food boxes to them. As she tells it:

> There was a lady from our church who is quite a bit older than I was and she wanted to participate, but she couldn't drive anymore. So, we worked it out that I went by and picked her up and we would go. And we developed just a wonderful friendship and relationship out of that, and it was something as simple as driving to the bank and making a few deliveries, but it's a very special feeling—not only helping those who are receiving it, but making those relationships with people who are looking for companionship and community.

Another member expressed how serving together in the community helps deepen the quality of friendships and relationships with other congregation members: "It is exciting when there is more to it than just the same theological views. There is something deeper, more substantial to hang your friendships on." A volunteer at another church similarly talked about building friendships through service, saying, "I enjoy feeding the homeless. We have four ladies that have been working together for some time. I enjoy the camaraderie with them. I enjoy working with them. We have a lot of fun and we're still helping someone. It's just a good feeling to be able to do something like this."

My conversation with one member really illustrated the reciprocal relationship between congregational warmth and service in a beautiful way. In speaking about the church community where she said she had developed lifelong friendships, she said, "Not only did we go to church together, but we were personal friends, our kids were friends with their kids—that also draws you in to want to serve, and give, and be part of that overall situation. You are in it together. . . . You are so interconnected it makes you want to give and participate in the church. It makes you want to give back."

Thus, the qualitative data indicate that the key to developing congregational warmth through service seems to be serving *together* as a congregation. To look at this from another angle, we return again to the quantitative data to model both service to congregations and service outside of congregations and compare the differences. When we are talking about service to the congregation here, we are thinking of things like volunteering for fellowship events, setting up chairs for a shared meal, or vacuuming the worship hall. Service outside the congregation might be anything from participating in a litter pickup to serving on the PTA. It is the recipient of the service that is the key difference here. Is the respondent serving at their place of worship or somewhere else?

The full models are available in Table C.13 in the appendix, but the variables that are significant predictors of service in each context are presented in Table 4.3, illustrating some key similarities and differences between service to and service outside of congregations.

The first variable under comparison in Table 4.3 is reciprocal service. In the model of service to congregations, service outside of congregations is included, and vice versa. Importantly, the two kinds of service significantly predict one another. One way of thinking about service is that it is a finite resource. For every hour of service a member gives *outside* the congregation, that is one less hour of service available to give *to* the congregation. These results suggest that this zero-sum mentality is not an accurate way to think about service. Instead, service in either capacity increases the likelihood of service in the other. Service begets service.

When it comes to the community variables, belonging to a community group at the congregation is a positive and significant predictor of service in both contexts; however, community engagement and hearing community sermons only significantly predicts service outside the congregation, not service to the congregation.

Interestingly, the two religion measures affect the two different service dependent variables differently. Increased attendance leads to more service

TABLE 4.3 VARIABLES PREDICTING SERVICE TO CONGREGATIONS AND SERVICE OUTSIDE OF CONGREGATIONS

Service to the congregation			Service outside the congregation		
Variable	Direction	Significant?	Variable	Direction	Significant?
Service outside the congregation	Positive	Yes	Service to the congregation	Positive	Yes
Belonging to a community group at congregation	Positive	Yes	Belonging to a community group at congregation	Positive	Yes
Community engagement	—	No	Community engagement	Positive	Yes
Community sermons	—	No	Community sermons	Positive	Yes
Political sermons	Negative	Yes	Political sermons	—	No
Attendance	Positive	Yes	Attendance	—	No
Religiosity	—	No	Religiosity	Positive	Yes
Giving	Positive	Yes	Giving	—	No
Congregation warmth	—	No	Congregation warmth	Negative	Yes
Ideological diversity	Positive	Yes	Ideological diversity	—	No

to the congregation—a relationship we first saw in the previous section. A close connection to the congregation through service leads to more attendance, so it is no surprise that more attendance leads to a desire to serve. Of course, attending worship services provides more opportunities to be asked to serve, as well. Increased giving also leads to more congregational service. But the religiosity measure is positively associated with service both to the congregation and outside the congregation. Greater time spent in prayer and scripture reading leads to greater service in general, no matter the recipient.

The ideological diversity variable is associated with more service to the congregation but not outside the congregation. The finding that greater ideological diversity increases service is in line with our broader argument that congregations are a place where people can interact with those who believe differently from them, performing an important function for democracy.

Finally, Table 4.3 lists two variables with negative effects on service. For congregational service, political sermons tend to discourage it, perhaps because they are seen as polarizing. This finding supports the idea that there may be a trade-off between political and community engagement. Indeed, research indicates that most congregations choose to specialize in one or the other when it comes to engagement (Glazier 2019a). The second significant and negative variable for service outside the congregation is congregational warmth. This result might be more helpfully read as warmer congregations, or those that are more tight knit, as being less likely to engage in external community service, perhaps because they are more focused inward on caring for and serving their own members in a close community.

When we look at the correlation between political sermons and service to the congregation, it is only 0.05, so there isn't a substantive bivariate relationship there. No strong direct effect is happening. Contrast that with belonging to a community group at the congregation, which is correlated with service to the congregation at 0.32, a much stronger direct relationship. Looking at the overall picture presented by the quantitative data, hours of service given to a congregation may be best explained through some combination of religious commitment to serving itself, strength of connection to the congregation, and being present often enough to be asked. It is somewhat surprising that the congregation warmth variable is not significant in this model, but it may be a combined effect of the other variables accounting for congregational warmth and political sermons accounting for its opposite.

Although Table 4.3 neatly divides service to and service outside of congregations, when clergy and volunteers talk about the link between congregational and community service, they sometimes talk about how the line dividing the two can get blurry. Take, for instance, Pastor Shirlee, the congregational care minister at Saint Mark, who ministers not just to the sick in the church but to their families and friends. For him, the congregation is much bigger than the walls of his church—it reaches much further into the community. People will call him and say, "My friend is in the hospital, will you come pray over him?" As Pastor Shirlee describes it, Saint Mark wants them to know that "your family is our family" so that feeling of congregational warmth stretches beyond the church and into the community. He shares a story of driving more than two and a half hours to Memphis for the funeral of a congregation member's grandson who had been murdered. She didn't know he was coming, and as he tells it, "The look on her face to see me, representing Saint Mark, and coming to Memphis, to support her was priceless. And the beautiful part about it, not only did I show up, I was asked to officiate the Family Hour and provide words of comfort and prayer for the family, praying for the family. That was my real sense of fulfillment, if you will, in terms of: this is what I have been called to do."

The most important message for congregations to take away from this section is that the data don't support a service trade-off. Whether it is service to the congregation or service out in the community, service is self-reinforcing. Once people get serving, it creates in them a heart to serve. And for many congregations, that is what they want to foster in their members. Serving together is what leads to a close and flourishing congregation. In what might be a somewhat surprising finding to some, volunteering is especially important to younger members. Those who were born after 1980, Millennials and Gen Zers, are statistically significantly more likely to give service to their congregation (4.05, compared to 3.81, on a 1 to 5 scale) and outside their congregation (3.93, compared to 3.82, on a 1 to 5 scale) than other generational cohorts. In our 2020 LRCS survey, when we asked about willingness to volunteer on a variety of community issues, it was younger respondents who were significantly more likely to say they would volunteer for most issues, a finding discussed in more depth in Chapter 5. If places of worship want to attract younger members, offering meaningful opportunities for service is a great start.

Community Engagement Leads to Spiritually Flourishing Members

Chapter 3 presented data to demonstrate that community engagement has many benefits for individual members, including spiritual benefits. For instance, higher levels of community engagement predicted feeling closer to God today than a year ago and feeling God's love more often. These are the kinds of spiritual experiences that most clergy want for their members. They want the members of their congregations to be developing deep and rich spiritual lives for important theological reasons and also so that they can contribute to the spiritual life of the congregational community.

In addition to the individual spiritual benefits presented in Chapter 3, in this section we look at some further measures to assess the spiritual benefits of community engagement. These are benefits that accrue not just to individuals but aggregate up to the congregation. Take, for instance, the first variable that we examine: religiosity.

In these data, we measure private religiosity with a combination of two questions: one about frequency of prayer and one about frequency of reading holy texts, like scriptures. Many measures of religiosity also include attendance, but as we already examined attendance separately and are more interested in personal devotional religious measures here, we exclude attendance. The full question wording and summary statistics are available in Appendix A. Most clergy probably want higher levels of religiosity among their members for its own sake—they see it as good for the members' souls—but as the models in this chapter have already demonstrated, religiosity is also associated with higher levels of worship service attendance, more generous giving, and greater service outside the congregation. A more religious membership is pretty good in all kinds of ways for a congregation.

Our statistical model of religiosity shows that higher levels of community engagement and belonging to a community group at one's congregation both predict greater religiosity (full model results are presented in Table C.14 in the appendix). Religious variables, like providential religious beliefs—believing that God has a plan that you can help bring about—and attending worship services more frequently, are the strongest predictors in this model, but even when they are accounted for, community engagement still has a significant influence on religiosity.

Because our Clergy Advisory Board was interested in having more questions about the spiritual well-being of members on the 2020 survey, we have an additional way to assess how members are doing spiritually through the question: "How often do you feel a deep sense of spiritual peace and well-being?" Response options range from "Never or almost never" (1) to "Several times a day" (7). Full question wording and summary statistics are in Table A.1 in the appendix. As a deep sense of spiritual peace and well-being is something that most clergy want for their congregations, we ran a statistical model to see how community engagement might influence such feelings, with the full model results in Table C.15 in the appendix.

The key community engagement finding to emerge from this model is that the more service one gives outside their congregation, the more likely they are to express feeling a deep sense of spiritual peace and well-being. For our hypothetical average respondent, Ms. Mary, that means that if she gives no service outside of her congregation, she will feel a deep sense of spiritual peace at a score of about 4.9 on a 1 to 7 scale, or on the high end of "At least once a week." If she gives fifteen or more hours a month to serving outside her congregation, however, she is predicted to feel that spiritual peace at a score of 5.3, or solidly into the "Most days" territory.

The full model results, presented in Table C.15 in the appendix, show that being at a smaller congregation, having higher levels of private religiosity (prayer and scripture reading), being older, and being Black are also associated with more regularly feeling a deep sense of spiritual peace and well-being. But the finding about service is the one that is particularly interesting for our research here, and it is bolstered by the qualitative data as well.

Take, for instance, Pastor Phillip Pointer of Saint Mark Baptist Church, who regularly tells his congregation that it is "more blessed to give than to receive" and then is also quick to point out that he is just echoing the sentiments of Jesus and sharing his own personal experiences as he encourages them to give. In speaking of the community projects of Saint Mark in particular, Pastor Pointer says, "Those who are involved in our outreach efforts, in Tendaji, in things like the Restoration Project, they benefit, but it also buoys our communal sense of well-being and satisfaction. We have better church when the Restoration Project is going on. I believe it is a spiritual law."

From clergy and congregants alike, we heard about how community engagement, especially offering service and relief to those most in need, was a spiritual practice, even a form of worship. As one member said:

> It is essential to the church, for the longevity of the church, otherwise it becomes about programs and children's programs and daycare, and the church is just competing with shallow things that are offered everywhere. There is a substance and an awareness of God's presence that you miss out on if you don't go experience it with people who are truly suffering. There is something about doing it with other people. It becomes a form of worship that you can't experience otherwise.

One interesting finding from our data is that none of the religious traditions is significantly more community involved, based on means of member involvement, than any other. Nor is there any statistically significant difference in terms of the number of social programs offered, based on the 2018 LRCS clergy survey ($n = 112$). Although some research indicates that there are differences in levels of engagement across religious traditions—for instance, evangelicals are less likely to engage (Beyerlein and Hipp 2006; Chaves and Tsitsos 2001; Driskell, Lyon, and Embry 2008) and Black Protestants have a historical and cultural tradition of engagement (Barnes 2005; Chaves and Higgins 1992; Pattillo-McCoy 1998)—we don't see differences in engagement here. There may be important reasons why there aren't distinctions in terms of community engagement across religious tradition in the LRCS data.

First, some of these historical differences may be fading. For instance, evangelicals are increasingly engaging (Djupe and Gwiasda 2010; Fulton 2016; Kerley et al. 2010; Mulder and Jonason 2017; Steensland and Goff 2013), the distinction between worldly and otherworldly orientations among congregations is fading (McRoberts 2003), and community engagement has become almost institutionalized (Fulton 2016). Take this statement, from an evangelical pastor in California, who says that when he was younger, the messaging was mostly about how churches "should stay out of politics." But the view has changed over time. He goes on to say, "Now it seems almost a sin not to get involved" (quoted in Friedland 1998, 241). Previous multimethod analysis of clergy interviews from the LRCS ($n = 64$) regarding how they view their community engagement reveals that a significant minority (about one-third) see their engagement as intimately connected to their religious practice; they see no difference between the material and the spiritual (Glazier and Street 2020), with no significant differences by religious tradition.

Additionally, the unique nature of the LRCS data may contribute to muting some differences that do still exist. Our definition of community engagement is expansive and includes efforts that might be considered by some more religious than social service oriented. For instance, we included marriage and family counseling as a social service on our 2018 survey of clergy and also left space for clergy to tell us about additional social programs or services they provided. Some filled in services like "grief counseling," "anger management," and "spiritual guidance." Because the clergy counted these as social programs, we counted them as social programs.

Similarly, the congregations who opted into participating in our 2020 survey of congregation members, and the individual members of the congregations who completed the surveys, may be more community involved than other members of the congregation, so some response bias may mute differences across religious traditions, as well. However, Table 2.3 in Chapter 2 provides the distribution of respondents across religious traditions in our sample, indicating a diverse respondent base. Additionally, if the most engaged people are responding from each congregation, and if there are fundamental differences in the levels of engagement across religious traditions, there should be different baselines for the most engaged people in different religious traditions. But we don't see these differences by religious tradition. Thus, one tentative conclusion to draw from the data in this chapter and the broader study is that religious tradition matters less than we might expect when it comes to community engagement. All kinds of congregations are engaged in their communities. This engagement may look different for different faith traditions, but no single tradition is opting out of engagement. Indeed, the LRCS data indicates that all traditions are benefiting from engagement.

Linking Community Engagement and Congregational Benefits

As both the qualitative and quantitative data have shown, community engagement has many benefits for congregations. The benefits we have outlined are directly derived from the data of the LRCS, but we could imagine, and research supports, other benefits as well. For instance, community engagement leads to reputational benefits for the congregation, future partnership opportunities, and perhaps even evangelism benefits (Ammerman 2001; Mulder and Jonason 2017; Owens 2008). Figure 4.3 attempts the somewhat daunting task of capturing the directional influence of how exactly the different community-minded behaviors congregations and their members might engage in influence specific outcomes that are beneficial to the congregations themselves. Fair warning, there are a lot of directional arrows in Figure 4.3.

On the left-hand side of the figure, we have the community-centered behaviors. There are many ways that congregations influence the community engagement of individuals, including through overt ways like delivering community-oriented sermons or creating small groups that are specifically designed to address community issues (both of which are community-centered behaviors listed on the left-hand side of Figure 4.3).

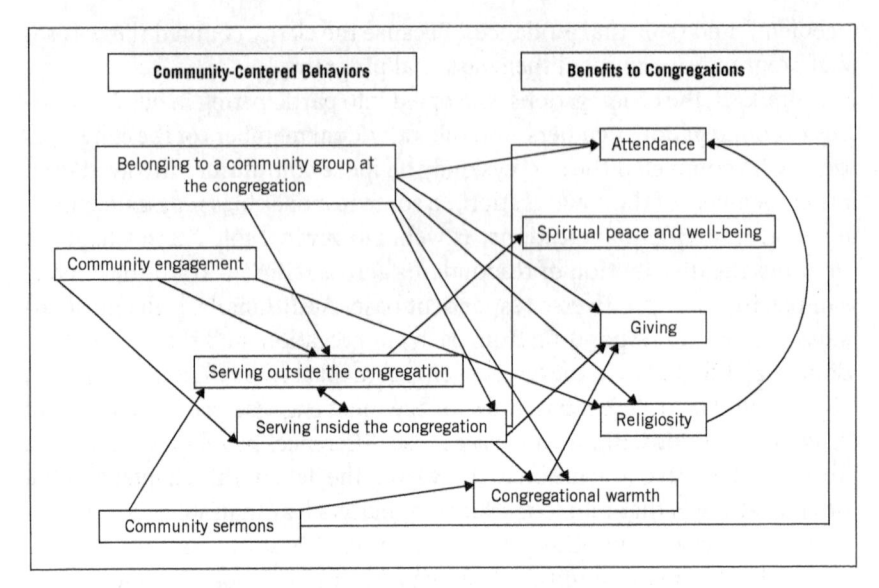

Figure 4.3 How Community-Centered Behaviors Benefit Congregations

On the right-hand side of the figure are the benefits to congregations—everything from higher attendance to members who have greater spiritual peace and well-being. Congregational warmth is slightly offset, holding a place that is somewhat in the middle, because it serves as a kind of mediating variable. Community sermons, service to the congregation, and belonging to a congregational community group all contribute to greater congregational warmth, which in turn contributes to greater giving. Service inside the congregation is also more toward the middle space because, while we have been counting it as a community-centered behavior because it is service, it also directly benefits the congregation.

If one looks too long at Figure 4.3, it can start to look like a pile of spaghetti noodles all tangled up. The main messages we hope readers take away from it, and the reason we wanted to visually represent the relationships between community engagement and congregational benefits, are twofold. First, the many community-centered behaviors reinforce one another. On the left-hand side of the figure alone, many of the variables influence and strengthen each other. Second, there are many paths by which community engagement benefits congregations. Seeing so many directional arrows tells us that there are lots of ways that congregations benefit from the many forms that community engagement can take. The resulting figure may not be very pretty, but the complexity itself is part of the point. These two concepts—community engagement and congregational benefits—are closely intertwined in many different ways.

To see what this looks like in practice—how a place of worship actually benefits from their engagement in the community—we take a close look at one Little Rock congregation that has focused their engagement efforts on inclusion and racial justice: Second Baptist Church Downtown.

2BC: Second Baptist Church Downtown

The desegregation crisis of the 1950s came to Little Rock with a fury that left scars that linger to the present day. Most white churches at the time were firmly on the side of segregation. Second Baptist Church Downtown, one of a handful of "Second Baptist" churches in a city full of churches and affectionately known as 2BC, was an exception in 1957 and remains exceptional today. Second Baptist Church Downtown took the side of integration in 1957, when it was profoundly unpopular among white Christians in Little Rock, and committed the church to the work of racial justice and reconciliation—both inside and out. It is this legacy that has come to form a core component of the identity of 2BC today.

Although Second Baptist Church Downtown remains a majority-white congregation, the history of the church's work on racial justice is something they are proud of. As one member described it to me, "The spirit of this is in our bones, and it drives our worldview as we move forward." In 2018, the church partnered with Arkansas Baptist College, one of the three historically Black colleges and universities (HBCUs) in Little Rock, for a Wednesday night lecture series, "Race in the Rock," on the history of racism in the Christian church in America. The series was based on Rev. Dr. Jemar Tisby's book *The Color of Compromise: The Truth about the American Church's Complicity in Racism* and featured Tisby as a speaker. Alternating between locations at 2BC and Arkansas Baptist College, this series engaged church members, college students, and the broader community in challenging conversations about history, practices, and beliefs that continue to this day.

This lecture series came about, in part, because, in the summer of 2018, the lead pastor of 2BC, Preston Clegg, took a thirteen-week sabbatical, which he used to study systemic racism. This sabbatical was funded by the Lily Foundation in part because of 2BC's legacy of engagement in racial justice. Pastor Clegg's continuation of that legacy was natural, but his appointment as the lead pastor in 2013 and the sabbatical to study systemic racism are seen by both pastor and congregation as key points in the life of the church when racial justice became more prominent.

Thus, the leadership and the congregation of 2BC had already prioritized race relations in a city divided by race when the murder of George Floyd rocked the nation during the summer of 2020. Many churches found their attendance waning during this time because of the pandemic. Local and national racial strife added another complicating element, one that some would prefer to avoid. One member who came to 2BC in recent years spoke about feeling confused and frustrated by the silence in her church circles during this time before her move to 2BC and recalled feeling that "we need to address this" but being told "that's way too divisive." At 2BC, the view is quite different; racial justice is very much seen as a religious issue. Sermons from the time not only note the connection between faith and justice but also call for that justice to be deep and profound and soul stretching.

Following George Floyd's murder, Pastor Clegg preached, "The protesters all over this country are saying 'No justice, no peace.' And that's not just a yearning and a heart cry, it's just a matter of fact. We will never be in the stratosphere of God's peace, so long as we're apart from justice." Pastor Clegg called on the members of 2BC to not only believe but to act, saying, "If we are faithful in this work, church, then our very lives might be something of a revelation from God and the day might just come when everything is prayer and praise and all God's children look each other in their eyes as equals." These are faith-filled, even prophetic, words of hope directed to a topic that was tearing open a city and a nation.

During this summer of racial discontent, city leaders, law enforcement officers, and others reached out to 2BC. As Pastor Clegg said in a sermon on June 14, 2020, "All of them have begged me and Second Baptist Church to let our light shine brightly in these days. I intend to, I know we intend to, and the gospel of Christ demands nothing short of us. . . . And let us be praying over how we as a church might be a redemptive influence in our city and beyond, in the days and weeks to come. We're also going to think about how our church can be advocates publicly for racial justice, how our voice can be leveraged for the good of all people in our city, and how we might bear witness to the way of Jesus in these days."

Additionally, the deacons of 2BC approved a formal and public statement on the church's stance regarding systemic racism. The statement includes specific religious language about repentance but also enumerates policy priorities, like removing Confederate monuments, teaching about African American history in schools, and increasing funding for public defenders. Throughout, racial justice reforms are supported with religious language. For instance, calls to reform the justice system include the statement, "Because we believe the Gospel of Jesus releases captives rather than perpetuates their captivity, we believe that the criminal justice system needs a massive repurposing" (2). And in the section on social reforms, there is a paragraph that reads: "Whereas the biblical notion of repentance—as illustrated in the story of Zacchaeus (Luke 19:1–9)—involves correction and not just contrition, restitution instead of merely remorse, we ask our state legislators to begin working with the

Black Legislative Caucus to study and recommend a course for reparations for the state of Arkansas" (5).

The commitment to racial justice is long term at 2BC. Pastors preach on the topic and urge members to protest, and in 2020 they even worked with Arkansas Baptist College to establish a fund for Black entrepreneurs with a $150,000 gift. Although Second Baptist Church remains a majority-white congregation, Pastor Clegg says they are "trying to justice our way to diversity" instead of "trying to diversify our way to justice," and he says he regularly asks the Lord why the work is going so slowly.

It is clearly work that matters across the board at 2BC. Whereas some congregations hesitate to get involved in what might be viewed as political or hot-button issues, for 2BC, racial justice is their legacy, and advocating for it fits naturally with their theology. One member of the Deaconate, a third-generation member at 2BC, said that racial justice work is just "following Jesus . . . there is a very clear scriptural mandate . . . it's not optional, in my opinion."

Pastor Clegg says that he saw new members coming to 2BC in recent years because, after the murder of George Floyd, "their churches were conspicuously silent and they couldn't stay there any longer." They were hungering for a church with something to say about matters of social justice related to Jesus. Pastor Clegg said, "Here are people who are in the pews at Second right now, because in the pandemic their church had nothing to say about racial justice when everyone else in the world was talking about it." One such member told me about nearly feeling done with church because of hypocrisy and disconnection from people who are really suffering at the margins but then finding 2BC and realizing "I don't have to settle. . . . I don't have to quit church altogether."

I spoke with one of these members, who told me about feeling disillusioned with her church experience because of the lack of response following George Floyd's murder and also because of how they handled LGBTQ issues. A friend told her about 2BC, and when she checked out the website, she liked what she saw right away because "they were bold about inclusion [and] racial justice." She felt like her church and private Christian school were more worried about offending big donors than speaking the truth, which, as she put it, goes against "all the things that I had been raised to believe and understand about Jesus Christ and how he treats people." She didn't find that cognitive dissonance at 2BC, where the church lived out the example of what she saw in Christ's life of loving and advocating for the marginalized.

Another recent member at 2BC told a similar story of wanting to find a new kind of church: "We really felt strongly about an inclusive culture. Racial inclusivity was a big part of that, but LGBTQ was a part of that, too." The first

Sunday they attended 2BC was during the pandemic, and the services were held outdoors on a beautiful fall day at Lake Nixon. And Rev. Dr. Jemar Tisby was a guest speaker. This new member told me they had been looking for a place "where there is a seat for everyone and I feel like that is what we found."

The kind of high-profile engagement 2BC has with political or controversial issues may not be the right fit for every congregation. But for 2BC, racial justice is very much a religious and moral issue. Pastor Clegg says, "My convictions about racial justice are intrinsic to my faith. I don't know how to separate those." On the Sunday of Juneteenth in 2022, Rev. Dr. Jemar Tisby returned to 2BC, this time to preach a sermon. The sermon he preached was about "Freedom as Rest," and he explicitly connected spirituality with racial justice, saying at one point, "Maybe, brothers and sisters, when we struggle to feel freedom, when we struggle to experience freedom, maybe that's because there's a lack of the presence of the Spirit in our lives." He pointed to the passages that Jesus chose to read to announce his ministry, taken from Isaiah 58 and 61, which are recounted in Luke 4. Reverend Tisby called for these passages, about letting the oppressed go free and proclaiming liberty to the captives, to not just be spiritualized. That is not how Isaiah meant them, that is not how Jesus meant them, and that is not how we should treat them. Just like Reverend Tisby, Pastor Clegg sees a deep spiritual connection between racial justice and faith, saying that his "faith demands, not just invites, but demands that I see the work of racial justice as faith-based work. Not as an appendix to it, not as something that is a liberal tack-on to the faith, but as something that is intrinsic to my faith."

Centering the issue of racial justice in the life of the church means that it comes up in many sermons—not just the Sunday before Martin Luther King Jr. Day. It means that 2BC has many partnerships in the community. They held a joint service with a major Black Protestant church, Saint Mark Baptist Church (featured as a case study in Chapter 6), for Juneteenth. Upon leaving the joint service, some members of 2BC were heard to say that "this is what the Kingdom of God feels like." It means working with the Little Rock Police Department to host one of a series of "Courageous Conversations" about violence in the city, partnering with the Mosaic Templars for panel discussions, and Pastor Clegg receiving the Racial Justice Trailblazer Award from the Cooperative Baptist Fellowship.

The growing emphasis on racial justice in recent years has built on and strengthened the legacy that was already at 2BC. In late September 2022, the church held a retreat for members, especially all the new members, to get to know each other. The theme for the retreat was "Continuing the Legacy of 2BC." The same fervor that motivated the church in 1957 remains to this day, but the understanding of the nature of racism today is much more structural. It is more than just interpersonal relationships. And the congregation at 2BC is growing—in their understanding, advocacy, and numbers. Some members at 2BC even talk about the pandemic as a "blessing in disguise" for the congregation because it enabled services to be held both in person and online, so some members of the community "who didn't know about 2BC were able to find out about it online and join us."

The congregation today is more inclusive in a number of ways than it was even a decade ago. Printed in the worship service programs is a statement reading, "Because our identity is found in Christ, we welcome all people, regardless of race, gender, gender identity, sexual orientation, marital status, physical and mental ability, and nationality into full participation in the life of this congregation." The result has been an influx of members who want to engage on social justice issues, including race and LGBTQ issues. Because 2BC has spoken out, they have lost some members, even long-standing members, but those who remained say that what has been gained—both qualitatively and quantitatively—outweighs what has been lost.

No congregation exists in a vacuum. The particular history that Second Baptist Church Downtown has, in the particular city that it inhabits, with the particular pastor that currently leads it, all come together to create a church that is active and engaged on racial justice issues. For 2BC, it is not political; it is very much religious. Some of the solutions may be policy solutions because the problems of racism are systemic, but racism is spoken of as a sin, as "an affront to the image of God in all people," as Pastor Clegg puts it. He goes on to say that "I like to frame racism and racial justice as redemptive work, that is, to recover the image of God in all people, or . . . to recover our ability to see the image of God in all people." This is spiritual work at 2BC; as they are engaged in the community, they are growing the spiritual lives of their members.

Conclusion

There are many reasons why congregations should prioritize community engagement. This chapter demonstrated, through statistical models and qualitative data, that doing so directly benefits congregations. Some congregation leaders may be concerned that if they encourage their members to get involved in community service and community projects, those members won't have the time or energy left to help out with the church fish fry or set up chairs for the Iftar meal. Our data suggests just the opposite. Table 4.3 shows that there is no trade-off at all between community and congregational service. In fact, the two predict one another. Congregations with higher outside service also have higher inside service. When congregations get involved in serving the community, they are creating a culture of service that leads to higher overall levels of service. By prioritizing community engagement through hosting community groups and giving community sermons, congregations will also see stronger attendance numbers, places of worship that feel warmer and more welcoming, and members who are spiritually strong. In short, the payoffs of community engagement are significant for congregations.

As one leader put it in an interview, "A church's desire to live in perpetuity means you need to be cultivating relationships with those outside of your congregation. So, I think embedded in the very faith itself, is community engagement. I think people bring those partnerships to the pews, and then take the church into their other spheres of belonging when they leave. And then I think it's in the church's best interest to have community engagement to outlive itself."

5

How Engagement Helps Democracy

On the third Tuesday of each month, the fellowship hall of Life Line Baptist Church is filled with around sixty business, religious, and community leaders from Southwest Little Rock. On the third Tuesday of September 2022, folks started arriving about ten minutes before noon, signing in at the door and making donations for a lunch of fried chicken, salad, veggies, potatoes, a roll, dessert, and, of course, sweet tea. Attendees were welcomed by the pastor of Life Line Baptist Church and organizer of the lunch, Pastor Jeff Dial, who begins by telling everyone that "community is communicating unity, so let's do that today." Every lunch begins with prayer and the Pledge of Allegiance, followed by reports from local schools, updates from elected officials on any rezoning or political matters, crime numbers from the police department, announcements of community events, and a real estate report. There is also a featured speaker at each lunch—today it is Principal Nancy Russo of Little Rock's Central High School, as the desegregation anniversary is around the corner—and new attendees are invited to stand and introduce themselves.

The monthly lunches at Life Line Baptist Church are a great example of how engagement benefits the community. During this one hour, attendees learn about political, safety, business, and community updates across their section of the city of Little Rock. Judges might speak and urge people to fulfill jury duty if they get a summons. The fire marshal might talk about vacant buildings and whom to contact if something dangerous is happening in one. Crime is an especially big concern in Little Rock. In our 2020 survey, 84.2

percent of respondents said that crime was an important or very important issue to them. Homicides were almost twice as high in 2022 as in 2018 (81 in 2022 compared to 42 in 2018) (Little Rock Police Department 2023). At this very lunch, the police were questioned about a homicide that took place just down the street from the church only two days earlier. When the police finished giving their report and reminded people "if you see something, say something, call the police," along with their nonemergency number, Pastor Dial asked everyone to repeat the number together and implored, "The police can't do it on their own, and we've got to work together to make, especially Southwest Little Rock, a better place to live, and police help us with that."

The spirit of unity at the Life Line lunch brings something intangible to the community of Southwest Little Rock. Pastor Dial and the people who come together for these lunches are making connections with one another, staying informed on community issues, and developing a real sense that they are in this together as a community. Alexis de Tocqueville considered religion "the first of [America's] political institutions" (1969, 292), and the monthly lunches are one means by which religion is present in many facets of community and political life in Little Rock. One reason for this strong presence is Pastor Dial's outreach to the business community. The lunches at Life Line are not just for clergy and community leaders. He even invited the local liquor store to attend. The Edwards Food Giant grocery store down the street attends and helps sponsor Life Line's trunk-or-treat event for the community on Halloween. With the police also helping out, Pastor Dial announces that it will be "the safest place to be Halloween night." The feeling at the Life Line lunches is that they are all one community and have to work together. Life Line is helping facilitate that positive impact.

It can be relatively easy to see the impact that congregational community engagement has through the direct social services that places of worship provide via food programs or job-placement services. But the positive impact of congregational community engagement is so much broader than direct service provision. This chapter shows how the benefits of engagement that flow to individuals and places of worship aggregate to make for a healthier and more robust democracy.

Aggregating the Benefits of Engagement

The LRCS mostly measures the benefits of community engagement at the individual level; we survey and have conversations with individual leaders and individual congregants. But just as Chapter 4 showed that there are some individual benefits that actually benefit the whole congregation, there are also some individual benefits that end up helping communities and societies, as well. Two such benefits are particularly important for a well-functioning democracy: social capital and political efficacy.

Social capital is about the connections between people—the social networks that bond similar people and bridge diverse people (Dekker and Uslaner 2003). This academic concept was popularized by Robert Putnam's (2000) book *Bowling Alone*, which argued that the decline of voluntary associations in America, like bowling leagues, along with other changes, contributed to a dramatic drop in social capital. The result is a much more disconnected society, with negative outcomes for democracy—fewer petitions signed, less political engagement, and lower voter turnout.

Social capital is important for democracy because it is the basis for a great deal of cooperation, trust, and reciprocity (Putnam 1993); thus, social capital is central to how modern economies and liberal democracies run (Fukuyama 2001; Kenworthy 1997). Social capital contributes to greater political participation (La Due Lake and Huckfeldt 1998) and better community governance (Bowles and Gintis 2002). Social capital can have a dark side, however. When communities are closely bonded, they can become insular and even restrictive (Portes 1998). Despite the potential for these drawbacks, most people agree that social capital is a public good worth pursuing.

Social capital is about the relationships among individuals; a society high in social capital is one where people know their neighbors, trust that favors will be returned, and have dense networks of friends and colleagues. Such well-connected societies are normatively good—the people living in them are more optimistic and satisfied with their lives—but they are also better for democracy, as the people in them are better informed, more connected to the functions of government, and more likely to be politically involved (Narayan and Cassidy 2001). Thus, the benefits of social capital extend far beyond individuals.

Political efficacy is similarly both a personal and a public good. As first defined in Chapter 3, political efficacy is believing that one can make a difference and one's voice matters; it is believing that political change is possible and that one can be a part of making that change happen (Campbell, Gurin, and Miller 1954). And, just as with social capital, political efficacy is both important for democracy and on the decline.

When people believe they can contribute to political change, they are more likely to participate in politics through things like attending community meetings, signing petitions, or voting (Almond and Verba 1963; Uslaner 2002), and they may be less likely to go outside the political system by choosing to participate in violent extremism (Iqbal, O'Brien, and Bliuc 2022). With more people participating in politics (Abramson and Aldrich 1982; Rosenstone and Hansen 1993; Verba, Schlozman, and Brady 1995), the result is a positive feedback loop that leads to greater participation in the future (Finkel 1985), which can reinforce democratic stability if demands on the system remain reasonable.

Citizens' efficacy and political involvement also predict trust in government (Parent, Vandebeek, and Gemino 2005), something that is near historic lows in the United States in the early 2020s. Only 21 percent of Americans say they trust the government in Washington to do the right thing "just about always" (2 percent) or "most of the time" (19 percent) (Pew Research Center 2022b). More specific measures of efficacy are similarly discouraging. A recent Harvard Youth Poll (Harvard Kennedy School Institute of Politics 2022) showed that 36 percent of young people believe that "political involvement rarely has tangible results" and 42 percent believe that their vote "doesn't make a difference." The good news is that community engagement can make a positive difference in both social capital and political efficacy, in addition to making other contributions to society and democracy. The next section details those benefits.

Benefits to Society from Community Engagement

What can the data of the LRCS tell us about how community engagement contributes to these valuable concepts of social capital and political efficacy? We can look for ways that community engagement contributes to social capital and political efficacy in both qualitative and quantitative data, in addition to looking for other benefits of community engagement, like encouraging political participation.

Improving Social Capital

How do congregations contribute to social capital? Places of worship are often "social anchors" in the community, and as such they facilitate both bonding social capital within their membership and bridging social capital as they connect people across racial, economic, and gender lines (Clopton and Finch 2011; Putnam and Campbell 2012). Congregations bring people together for worship and fellowship; as they do so, they provide a space to build and grow social connections (Cnaan, Boddie, and Yancey 2003). Indeed, "no voluntary or cultural institution in American society gathers more people more regularly than religious congregations" (Chaves 2004, 1). Attendance at religious services leads to more connections and friendships (Schwadel et al. 2016), and people who have more friends at their places of worship are more likely to engage in both religious and secular civic activity (see also Lewis, MacGregor, and Putnam 2013; McClure 2015). Congregations are helping to build social capital by increasing trust and providing opportunities for people to make connections with their fellow citizens (Brown and Brown 2003; Cassel 1999; Putnam 2000). In fact, just the act of participating in worship itself can provide members with a pattern for life and how to act in the world—it establishes relationships with divinity and teaches them about character and virtue in a way that builds social capital (Bellah et al. 2007, 227).

There are many potential ways to measure social capital (for a review, see Claridge 2004). We begin by considering congregational warmth as a proxy. The congregational warmth measure, first introduced in Chapter 4, is a single measure made up of combining agreement with four items from the 2020 LRCS survey of congregation members. These items are what social capital is about—connections and networks with other people—except for a question about the congregation meeting the respondents' spiritual needs. Thus, we dropped that item and are left with a new, three-item scale of congregational social capital:

- My congregation feels like family to me.
- I feel like an outsider in my congregation (reversed).
- I would be prepared to invite friends or relatives to a worship service here.

From our statistical model of this social capital measure, the results indicate that both hearing community sermons and belonging to a community group at one's congregation are associated with higher levels of congregational social capital. Providential religious believers also have higher levels, as do those who belong to congregations with higher average levels of congregational warmth. The results of the full model are in Table C.16 in the appendix. This new congregational social capital measure has been rescaled to run from 0 to 1, and if we calculate predicted probabilities, using an average congregation member, Ms. Mary, first introduced in Chapter 3, we can really see the effects of congregations on social capital. Ms. Mary is an average member from our 2020 sample: a white female, politically moderate, with average religiosity and political engagement. If she hears no community-minded sermons at her place of worship, she will have a congregational social capital score of 0.65 (on the 0 to 1 scale), but if she hears community-minded sermons frequently, her congregational social capital score rises to 0.82—a 26 percent increase. Being part of a community-oriented group at one's congregation has a smaller but also significant effect, increasing congregational social capital from 0.73 to 0.80.

These findings illustrate how mobilizing congregants to action in the community—through the congregation—can help bond the congregation itself. Importantly, our measure of social capital is focused on connections and networks *within* the congregation. Ideally, these would also lead to improved social capital beyond the congregation, but that is not something our quantitative data can capture. Interviews with clergy and volunteers, however, indicate that this process is at work in congregations.

Take, for instance, one Little Rock congregation that began an effort to connect with the community around their church and to provide food aid to those who were homebound. One volunteer told me about an elderly woman she regularly visited, saying, "Ms. Jenny[1] is always so appreciative. She always sticks five dollars in our hand and insists that we take it." When this church did a back-to-school event, Ms. Jenny brought her grandson, but by the time they arrived, all the school supplies had been distributed. Because the church volunteer had built a relationship with Ms. Jenny, she went out and bought a backpack, filled it with supplies, and dropped it off at Ms. Jenny's home for her grandson. This act of service came naturally because, as the volunteer said, "She's not just a lady on our walking route anymore; she's a friend. . . . I live right next to Walmart. It is not a big deal. And especially because we know her so well." Thus, social capital is growing within and beyond congregations as they prioritize community engagement.

Boosting Political Efficacy

The public is somewhat ambivalent about political involvement by places of worship, with one survey showing only 35 percent of Protestants saying congregations should keep out of political matters (Djupe 2019), while a nationally representative sample of U.S. adults shows an increasing number want houses of worship to keep out of politics—up to 70 percent in 2021 (Nortey and Lipka 2021). Despite this ambivalence, political efficacy is not partisan. In fact, many congregations are probably building political efficacy in their members without even knowing it. When members help organize social events, teach Sunday School, run meetings, or speak at gatherings, they are not only helping out their congregation, they are learning important civic skills and gaining a greater sense that their voice matters (Brady, Verba, and Schlozman 1995; Calhoun-Brown 1998; F. Harris 1994). Experimental studies have even shown that religious messages can directly increase political efficacy and political participation (McClendon and Riedl 2015).

We measure political efficacy through agreement with a battery of three questions, focused largely on community influence, first introduced in Chapter 3:

- Becoming involved in political or social issues is a good way to improve the community.

---

1. Name has been changed for privacy.

- Government is too complicated for me to understand (reversed).
- I believe that I can personally make a difference in my community.

In our statistical model of efficacy, both political and community activity predicted greater political efficacy, as did service outside one's congregation. Religiosity (more frequent prayer and scripture reading) and stronger feelings of warmth toward one's congregation also contribute to higher levels of political efficacy. The full model is available in Table C.7 in the appendix. Once again, we can see the substantive effects by turning to our hypothetical Ms. Mary. The political efficacy battery has been rescaled to run from 0 to 1. Moving Ms. Mary from the lowest level of community activity to the highest would change her predicted level of political efficacy from 0.54 to 0.86, or an over 59 percent increase in political efficacy. With this higher political efficacy, Ms. Mary and others like her will be more likely to vote, less likely to be cynical about and check out of their duties as citizens, and more likely to contribute to the health of democracy. Being part of a community-engaged congregation contributes to those benefits, which are collective goods that help society as a whole.

Encouraging Political Participation

More than teaching people civic skills and fostering social capital, can congregations directly encourage political participation? For decades, the research on religion and politics has shown that there is a positive relationship between religion and political participation. People who regularly attend worship services are more likely to be politically active—to vote, donate to candidates, and volunteer for campaigns (Beyerlein and Chaves 2003; Brady, Verba, and Schlozman 1995; F. Harris 1994; Hougland and Christenson 1983; Jones-Correa and Leal 2001; Liu, Austin, and Orey 2009; Macaluso and Wanat 1979; Norris 2013). Worship service attendance is also associated with participation in civic and community organizations (Beyerlein and Hipp 2006; Lewis, MacGregor, and Putnam 2013).

Beyond attending religious services, research also indicates that being active in small groups, participating in additional congregational activities, or taking on a lay leadership role at one's place of worship further encourages political and community engagement (Djupe and Gilbert 2006; Polson 2016; Sarkissian 2012; Sinha, Greenspan, and Handy 2011), with some variation by ethnicity (Djupe and Neiheisel 2012).

Just as with the other variables, we ran a statistical model of political participation. The full model results are available in Table C.17 in the appendix. Individual community engagement and education are the only positive and significant predictors of political participation in the model (holding providential religious beliefs and feeling ideologically close to fellow congregants both tend to decrease political participation).

Who participates in politics has significant consequences for the classic political science question of "who gets what when." Elected officials have no incentive to be responsive to people who don't vote, campaign, attend meetings, or write letters (Verba and Nie 1987). When citizens get involved in politics, especially on a local level, they feel more responsibility for public matters, see decisions as more legitimate, and listen to diverse opinions (Halvorsen 2003; Michels and De Graaf 2010). Political participation is good for democracy, and community engagement helps encourage it.

Some congregations are more invested in encouraging political participation than others. On Saturday, October 29, 2022—the first Saturday of early voting in the 2022 midterm elections in Arkansas—four Black Protestant congregations joined together to encourage their members to get out and vote. Clergy from Saint Mark Baptist Church, Second Baptist Church, Longley Baptist Church, and New Hope Baptist Church met at Parkview High School—an early voting location—and spoke to their gathered members about the importance of voting before casting their ballots. Some churches even provided rides to the polling location. LRCS researchers spoke with people at the event, who were excited to vote and felt like the churches were doing the right thing by encouraging voting. One said, "I feel like it's a responsibility of the church to inform, or not even inform, but *encourage* people to vote." Another person said, "I think it's important that congregations remind people of their social responsibility," and a third commented, "We have a civic responsibility to get out and take advantage of the right to vote. People fought for that, for that right."

Table 5.1 summarizes the societal benefits that aggregate from the community-oriented behaviors of individuals and congregations, as described in the prior models. Through community engagement—from sermons to serving—democracy and societies are strengthened.

TABLE 5.1 THE STATISTICALLY SIGNIFICANT BENEFITS TO SOCIETY OF COMMUNITY ENGAGEMENT	
Community-oriented behavior	Societal benefit
Community engagement (six-question battery)	More political participation
Community action (three questions from the six-question battery; only tested on efficacy)	Greater political efficacy
Hearing community sermons	Higher levels of congregational social capital
Serving outside the congregation	Greater political efficacy
Belonging to a community group at the congregation	Higher levels of congregational social capital

Providing Direct Social Services

The individual benefits of congregational community engagement "level up" to benefit communities and society as a whole, as we saw in the previous section with social capital, political efficacy, and political participation. But communities also receive direct social service benefits when congregations are engaged in the community. Consider the opening story about the monthly lunches at Life Line Baptist Church. People attending lunch in September heard about the community trunk-or-treat event the church hosted: a free event for anyone in the community to attend with their children on Halloween night. This example may seem somewhat fun or even frivolous, but many places of worship provide vital social services in communities—everything from marriage counseling to health fairs to after-school programs. Sometimes they step into the gap to provide a safety net when family or government are not able to do so.

Although the research presented in this book mostly focuses on individual-level data on how the benefits to individuals aggregate to congregations and society, other research has demonstrated that the social services congregations provide have significant and positive impacts on their communities (Cnaan, Sinha, and McGrew 2004). To take just two examples, church-based health promotion interventions are associated with better health outcomes (Campbell et al. 2007), and faith-based community substance abuse prevention programs lead to lower drug use among teens (Marcus et al. 2004).

Congregations that engage in these kinds of gap-filling social programs have been even more common in recent years due to two key factors: government support for faith-based social service provision and the COVID-19 pandemic. From the enactment of Charitable Choice legislation under President Clinton to the establishment of the White House Office of Faith-Based and Community Initiatives under President Bush, which was then repurposed as the Office of Faith-Based and Neighborhood Partnerships under President Obama (Levin 2014), government support for faith-based social service provision has continued to grow. This has provided resources and opportunities for religious organizations, including facilitating partnerships with nonprofit social service providers (Cnaan, Sinha, and McGrew 2004b). Additionally, the trust that places of worship hold in communities can be critical for meeting public needs and overcoming disparities. Take, for instance, COVID-19 vaccines. Public health messages from clergy and using congregations as vaccine distribution sites helped get more people vaccinated and also helped address racial disparities in vaccination rates (Dada et al. 2022).

In 2018, we surveyed clergy in Little Rock and asked them about the social services they provide. Of the 112 clergy who responded (of a total of 358 congregations in Little Rock, contacted via email, Facebook message, website form,

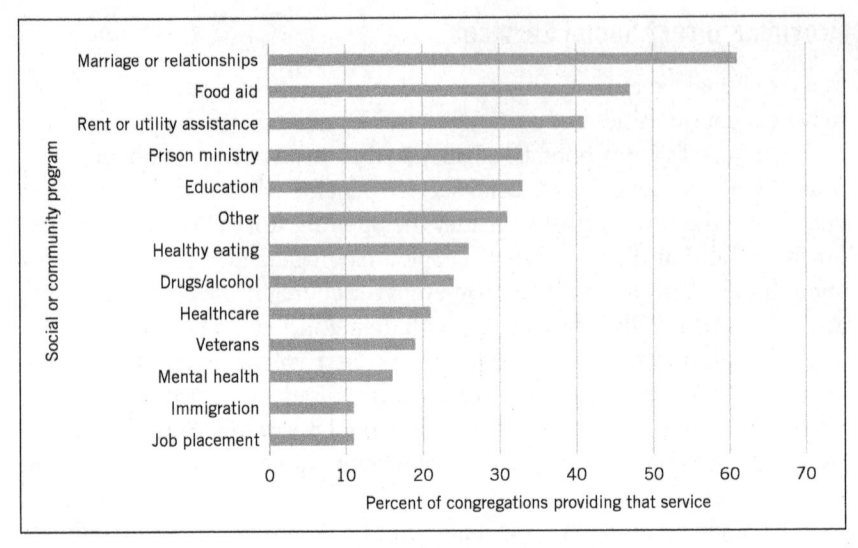

Figure 5.1 Social or Community Programs Provided by Little Rock Congregations, Percent Self-Reporting Providing Each, According to the 2018 LRCS Survey of Clergy

phone call, and mail, resulting in a 31 percent response rate), the average number of distinct social programs provided per congregation was 3.8 (standard deviation = 2.8). The most popular was marriage or relationship support, with 62 percent of all congregations reporting that they provided such support as a direct community program, followed by food aid at 47 percent. Figure 5.1 shows the programs provided by all of the congregations that responded to our 2018 survey.

The sixth most popular category of response is "Other," with more than 30 percent of congregations saying that they provide some other kind of community program. What do these services look like? Of the twenty-six clergy who told us about their "other" programs, seven (27 percent) had to do with families or foster care, five (19 percent) were programs for the homeless, four (15 percent) said they had no formal programs but tried to minister on a case-by-case basis, and three (11.5 percent) said their programs were spiritual or worship based.[2]

Our survey focusing specifically on social service provision was conducted before the COVID-19 pandemic, but we have reason to believe that community needs and congregation social service provision have both increased since the pandemic's onset in March 2020. For instance, a national study of

---

2. The remaining eight responses either fit into the prior categories (e.g., "hot meals" would be considered food aid and "diabetes" would be considered health care) or were not similar to any others (e.g., "transportation assistance").

thirty-eight Christian denominational groups shows that 45 percent of congregations made "permanent changes to their community outreach" during the pandemic, including things like expanding services to reach elderly and shut-in members of the community, creating relief funds for those in need, and establishing phone trees to check in on people (Hartford Institute for Religion Research 2021, 1).

These expanded services were often in response to direct community needs since the onset of the COVID-19 pandemic; 25 percent of churches reported an increase in the number of people seeking food aid, and 37 percent reported an increase in the number of people seeking mental health counseling (Tevington 2022). Some congregations got creative with their use of space, as there was a greater need for families and children who couldn't be in school to access outdoor space. As one congregation reported, "We expanded our outdoor space to offer families in the community an outdoor area to bring their children—a playground, walking trail, and little free library, with plans to add a picnic shelter" (Hartford Institute for Religion Research 2021, 3). Congregations are so much more than worship spaces. They provide direct services that benefit communities.

Just consider what communities would be like without the services that congregations provide. Nationally, nearly 80 percent of congregations participate in some kind of social services program (Chaves et al. 2021, 81). For instance, in a country where drug overdose deaths increased fivefold from 2000 to 2020 (National Institutes of Health 2023), 43 percent of congregations report that they provide support for people struggling with drug or alcohol abuse (Chaves et al. 2021, 79). More than 50 percent of people will be diagnosed with a mental illness at some point in their lives (Kessler et al. 2007), and 26 percent of congregations provide support for people with mental illness (Chaves et al. 2021, 79), helping reduce the stigma in faith communities (A. Campbell 2021; Costello, Hays, and Gamez 2021).

On March 31, 2023, Little Rock was hit by a powerful series of tornadoes, including one rated EF3, that destroyed homes and businesses throughout the city and left one person dead (Bass 2023). With winds up to 165 miles per hour, the twisters ripped out trees and tossed cars, devastating homes and lives in the city. Almost immediately, cleanup efforts began, many of them organized by local congregations. By the morning after the tornadoes, City Connections, a nonprofit that works to connect churches and community, had compiled a list of congregations and the resources they were providing—from shelter to food, hygiene kits, or a place to charge devices. Later that day, one place of worship, Immanuel Baptist Church, had become a hub for organizing volunteers and supplies (Snyder 2023). They already had the infrastructure for food distribution, a clothes closet, and a dental clinic, so, as Matt Hubbard, the missions pastor at Immanuel Baptist, put it, they were ready to "go from one to one thousand real quick" (quoted in Snyder 2023). Many other individuals and community groups contributed to the recovery efforts in Little Rock, but without the organization and infrastructure of the congregations, the work certainly would have progressed more slowly.

Collaborating to Help Communities

As they seek to serve the communities where they reside, congregations may look for partnerships in the community. Collaboration can be a great way to more effectively and efficiently provide services. When congregations look around, they may find that many nonprofits are trying to solve the same problems that they are.

Faith-based and secular social service providers are often complementary—differing in important ways that make partnerships more beneficial (Ebaugh et al. 2003). Social service provision through congregations tends to be narrower, and their primary focus on religion means congregations may experience more management challenges than nonprofit organizations (Clerkin and Grønbjerg 2007). At the same time, partnerships tend to reduce the costs of service provision and expand the base of volunteers from which organizations can draw, so facilitating partnerships is generally seen as in the best interest of both nonprofit organizations and congregations (Bryson, Crosby, and Stone 2006; McGuire 2006). Indeed, innovation and collaboration across organizations can be vital to improving outcomes on important community problems—helping prevent child abuse, combat poverty, and address homelessness (Costello et al. 2022; Mulroy and Shay 1997).

Although partnerships between nonprofits and congregations occur somewhat regularly (e.g., Ammerman 2001; Cnaan, Sinha, and McGrew 2004b), there are many cases in which they do not. When religious organizations and nonprofits do collaborate in unique and creative ways, the result is often better community outcomes (e.g., Netting et al. 2005; Tripses and Scroggs 2009). For instance, when academics and doctors wanted to help more Hispanic women get screened for breast cancer, it was Spanish-language churches that encouraged their female congregants and women in the community to participate, ultimately leading to better health outcomes (Colon-Otero et al. 2014).

Despite the benefits of partnerships, they may not always serve the public interest. Sometimes partnerships fail (Andreasen 1996; Anderson and Jap 2005; Gray 1989). Power imbalances between partners (DeFilippis 2008; Rich, Giles, and Stern 2001) or co-optation by political power brokers within the community (Harris 2016; Leach 2016) can negatively impact partnership arrangements. Sometimes partnerships or projects don't serve those most in need but may serve the egos of those running them or just make those providing the service feel good (Lupton and Lawlor 2011).

Why congregations partner with others and why those collaborations may run into barriers is a complex topic, but it is one that we know congregations care about. In interviews with clergy in 2018 ($n = 47$), we asked, "Are there characteristics of the local nonprofit environment that weaken an organization's ability to form partnerships?" In interviews with clergy in 2020 ($n = 38$), we asked, "What do you see as the biggest barriers to more organizations working together to address problems in Little Rock?" Using an inductive process involving multiple teams of student researchers, we read through all the interviews and identified four main challenges to collaboration. As these two questions were slightly different and each leader often provided multiple, overlapping reasons why collaboration might be difficult, we do not provide statistical summaries of how many times each challenge was mentioned, but the challenges are described in the following list, with illustrative quotes from clergy interviews. These qualitative data can help us see the many challenges that congregations might face in this area.

1. **Credit claiming:** Each congregation wants to be the one that is known for doing the project—they each want to have their name on it—so sharing credit through collaboration is difficult.

   "Congregations become very territorial. . . . I just think again, ego, that they just want to get the praise. They want to be the ones that are like 'hey, we're doing this' and 'look at what we're doing.' So I think that's really the biggest issue and it shouldn't be, but that's really what it comes down to. People are human at the end of the day."

   "I would think the first thing, you know, for real, just transparent, would be competition. I think a sense of competition between churches is a barrier."

2. **Theological/political/social differences:** Some congregations may be hesitant to work with those whom they have significant theological or political disagreements with, some may also be uncomfortable working with a congregation from a different socioeconomic class or racial background, and some congregations may not have any contacts across denominations. These differences can hamper collaboration.

   "I don't have the first clue how to get a truly interfaith effort going here that crosses racial lines."

   "I think there's a fear that 'what if things change?' What if we do get a big influx of people who were thinking differently than us, who believe differently than us, who have different spiritual practices than we do? You know, are they going to change the place?"

3. **Logistical challenges:** Identifying the right issue, knowing where to go to get information, or having sufficient resources to engage can all make collaboration difficult.

"There's a complete and total lack of coordination among community-based organizations."

"Four walls are extremely comfortable. You know what to expect within your own four walls. So that's comfortable. And I think that hinders collaboration."

4. **Resistance within the congregation:** Some members may struggle with the idea of change, or there may be disagreements over which issue to engage on or how to address it. These issues within a congregation would need to be resolved first before collaboration could be considered.

"We're a church that is very diverse politically and so you're always going to have differing opinions on the cause of the issues—like of homelessness, for example. You're going to have different people who believe different reasons why people are homeless, and how to get them out of homelessness, and how they got there, and what to do about those things."

"We've always done it this way, so why change?"

As congregations ponder the best way to engage and serve, they may want to consider collaboration with other congregations or with nonprofits. Doing so is not always easy. Just as interest groups may find that joining coalitions may be helpful in some circumstances, incongruent ideologies or competition may make it difficult in others (Newmark and Nownes 2019). Thus, it can be helpful to be aware of the potential barriers that might arise in pursuing collaboration. As I personally texted with clergy to coordinate tornado relief efforts in April 2023 and joined them in hauling away debris, I experienced both collaboration and resistance. I saw congregations working together to help families in need. And, as I communicated with clergy about opportunities to serve, I received some pushback about joining in recovery efforts organized by other congregations. For instance, one text message read, in part, "Generally we organize into self-contained teams," and a response to an invitation to join with another congregation's efforts one Saturday morning was, "I'll float the idea and see what the response is." That congregation did not show up at the joint effort.

Although the barriers listed here may be challenging, they are far from insurmountable. In a 2018 survey of nonprofit organizations in the Little Rock area ($n = 329$), we found that the vast majority view partnerships with religious congregations favorably. In fact, 70 percent reported that they had partnered with a congregation in the past, and all of those said they would be willing to do so again. None of them had a negative experience that would prevent partnering in the future. Of the remaining 30 percent, 20 percent expressed interest in partnering in the future; only 7 percent said they were not interested in partnering, and 3 percent said their policies prevented them from partnering with a religious organization (Glazier 2019b). Research into congregations' social service involvement following the expansion of faith-based initiatives shows that there was no significant increase, despite changes to laws and increases in government incentives (Chaves and Wineburg 2010). People and places of faith are intrinsically motivated to help their communities and are often operating at capacity—adjustments to government regulations don't move the needle much on their involvement, but collaboration just might.

Choosing a Community Issue

There are many community issues that congregations could get involved in and only so many hours in the day and dollars in the budget. What kinds of issues do the most and least engaged congregations care about? We asked about the importance of six community issues in the 2016 and 2020 LRCS surveys of congregation members. Using the process introduced in Chapter 2, we divided these fifty-three congregation/year observations into categories at natural cut points, representing the most and least engaged congregations. Recall that these are congregation-level averages, so we are talking about entire congregations that have high levels of community engagement among their members or low levels of community engagement among their members. Each category holds about 15 percent of the respondent population. For five of the six community issues we asked about (education, health, race relations, homelessness, and poverty/inequality), the most engaged congregations ranked the issue as significantly more important than the least engaged congregations. Only the importance ranking for crime was statistically indistinguishable.

We can dig deeper into these six issues, plus two more—marriage and family and foster care and children—by looking more closely at just the 2020 LRCS data. Conducted in October 2020, our electronic surveys allowed us to ask follow-up questions, so anyone who rated an issue "Very important" was asked whether they would like to see their congregation get involved in addressing that community issue and whether they would be interested in volunteering to help with that issue. Figure 5.2 again compares the most and least engaged congregations, this time looking only at the 2020 respondents, with each category representing about 10 percent of the sample.

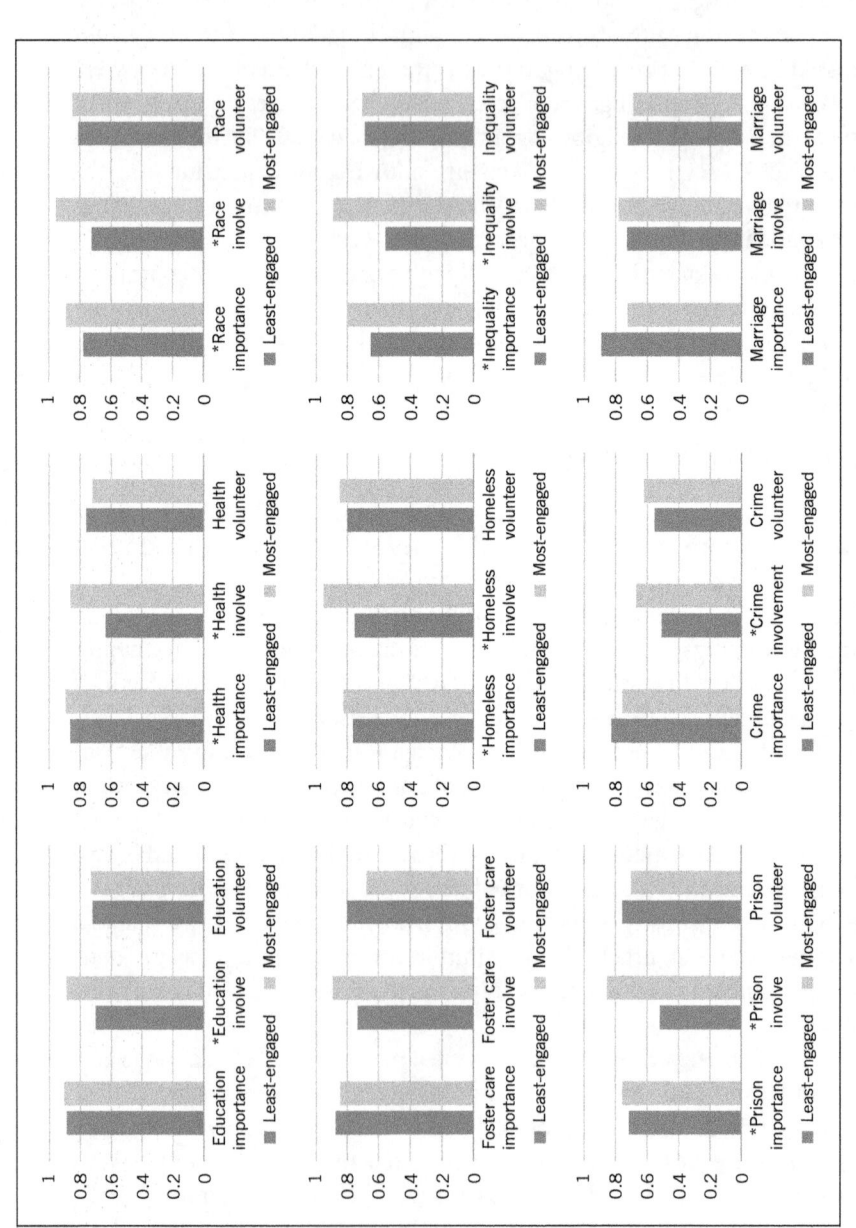

Figure 5.2 Importance of, Interest in Congregational Involvement with, and Willingness to Volunteer on Community Issues, Comparing the Most Community Engaged and Least Community Engaged Congregations in the 2020 LRCS Data

Note: The community issues for which the differences between the least engaged and most engaged congregation categories are statistically significant are marked with an asterisk.

In the 2020 data, we again see a trend toward the most community-engaged congregations saying that community issues are more important to them. But we also see a trend toward wanting their place of worship to get involved in helping to address these community issues. In Figure 5.2 all the data have been normalized to run between 0 and 1. Even though the original scale for issue importance was 1 to 5 ("Not at all important" to "Very important") and the original scale for congregational involvement was 0 to 2 ("No," "Maybe," or "Yes"), all of the variables in Figures 5.2 are scaled 0 to 1 so they can be directly compared. This allows us to see how, even for issues like education and crime, where the most community-engaged congregations do not think the issue is more important than the least community-engaged congregations, the most community-engaged congregations are still more likely to want to get involved. This finding matters because it shows that community-engaged congregations translate issue importance into action. The members of these congregations want to help their communities. They want to do something because they believe they can make a difference—that is efficacy in practice.

The 2020 LRCS survey also asked about volunteering to help with each community issue, and we found no statistically significant differences between the two categories of congregations on this question for any of the community issues. The most and least engaged congregations are just as likely to have their members say they would volunteer to help address a community issue. Still looking at a congregational and not an individual level, we know from the results in Chapter 2 that the least engaged congregations were more likely to give service to their congregations, while the most engaged congregations were more likely to give service outside their congregations. Perhaps the question about volunteering to help with a community issue is hitting a kind of sweet spot that taps into both kinds of service: the place of worship getting involved in a community issue. This finding bodes well for any type of congregation that is considering community engagement. Even if they haven't done much community work before, these data indicate that at least some of their members—around 60 to 85 percent of those who say an issue is very important—will be willing to volunteer to help out.

Of particular interest to places of worship that are hoping to counter the trend toward aging and shrinking congregations is the enthusiasm that young people show for volunteering. Respondents under forty, who make up about 14 percent of our 2020 LRCS sample, are significantly more likely than those over forty to say they would volunteer on the community issues of race, health care, education, marriage and family, foster care, and prison/criminal justice. This finding is somewhat surprising, since the literature on volunteering indicates that older people are usually more likely to volunteer, particularly after children leave home or they retire from the workforce, because they have more time to dedicate to it (Verba, Schlozman, and Brady 1995; Wilson 2000). The fact that younger people are so eager to get engaged in community volunteering through their place of worship speaks directly to the argument of Chapter 4: congregations can be strengthened through community engagement.

The specific issue any one place of worship chooses to get involved with will depend on many factors—everything from member interest to congregational resources to collaboration opportunities. The LRCS data show that different congregations have different priorities but that diverse congregations and many different kinds of members are interested in getting involved and volunteering.

The Benefits of Ideological Diversity in Congregations

For years, social scientists have been tracking trends of "self-sorting" as Americans have moved to cities and neighborhoods that align with their preferences—public transportation and a good art scene for liberals; more space and churches for conservatives (Mekouar 2022; Tam Cho, Gimpel, and Hui 2013). This divide is not easily distilled into individual-level differences, however (Gimpel et al. 2020). There is something about living in densely populated areas or away from major cities that influences how we see the world—and people are increasingly making choices to be near those who see the world like they do.

Thus, this "Big Sort," as it is popularly known thanks to the book by Bill Bishop (2009), may be becoming more purposeful. The COVID-19 pandemic made remote work more common, enabling people to live where they want, not where they are geographically constrained for employment (Mekouar 2022). A 2021 real estate survey showed that more people are specifically limiting their searches based on politics (Fairweather 2021); between 12 and 15 percent will not live somewhere that doesn't align with their views on abortion. And the divide is not just urban versus rural or along racial lines. Research by Brown and Enos (2021) calculating the residential segregation of every registered voter in the United States finds that there is "substantially lower cross-party exposure than would be expected if partisans were not segregated into different residential environments" (1002). Basically, if we were randomly encountering people, we would run into a member of another party about half the time, but with the residential sorting Americans are doing, we encounter people from another party only about a third of the time.

Can congregations help address this? Republicans are more likely to be religious and attend church, compared to Democrats (Pew Research Center 2020), so places of worship begin with a partisan skew. Additionally, congregations maintain and transmit social norms (Wald, Owen, and Hill 1988), providing a space where frequent social interactions, information exchanges, and similar message exposure can lead members to align their political views and behaviors (Mangum 2008; Stroope and Baker 2014). Thus, building or maintaining ideological diversity at a congregation may be an uphill battle. But doing so can be beneficial, not just for the congregation but for democracy as well (Mettler and Brown 2022). Research shows that when religion becomes politicized in a way that is salient in the context of the congregation people are worshipping in, it can drive them out—even if they identify with same political party (Djupe, Neiheisel, and Sokhey 2018). Politics can drive people away from religion even without hyperpartisanship. Our data indicate that greater ideological diversity can help make for a stronger congregation.

How can we know if a congregation is providing a space where people from diverse ideological perspectives are worshipping together? In our surveys, respondents are asked to place themselves on an ideological scale of 0 to 6, liberal to conservative. Thus, we can calculate an average ideology score for each congregation. The overall average for the sample is 3.34, or pretty close to the middle with a slight conservative lean, but individual congregations range from 0.82 to 4.91. But looking just at the average for a congregation might mask the ideological diversity of it. A congregation where everyone placed themselves at 3 would look the same as a congregation that was evenly divided between extreme liberals who placed themselves at 0 and extreme conservatives who placed themselves at 6.

Thus, we can use another statistical measure, the standard deviation, to calculate how widely distributed along the scale the responses for a given congregation are. For the entire sample, the standard deviation is 1.91, but each congregation is much more similar within its own membership, ranging from 0.06 to 0.56 for a standard deviation. A congregation with a higher standard deviation will have members who are more widely distributed along the ideological spectrum. In that kind of congregation, both liberals and conservatives will be worshipping together. And we do see some congregations that fit this pattern. As one leader put it, "We aspire to be a vibrant community where conservatives and progressives can accept, respect, and love each other in Christ in spite of our differing political views." This can be a challenging balance for clergy to achieve. As one leader told me, "I'm reluctant to get entangled in the political space as a church . . . there's a place for people at [our church] who vote blue and red, and I'd be careful about alienating either—there are too few places in our society where they mingle as it is!"

When we look at the statistical models we have used throughout the book, there aren't many where ideological diversity has made a significant difference, but for two important variables it has: political efficacy and service to the congregation.

In our statistical model of efficacy, individuals who worship in congregations that have more ideological diversity are more likely to feel politically efficacious—like their voice matters and they can make a difference ($p = 0.06$). The substantive effect of this, when we consider our average congregant, Ms. Mary, through the statistical tool of predicted probabilities, is about a 9 percent increase in political efficacy. In the most ideologically similar congregation, her efficacy score is predicted to be 0.72, but in the most ideological diverse congregation in our sample, it increases to 0.79. What is the mechanism at work here?

In a diverse congregation, members have opportunities to come into positive contact with those who hold political views that are different from their own. They serve together, worship together, and raise kids together. There is likely a fine line between an ideologically diverse congregation and one that is politically divided. In a divided congregation, people may keep their guards up and specifically avoid that kind of contact—opting not to volunteer for a committee someone from another party is chairing, choosing not to sing in the choir someone different from them is directing, or choosing not to help with a booth at the fall festival a political rival is organizing. In a diverse congregation, these kinds of opportunities for positive contact abound and contribute to political efficacy. When members have opportunities to connect with people who are different from them in meaningful and positive ways, they come away feeling less cynical and more optimistic about their ability to make a difference. Ideological diversity also contributes to another measure that matters to congregations: volunteering.

Ideologically diverse congregations have members who are more likely to volunteer their time to serve at their place of worship. Most of the significant variables in our model of congregational service, first introduced in Chapter 4 and the full model for which is available in Table C.13 in the appendix, have to do with how closely connected one feels to one's place of worship. Belonging to a community group at one's congregation, attending more often, feeling a stronger sense of congregational warmth, and being a more religious person in general are all associated with giving more service to one's place of worship. But when we look at the predicted probability that a respondent would give the highest category of service—fifteen or more hours of service in the past month—the strongest effect by far comes from the ideological diversity of the congregation. These results are presented in Table 5.2.

It seems as if, in ideologically diverse congregations, members are connecting with those who are different from them and building a stronger congregation. We see this in literature from sociology, organizations, and business (Frémeaux 2020; Herring 2009; Sheppard 2018). Diversity makes for stronger organizations as more perspectives are shared, new ideas are brought forward, and minds are changed. In the LRCS data, ideological diversity is

TABLE 5.2 PREDICTED PROBABILITY OF RESPONDENT GIVING FIFTEEN OR MORE HOURS OF SERVICE TO THEIR CONGREGATION IN A MONTH, VARIANCE BY EACH SIGNIFICANT VARIABLE, AND INCREASE			
Variables	Lowest (%)	Highest (%)	Increase (%)
Community group at congregation	2.5	5.0	100
Religiosity	2.1	4.7	123
Congregation warmth	1.6	4.4	175
Worship service attendance	0.9	5.6	522
Ideological diversity	1.9	19.7	936

correlated with congregational warmth at 0.47, a fairly strong correlation, and clergy-perceived political division is negatively correlated with congregational warmth at −0.52. Thus, having an ideologically diverse congregation has about the same positive relationship to the warmth and positive feelings within a congregation as political division does harm to it. These data clearly show that diversity and division are measuring different things. The simple presence of people who hold different political views in a congregation can be a very positive thing, but when there is animosity among them—perhaps even infighting on congregational councils, refusal to work with each other, and hard feelings—it can be detrimental.

What might an ideologically diverse congregation look like? From the 2020 data, I pulled one Black and one white congregation that were high on the ideological diversity measure and compared them against the sample averages on a number of key variables. These comparisons are presented in Table 5.3 as illustrative examples of what ideologically diverse congregations might look like.

While the ideological diversity scores of these two congregations are quite similar and well above the average for the full sample, Congregation 1 is much more evenly distributed along the ideological spectrum, with Congregation 2 having a higher concentration of liberal members with only a few conservatives and moderates. For both congregations, there is higher congregational warmth and service. It is also interesting to note that these are both relatively small congregations, with respondent n's of 71 and 49, respectively, compared to the average of 207 for the broader sample. Ideological diversity may be easier to maintain in smaller congregations, where personal relationships are a more central part of the worship experience. In fact, congregation size and ideological diversity are negatively correlated at −0.73, quite a strong relationship.

Just as with community engagement, ideological diversity doesn't look the same for all congregations, but this is one area where places of worship can counter the tide of polarization and self-sorting in America. As one leader said, "I believe strong churches are the backbone of a community. . . . Good-

Variables	Congregation 1	Congregation 2	Full sample
Respondent n	71	49	2,294
Percentage of the congregation with Black racial identity	81.5% Black	5.8% Black	8.6% Black
Ideological diversity	0.35	0.37	0.14
Ideology (0–6, liberal to conservative)	3.5	1.58	3.34
Conservatives (including leaners)	15 (21%)	5 (10%)	963 (42%)
Liberals (including leaners)	15 (21%)	36 (75%)	757 (33%)
Congregational warmth (rescaled 0 to 1)	0.800	0.866	0.792
Attendance (1 = Never, 6 = More than once a week)	5.03	4	4.64
Community engagement (rescaled 0 to 1)	0.677	0.703	0.728
Service to the congregation (hours in the past month: 1 = None, 5 = Fifteen or more)	1.97	2.22	1.92

TABLE 5.3 COMPARING TWO IDEOLOGICALLY DIVERSE CONGREGATIONS TO THE FULL SAMPLE

ness knows we have a world now where it is too much talk about hate and division and we need a lot of people to stand up and say, 'No, that ain't the way. Love is the way.'" By providing congregants with a place to meet, worship, work, and engage with people who believe differently from them, churches, mosques, temples, and synagogues can help them create positive bonds, dispel misinformation, and strengthen congregational ties (Patterson, Madsen, and Alleman 2022; Shi et al. 2019; Vraga and Bode 2017). The end result is good for both places of worship and democracy—greater service to congregations and greater political efficacy.

Case Study: Second Presbyterian Church

Few congregations are as committed to community service and engagement as Second Presbyterian Church in Little Rock. There is a true culture of service at the church, reflected through the church's teachings and funding priorities. Although the theology of Second Presbyterian supports these choices, the case study of this church also illustrates how their community service is mutually beneficial—the church leaders involve members in making decisions about priorities, they partner with organizations throughout the community, and thus they can serve the community better and direct their mission dollars better. In the case study that follows, Second Presbyterian serves as an example of how congregational community engagement can truly have wide-ranging impacts for good.

Second Presbyterian has a long history in the community. Founded in 1882, service is central to the identity of Second Pres, as it is fondly known. This service is seen in a number of ways—from the active volunteers in the congregation, to the use of its buildings by many nonprofit and civic organizations, to the way the budget is allocated—but it is at the heart of how Second Presbyterian Church in Little Rock chooses to act. What is particularly unique about Second Pres is how that culture of service is so often aimed outward to serve the broader community in Little Rock and around the world.

Many congregations talk about community service, but one way that Second Pres really demonstrates their commitment to giving is through their budget decisions: 25 percent of money given each year by church members goes to the church's outreach ministry, which funds organizations and projects outside the walls of Second Presbyterian Church. Associate Pastor for Outreach Lindy Vogado says, "This financial commitment on the part of our congregation allows us to use our resources strategically so they can make the biggest impact possible. We are the largest congregational donor to several organizations in our community, and I am proud that we can partner with people and agencies that are doing such important work in our community."

One volunteer I spoke to said that, even in difficult budget discussions, "nobody wants to diminish that support." The 25 percent outreach giving commitment at Second Presbyterian Church is a significant part of the ethos of the church. Another described Second Presbyterian as "a very outreach-minded congregation," saying, "It's always been a thing here . . . it's drilled into you, it's part of the culture. Everybody buys into that." Even the building is a community ministry at Second Presbyterian—any given day of the week, it is being used by Boy Scouts, twelve-step programs, volleyball teams, or LifeQuest, an adult education program for seniors, free of charge as a service to the community.

The outreach ministry benefits a number of different community organizations. For many years now, Second Presbyterian has adopted a local elementary school, Bale Elementary. The members at Second Pres volunteer at the school, contribute to teacher appreciation, fund field trips, and tutor the kids. Before the COVID-19 pandemic slowed in-person efforts, there were forty volunteers involved in the engagement efforts at Bale. The students from Bale Elementary performed skits for church members to say thank you. One of the lay leaders of the outreach effort with Bale Elementary emphasized the value of this and other opportunities for "basic human connection" with the kids at the school, saying, "When you see, hear, meet, you get to understand better the kids you serve." The visits the students made to the church were really meaningful for the members, as well, even those who never made it to an on-site tutoring session or a teacher appreciation day. It helped the members at Second Pres see the people their church was helping. As one volunteer said, "They were so appreciative and so grateful and that makes for a good partnership, when you know what you're doing is making a difference and they appreciate what you're trying to accomplish."

In 2020, as racial tension increased across the country, Second Pres formed a racial justice task force to examine the issue and see what could be done at and through the church. Members talk about a real sense in the community consciousness at the time that, "Oh, we need to be doing something." As a result of this task force, some members at Second Presbyterian read books about racism and held small group discussions, as education is an important part of the culture at the church. But the task force also wanted to do more. As Pastor Vogado said, "We wanted to get a task force together to think about some long-term actionable items, as opposed to just talking about it and then not doing anything."

The task force actually used the 2020 report that the LRCS generated for Second Pres to identify that racial justice and health care were two major priorities for the congregation. One of the task force members had a master's in public health and had worked at the University of Arkansas for Medical Sciences Fay W. Boozeman College of Public Health before retiring a few years earlier. Using personal contacts at the school, the task force worked with them to identify needs and ultimately establish a scholarship for students of color and a speaker series about racial inequities in health. One task force member described a sense of "urgency about the work" of the task force both from the church and within the task force itself, even saying that "people are ready to spend more on this effort." In speaking about the racial justice efforts at Second Presbyterian Church, Pastor Vogado says, "We're trying hard but we're still a very affluent, predominantly white congregation. I would not want to project the idea that we feel like we've got it figured out because we don't, but I think we're starting to think about some things that are important to move forward."

And the members at Second Pres have many opportunities to serve— whether it's providing meals through Stewpot, helping to house families in transition through Our House, or reading to kids at Bale Elementary, there are service opportunities almost every day of the week. And the members at Second Pres are not shy about asking for volunteers! One member I spoke with, who helps organize volunteers for a local medical ministry, joked, "I could walk in on Sunday morning and there was not a physician in the congregation that would make eye contact with me." All the medical professionals knew she was coming—and many of them were already part of the volunteer staff at the clinic.

In 2021, after the United States withdrew from Afghanistan, Second Pres adopted two Afghan refugee families, helping them adapt to life in Little Rock, get around via carpool, acquire furniture for their new homes, and learn English. In total, over seventy members of Second Pres were involved in some part of the effort to help these families. One of the coordinators said it was really touching to see how much everyone wanted to help: "You had retired CEOs driving kindergarten carpool—they just wanted to contribute!" Another volunteer said they really appreciated this effort because they were able to get to know the families personally. Some community service projects, even building new homes or doing neighborhood cleanups, can feel impersonal, but as she put it, "These families were ours." Another volunteer similarly commented on how much a personal connection matters: "You have to personally see an issue to identify with it. It changes your perspective: the opportunity to see things on a personal level."

Church community is also built through organizations like Presbyterian Women, a weekly Bible study group that also meets once a month to have a "Together in Service" event. The group donates a portion of its budget each year to both local and national nonprofit organizations, meeting together to discuss what they would like to support. They also contribute to community service by supporting efforts like the projects at Bale Elementary or providing meals for the hungry. One member told me, "I love the intergenerational aspect of community through Presbyterian Women." Although her mother was no longer alive, she connected with "mother figures" she otherwise wouldn't get to know through her engagement with them in service through Presbyterian Women.

When I attended worship services at Second Presbyterian Church, I met some new members who had only recently joined. They told me that they had been seeking a more inclusive and community-involved church and were drawn to Second Pres. And they were put to work right away! Within a year of joining, members of the family had assumed lay leadership roles in the church, volunteered on the Zoo Walk for Alzheimer's support and awareness, and served as greeters in the congregation. The way this new family began contributing to both congregational and community service at Second Pres is a great illustration of one of the key findings in Chapter 4, where, for community-engaged congregations, there is no trade-off between service to the community and service to the congregation. They are mutually reinforcing. Thus, for this new family, service at Second Pres means service in all capacities.

On August 21, 2022, Second Presbyterian Church held their "Fall Kickoff" Sunday. This Sunday was special because not only were children encouraged to bring their backpacks to church that day to be blessed for the start of the new school year, but all members were invited to attend a "Time and

Talents" fair between services. At this fair, they could learn about the different ministries at Second Pres and the ways they could give service.

As I walked into the main hall where the fair was held, I could see that there were dozens of booths set up, staffed by eager volunteers who were signing people up to staff games at the church picnic, commit to helping the environmental ministry with a cleanup day, or give a few hours of their time to write cards to those who were sick or homebound. The enthusiastic commitment to service in the hall was infectious. It's possible that I left the "Time and Talents" fair having promised to help out with the church picnic a few weeks later . . .

The model of community service that Second Pres represents is not a model that every congregation can follow. More than one congregant told me that they are able to do so much because they have a number of affluent members who give generously and support the causes the church cares about. As one lay leader said, "We are very fortunate, in our congregation, we have people who have the resources to do that." The resources of both time and money are more abundant in this congregation than in many others; Second Pres recognizes that fact and chooses to use that privilege in community service.

Conclusion

Places of worship contribute so much when they reach outside themselves to get engaged in their communities. Not only do their efforts lead to benefits for their own members, as discussed in Chapter 3, and benefits for their own congregations, as discussed in Chapter 4, but those positive externalities aggregate to improve society and support democracy, as well. Additionally, many congregations provide direct social services that are needed and valued by people in their communities, even more so since the COVID-19 pandemic.

Talking with friends and family about community problems or attending neighborhood meetings may seem like small acts, but they matter for society and democracy (Andrews and Turner 2006; Nalbandian 1999; Putnam, Leonardi, and Nanetti 1994; Williams and Schoonvelde 2018). Congregations are just the kinds of organizations to foster these behaviors (Neiheisel, Djupe, and Sokhey 2009). In numerous small ways, religion serves a critical political function by putting limits on individuals and thus making the collective endeavor of democracy possible. As Bellah and colleagues (2007) put it, religion is constantly "hedging in self-interest with a proper concern for others" (223). By doing so, religion can help bolster democratic norms and improve civic skills. In response to increasing alarms regarding the fragility of American democracy (e.g., Gates 2022; Huq 2022; Mettler and Lieberman 2020), these efforts might be just what the country needs.

When congregations are engaged in the community, the response from community members is often very positive. As I chatted with one community member, she spoke with great enthusiasm about a local church's efforts to serve her community, saying, "It's beautiful. We love it, because they bring the community together and our community comes out and they support them and the church supports us and supports the community and they're good people." We saw the real, physical good that congregations can do in communities play out as places of worship became the default centers for donations and organizing in the aftermath of the tornadoes on March 31, 2023 (Snyder 2023). But beyond the on-the-ground service of congregations, they also help society by providing places where people can encounter ideological diversity, learn political efficacy, and build community.

One of the more politically relevant findings of this chapter is that ideologically diverse congregations, in particular, have added benefits for society and democracy. When congregations create welcoming environments where people are able to have positive interactions with those who hold different political views than they do—countering the increasing ideological isolation in America (Brown and Enos 2021)—they also boost political efficacy and create greater warmth in their own congregations.

As the last three chapters have shown, community engagement has a plethora of positive effects. But what does it look like in practice? In the next chapter, we take a close look at true stories of congregational community engagement in action. As congregations have different priorities, theologies, and resources, engagement looks different for different places of worship, but most congregations should be able to find examples that they can implement going forward.

What Engagement Looks Like

Four Different Examples

Community engagement looks different for different congregations. Resources—in terms of money, members, time, and theology—all play into the types of priorities congregations set and the kinds of engagement they choose. This chapter first looks at the big picture of what matters to congregations, in terms of the priorities they set, and then zooms in to examine in-depth case studies of four Little Rock congregations representing different examples of engagement.

Every congregation, even within the same religious tradition, is different. The context of a congregation plays an important role in influencing how it might engage with the community (Cavendish 2000; Glazier and Street 2020; Polson 2016). Smaller congregations may not have the resources to do the major projects that larger congregations can. Congregations with more grassroots organizational structures may need members to bring ideas for projects to the attention of committees or leaders.

Additionally, different congregations and different faith traditions may just value different things. When it comes to service, for instance, one congregation may be more focused on community cleanups while another may prioritize political advocacy and still another choose to spend its time visiting members in the hospital. Some of this "congregational culture" (Johnson, Cohen, and Okun 2013; McClure 2017; Polson 2016) may come from the history of the religious tradition itself (Beyerlein and Hipp 2006; Loveland, Stater, and Park 2008). For instance, the specific historical-political experiences and worship practices of Black Protestant churches tend to lead to greater community action (Barnes 2005; Calhoun-Brown 1996; F. Harris 1999; Lincoln and Mamiya 1990; Pattillo-McCoy 1998).

On the other hand, some churches have actively sought to steer clear of "worldly" matters like politics or social activism and have instead focused their energy on "otherworldly" concerns like saving souls (Iannaccone 1988; Leege and Kellstedt 1993), although this dichotomy certainly has its limitations (McRoberts 2003). For instance, in recent years, some evangelicals have begun to become more community minded, seeing community engagement and saving souls as two sides of the same coin (Steensland and Goff 2013). Differences certainly exist within religious traditions and among individuals who identifying as belonging to those traditions, but the culture of a religious tradition or a specific congregation can influence the community engagement of its members and how much the congregation itself prioritizes engagement.

Setting Congregational Priorities

How important is community engagement to congregations? In our 2020 data collection efforts, we asked both clergy and congregants about the priorities for their congregations. Instead of using the term "community engagement," which can be very open to interpretation, we asked both clergy and congregants to prioritize in rank order three things their congregation could be working on, roughly based on priorities identified by Nancy Ammerman (2005) in her foundational work, *Pillars of Faith*.

For clergy, this took place in interviews. We asked them which was their main priority: members (taking care of their members and fostering their spiritual growth), evangelism (sharing their faith and preparing for the next life), or action (serving the poor and needy and working for social change). Ammerman (2005) argues that, for most congregations, their own members come first. The secondary, and external, efforts tend to focus on either evangelism and a gospel of personal transformation or on offering immediate aid and comfort (131).

And we saw this play out for our congregations, as well. For the thirty-five clergy we interviewed in 2020, the mean ranking of the three priorities was as follows (with numbers closer to 1 indicating higher priorities for the congregations):

- Members: 1.51
- Action: 1.91
- Evangelism: 2.3

For some clergy, the decision to prioritize members was clear. As one leader put it, "The thing that my congregation does the best is take care of each other. So, I would have to say members." Other clergy struggled with choosing one over the other, however, seeing them as connected. For instance, one leader told us, "It's hard for me to distinguish between evangelism and action because evangelism is action." Another said, "I would say probably the members. It's tough because they are all interwoven and they're obviously self-reinforcing, but I think working with members and helping them spiritually progress would be my top priority."

In our survey of members in October 2020, we asked the question slightly differently, as members have a different perspective from leaders. We asked them to rank the priorities of their congregations according to what they would like to see them focus on. Specifically, we asked, "Places of worship have many different priorities during these challenging times. Please rank the following items according to what you would like to see your congregation focusing on right now." The respondents were then able to click and drag to reorder four options (presented in random order): spiritual growth and development, social connection and fellowship, helping those in need, and other. Once again, the closer the score each option is to 1, the more important it is to the respondent population:

- Spiritual growth and development: 1.99
- Helping those in need: 2.05
- Social connection and fellowship: 2.49
- Other: 3.45

Returning to the distinction between the most and least community-engaged congregations, as introduced in Chapter 2, we can compare how the priorities differ between them. In the 2020 data, the only data collection year when we asked the priorities question, the most engaged congregations make up about 9 percent of the sample with a congregation n of 8 and a respondent n of 214; the least engaged congregations make up about 11 percent of the sample with a congregation n of 9 and a respondent n of 252. The mean rankings for each priority for each category of congregation are presented in Table 6.1, keeping in mind that values closer to 1 are higher priorities.

Table 6.1 illustrates the differences in priorities between congregations that are highly community engaged and those that are not. The least community-minded congregations are, unsurprisingly, the most focused on spiritual matters. Helping those in need is their second priority, which may say something about how even congregations that aren't very community engaged see caring for those in need as a spiritual responsibility. The most com-

TABLE 6.1 PRIORITY RANKING BY LEAST AND MOST ENGAGED CONGREGATIONS		
Priority	Least engaged	Most engaged
Spiritual growth and development*	1.84	2.45
Helping those in need*	2.25	1.94
Social connection and fellowship*	2.50	2.20
Other	3.39	3.38
* $p < 0.05$		

munity-engaged congregations, on the other hand, have helping those in need as their most important priority, followed by social connection and fellowship, with spiritual growth coming in third. It is important to keep in mind that these are the numeric rankings of member respondents. They don't tell the whole story of a congregation. For many congregations, spiritual and material priorities may be inextricably linked (Glazier and Street 2020). Indeed, some of the open-ended responses to this question were, "My church already does all of these things," "All listed," and "How can you choose? All are important."

These responses were among the 255 "other" responses left by the congregational participants in the survey, in addition to the named rank categories. The "other" responses also included things as diverse as "gathering community together" and "needing to get back to in-person church" to "simpler instructions on use of Zoom" and "helping racial harmony." These open-ended responses were coded by the project director according to a codebook that is available in Appendix D in Table D.1 "Codebook for Open-Ended Responses of Congregation Priorities, 2020 LRCS Congregation Member Survey." A random sample of 56 responses (22 percent) were recoded for intercoder reliability (percent agreement = 97.9 percent, Krippendorf's alpha = 0.915). The categories of open-ended response are presented graphically in Figure 6.1.

For many of our congregations, helping those in need, the closest response option to community engagement, was a high priority. With a ranking of 2.05, compared to 1.99 for spiritual development, the two are statistically indistinguishable. The open-ended responses reflect this finding, as well: 78 of the 255 open-ended responses (30.5 percent) were about community involvement and advocacy, including on specific issues like racism, homelessness, and education. Comparatively, only 17 of the 255 (about 6 percent) were about evangelism.

Yet, in the open-ended responses, we again see reinforcement of Ammerman's foundational finding that, for most congregations, the well-being of their members comes first, followed by either an evangelical or an aid/service secondary priority. Although Figure 6.1 shows a great deal of interest

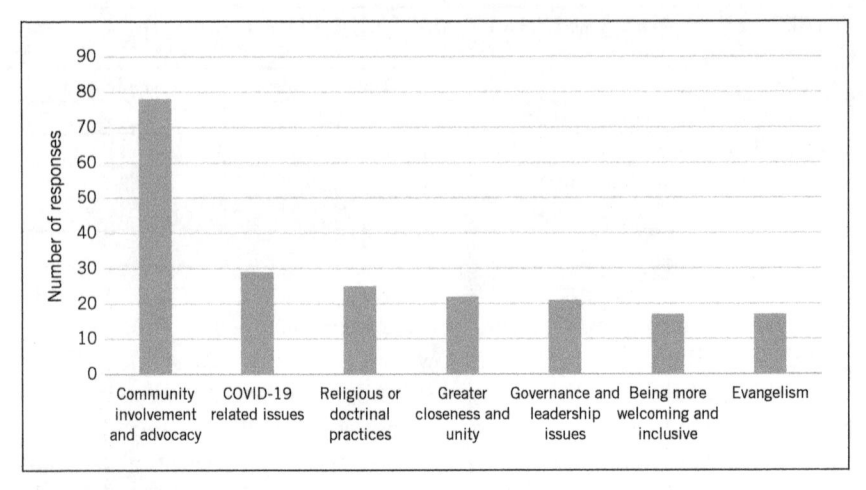

Figure 6.1 Categorical Coding of Open-Ended Responses about Priorities for the Respondent's Place of Worship, Responses to the "Other" Option

in community issues from the "other" responses, if we tally together all the categories that relate to the congregation and its members, they would encompass the majority of responses. These categories include: COVID-specific issues (29/255, 11 percent), specific religious or doctrinal practices (25/255, 10 percent), greater closeness and unity (22/255, 8 percent), and governance or leadership issues (21/255, 8 percent). There were 17 open-ended comments (about 6 percent) specifically about being more welcoming and inclusive, including to different racial groups and LGBTQ members. These responses indicate a strong concern for the congregational culture and well-being of members.

The open-ended comments also underscore just how different congregations are. One respondent said, "Anything not involving social justice and politics," while another said, "Advocating for justice." When congregants and leaders consider the best ways for their congregations to get engaged in the community, there are almost certainly going to be differences of opinion. Clergy have to keep that in mind and perhaps even have multiple options for engagement available for different members.

In their interviews, we saw clergy carefully considering these dynamics. For instance, one clergy member told us, "I think one of the things that we can do by engaging the community is showing that people of different backgrounds can coexist and love each other. That's one of the things we're looking for—new ways to be able to engage different parts of the city." There are theological and historical reasons for congregations to have different priorities, so community engagement can and should look different across congregations.

What Case Studies Contribute, for Researchers and for People of Faith

The previous three chapters presented ways that places of worship are engaging the community to benefit their members, their own congregations, and society. In line with the literature on the value of multimethod research, the case studies in those chapters helped validate the causal processes we saw working in the statistical models (Goertz 2016).

This chapter provides four additional case studies of congregations that are less closely linked to specific causal processes, although we do see many of the key statistical findings at play in their stories. However, the case studies in this chapter may be most useful for clergy and people who belong to faith communities. They present different ways of engaging in the community that might spark ideas and conversations at places of worship that are considering how to best engage. The culture, history, and theology of each congregation matters in making those choices.

For instance, at Bullock Temple CME, a historic Black Protestant church located across the street from Central High School, site of the Little Rock desegregation crisis in 1957, community engagement sometimes looks like helping keep that civil rights history and legacy alive. And as a key part of a small community, Bullock Temple is a central hub for news, health information, connection, aid, and fellowship.

At the Madina Institute, a Muslim congregation in a predominantly Christian area, they have focused their community-engagement efforts on interfaith work. They see their role in the community differently because of the place they hold as a minority religious tradition trying to encourage understanding, peace, and dialogue.

At Saint Mark Baptist Church, a large Black Protestant church with many resources to draw on, community engagement involves making important decisions about where to direct those resources. There are many needs in their area of the city, and they seek to help the most vulnerable—from kids who need after-school programs to unhoused people who need food aid to disaster victims who need relief—through their engagement efforts.

At Central Church of Christ, an evangelical congregation in downtown Little Rock, building relationships is the most important priority. They see community engagement and service as a way to connect with people and share the love of God. Their long-term efforts in the neighborhoods around their downtown church are based on a commitment to build relationships that last and demonstrate genuine love and care.

Even though all these congregations have community engagement and service as a major priority, it doesn't look the same at all places. In all these congregations I felt inspired and humbled by the people serving there. I hope the love these people have for their communities and their congregations comes through in their stories.

Bullock Temple Christian Methodist Episcopal Church

In a city with a long-standing history of racial division, Bullock Temple CME Church stands, as they put it, "at the corner of hope and healing." It also stands on a historical corner of the city of Little Rock, just across the street from Central High School, the infamous scene of the 1957 desegregation crisis for which President Eisenhower sent in the National Guard.

Founded in 1901, and in its present location since 1971, the church has seen a lot in the city of Little Rock. In 2022, they appointed a new pastor, Rev. Dr. Odessa Darrough, who attended Central High School herself in the 1960s. Reverend Darrough, who is now seventy-three years old, started pastoring in 2013 and calls herself a "newbie." The first time I met the new pastor, she was wearing a jaunty hat with "316" on the side—a conversation starter that allows her to tell people about the scripture found in John 3:16, "For God so loved the world that he gave his one and only Son, that whoever believes in him shall not perish but have eternal life."

Reverend Darrough looks much younger than her seventy-three years, and her approach to life and ministry is a holistic one—connecting mind, body, and soul—and, as she tells me, "that includes caring for each other and recognizing that I am my brother's keeper." That holistic approach is very apparent in the services at Bullock Temple, where members hear not just about Bible verses and scriptural exhortations but about upcoming elections and community events.

Bullock Temple CME is an example of a church that is at the heart of its community and a key source of community information. The programs for important church celebrations, like anniversaries, contain sections dedicated to "A Black History Moment" and "Health Corner." When I attended services at Bullock Temple, I heard announcements about booster shots, voter registration drives, the church's food pantry, and prostate cancer awareness. One week, the church was even raising funds for Lane College, an HBCU in Jackson, Tennessee, where Dr. Logan Hampton is now the president, after previously serving as the pastor of Bullock Temple.

In discussing this "whole person" approach to their ministry, Reverend Darrough says, "From a biblical perspective, our people perish for the lack of knowledge. So, we want to make sure that undergirding of the Word goes along with us wanting to inform, educate, and empower our people." Another member of the congregation elaborated by saying, "It feels like it's what God wants us to do. We heal the whole person. You're just not here on Sunday; there are things going on between Sunday and the next Sunday in your life that aren't necessarily focused at the church, but they still affect you as a person."

One great example of how Bullock Temple serves the whole person is through their food pantry. The food pantry originally began twenty years ago, and, as one of the key volunteers tells it, the idea came "from my grandmama. She's on a fixed income and around the twenty-fourth or twenty-fifth of the month, things start getting a little thin for her, so the idea was to help the sick and shut in to get through the month, but it's blossomed since then." In September 2022, Bullock Temple gave 82 food boxes to the needy, but during the winter months, they expect that number to reach as high as 150. Another volunteer told me that many churches in the area offer food pantries, due to the large of number of people who need help, but "one of the things that Bullock initiated was the effort by which we can coordinate" so that the different food pantries were open and available at the times that people needed them. When asked about the motivations driving Bullock Temple's food pantry, a volunteer told me that "as a church, that's what we're supposed to do, meet people where they are, spiritually and physically. It's hard to preach to people that are hungry."

The congregation at Bullock Temple, as is the trend for many congregations these days, is on the older side. But many of the members see this as an opportunity for mentorship and connection with younger generations. As one member said, "Bullock is in a good place to reach out to the community, through a mentoring program." Reverend Darrough calls the current church-going generation "the remnant" and is upfront about the challenges they face with a smaller and older congregation. She is used to leading smaller flocks, though, saying, "I truly live that, when two or three are gathered in my name, I'll be there," a reference to the scripture found in Matthew 18:20 in the Bible. "It's not about the numbers," she says, "it's who you can reach and touch." A church member echoed this focus on making connections and contributions, no matter the size, saying, "This is what God wants us to do. Go out and be with the people. Be a part of something."

For many at Bullock, there is a desire to keep the history of the church and the city, especially the civil rights struggle, alive for the younger generation. As one member put it, Bullock can help develop for young people "what's really important, what's really important about history, what's really important about what we *learn* from history and about how we can use it in the future."

And Bullock Temple CME Church has indeed been the scene of many historical moments, particularly as it relates to the civil rights movement in the city of Little Rock. Dr. Hampton, who served as the pastor of Bullock Temple for many years, said he always saw the church as well positioned to "engage the community around these notions of hope and history . . . as a place of restoration and reconciliation." Just a block away from Bullock Temple is the Little Rock Central High Museum and Visitors Center, opened in 2007 to mark the fiftieth anniversary of the 1957 Central High crisis. A lifetime member of Bullock Temple, Sanford Tolette sits on the board of the museum and is also one of the founders of Unity in the Community, an organization dedicated to affirming common humanity, celebrating diversity, and achieving unity.

Also in 2007, Unity in the Community buried a time capsule on the grounds of Bullock Temple. This time capsule contained numerous items, including the Little Rock Nine's hopes for the future. They also organized unity walks to promote the community coming together. These weren't protest marches, because, as Tolette puts it, "a walk is celebratory." On Sunday, October 29, 2017, a Unity Stone and Unity Park Garden were also dedicated on the same spot where the time capsule was buried, this time to honor the sixtieth anniversary. The dedication followed an interfaith service on unity in the community where representatives from different faith traditions and people of conscience offered prayers and thoughts for unity, particularly as it relates to the racial divides in Little Rock. Just as the Little Rock Nine had integrated Central High School, this interfaith service integrated people from different faith traditions, and people of no faith at all, together in recognizing their common humanity.

In 2018, a replica of the bench where Elizabeth Eckford's first attempts at integration ended on September 4, 1957, was dedicated directly south of Bullock Temple's church building. This bench is on the National Park Service's registry of historic places and marks where fifteen-year-old Elizabeth waited by herself to catch a bus home after meeting an angry mob when she attempted to integrate Central High School (National Park Service, 2020).

The now-famous image of Elizabeth, seemingly cool and composed in a pair of dark sunglasses and a white dress, facing down an angry mob while she waited for the bus, became emblematic of the "dignity and composure in the midst of convulsive bigotry" demonstrated by the students who integrated Central High School (Johnson 2019, 137). Elizabeth came to represent, for many, the courage of the Little Rock Nine.

On the occasion of the sixth-fifth anniversary of the desegregation crisis, surviving members of the Little Rock Nine again returned to Little Rock and Central High School to mark the event. The street in front of the school was renamed from Park Street to Little Rock Nine Way in a major celebratory event with elected officials and media coverage.

But the night before the celebration, members of the Little Rock Nine gathered in the fellowship hall at Bullock Temple CME Church to share a home-cooked meal with each other and the church family that has helped keep their legacy alive for so many years. While people enjoyed southern classics like okra and sweet potato pie, hugged each other, and exclaimed over how big grandchildren had gotten, Elizabeth Eckford slowly came to the microphone at the front of the room and spoke gratitude to the church she called "especially precious to me."

Afterward, Bishop Marvin Frank Thomas Sr. of the First Episcopal District of the Christian Methodist Episcopal Church, who had driven in from Memphis for the dinner, spoke of the importance of the story of the Little Rock Nine, comparing Bullock Temple to a "best supporting actor" in the civil rights history of the city. Bishop Thomas went on to say that Bullock Temple "did not ask God to place her on this corner, but when God placed this church on this corner many years ago, God already knew that God had a role for this church to play . . . and we are in no way tired yet."

The history of Bullock Temple CME—as a Black church in a city with a racially divided past, as a church physically located in a space that represents the heart of an iconic civil rights moment, and as a keeper of the memories of that past and as pressing toward a better future—is imbued in other, subtler ways in the church. For instance, the announcement that in-person Sunday School was returning was framed in historical and civil rights terms: "Sunday School is so important. It has been such a big part of the African American experience. Just think, our ancestors learned to read in Sunday School. We've grown from that, we're beyond reading, we're delving into the scriptures, and to life experiences."

However, for other members, the focus is more on the present and the needs of the students at Central High School and other schools in the area today. Bullock Temple calls this approach "One Church, One School," and it involves getting volunteers into schools, letting schools use their facilities when needed, and welcoming students in when they need a place to go. For instance, when Central High School was undergoing some renovations, the students used the fellowship hall at Bullock Temple for their theater rehearsals. The principal of Central High School, Dr. Nancy Russo, calls Bullock Temple "part of our school family." Bullock Temple feeds the Central High football team before every game, and, when Bullock needed a new stove, the PTA at Central High got together the money to help purchase one.

But this approach to serving schools in the community goes beyond just Central High School. One member tells the story of her great-niece, who was a facilitator in an after-school program that needed volunteers. She said, "We've got all these kids who are coming to this after-school program, and all of the volunteers are white. Will you please come?" Before COVID-19 made the logistics impossible, Bullock Temple held a Summer Academy for kids in the neighborhood—feeding, caring for, and teaching them throughout the summer weeks when many of their parents were working. Dr. Hampton remarked how the students would grow both spiritually and intellectually over the course of the summer as the church and the professional teachers they hired for the Summer Academy helped combat the summer "brain drain." The congregation of Bullock may be small in number, but the members are community minded. They are always ready to work together and answer the call. As one member told me, "We are better together. I truly believe that. You can do so much more with a community of people than you can without one."

Bullock Temple is a church that both preserves the past and looks to the future. You can hear this in Reverend Darrough's sermons on Sunday mornings as she reminds her congregants that "only when we stand for the promises of the past do we have the guarantee of God's rewards for tomorrow." With the "whole person" approach that Bullock Temple takes, members receive all kinds of community, health, financial, and spiritual information. And they are expected to use it to "govern themselves" and take action when necessary. Reverend Darrough exhorts them, "The call is for us to stand, stand for what is right, stand for others, those who can't stand for themselves, stand against the injustices of the world. We are the salt. And when we are at it, it should make a difference to the world."

The Madina Institute

Little Rock is the capital city of Arkansas and solidly situated in the southern Bible Belt. Muslims are a distinct religious minority in the city, where prejudice is not uncommon. Is it because of or in spite of these unique circumstances that the Madina Institute, a progressive Islamic mosque that was founded in 2016, spends so much time and effort on interfaith work? The more I tried to learn about the roots of Madina's interfaith work, the more it became clear that it was intrinsic to the organization and the people. Ms. Sophia Said, the cofounder of the Madina Institute in Little Rock, says that it was created to do what they believe "our faith mandates us to do, in terms of interfaith outreach, in terms of building bridges with humanity, in terms of having a shared vision of this community in Arkansas."

Dr. Sara Tariq, a board member at the Madina Institute and the other of its cofounders, similarly says that the impetus for its creation came from wanting to have a place where community connection was not just possible but part of the ethos. Dr. Tariq also speaks of wanting to worship somewhere that women were not peripheral, saying, "Most mosques in this country are run by the uncles—fifty-, sixty-, seventy-year-old men who come from the homeland and run things according to a worldview that doesn't necessarily include someone like me." For her, an important moment came when her thirteen-year-old daughter didn't want to go to the mosque. She says, "I put in all this work to make sure that my children develop a faith-based identity and I was losing it."

Because of founding members like Ms. Said and Dr. Tariq, who support the vision of a Muslim place of worship that bridges the generation gap to involve youth and the community outreach mission of interfaith work, the Madina Institute is flourishing today. Ms. Said repeatedly speaks of Madina as "still in the making." It is a young mosque, built on a vision of inclusion and nonjudgment.

Nowhere is this more evident than in the youth Friendship Camp, held for third through sixth graders for one week each summer. On the day LRCS researchers attended camp, it was filled with children from diverse faith backgrounds learning about the "superheroes" of each other's religious traditions. The goal of Friendship Camp is to give children both the resources to discuss religion and the space to ask questions about it, all while building friendships and having fun. The camp brings young people from different religious traditions—Christian, Jewish, and Muslim primarily, but also Buddhist, Baha'i, Hindu, and those who are questioning or don't consider themselves to have a specific faith—together to talk about and learn about religion.

In speaking at a major interfaith gathering in 2022, Ms. Said used Friendship Camp as an example of a story of "infinite hope" coming from interfaith work, saying, "The fifty-six children from our Friendship Camp—Jewish, Christian, Muslim children and children from no faith—they come together to write letters of hope to kids in Syria who have lost their parents in the war. And tell them that they are not alone; we are here for you; we are here with you."

The Friendship Camp is technically a project of the Interfaith Center, a 501(c)(3) nonprofit organization that is physically located in the same space as the Madina Institute and is also led by Ms. Sophia Said. Needless to say, the lines between the two organizations can get a little blurry at times, especially because the goals of promoting interfaith dialogue, unity, and collaboration are ones that both organizations share. As Lev Smyth, the administrator of the Friendship Camp, puts it, "Everyone at Madina is as committed to interfaith work as the Interfaith Center is."

One story that Lev tells about Friendship Camp is that on the last day of camp, the students attend worship services at different congregations in the city. When the students were gathered together for prayer at the Madina Institute, one little boy, who regularly worships at Madina with his family, leaned over to a new friend he had made that week and asked her, "Do you want me to translate [the call to prayer] for you?" She enthusiastically responded yes. Lev says, "That one small interaction, I think, perfectly encapsulated camp for me."

The Madina Institute's vision of peace and harmony can be challenging to achieve. The leaders are diligently working on at least two levels: first, those who are particularly engaged in the community, like Ms. Said and Dr. Tariq, are building bridges, holding dialogues, and fostering long-term relationships across religious lines. But in addition to these community relationships, the congregation's religious leaders, like Imam Mohammad Nawaz, are preparing the spiritual hearts of the people for this interfaith work. As Imam Nawaz says, "Usually mosques are limited to prayers," but the Madina Institute is doing so much more than prayer, particularly when it comes to interfaith work, which he sees as in line with the work of the Prophet Mohammed, "who allowed all people to worship in their own way."

Working with other faiths, particularly as a religious minority in the south, can be intimidating. One of the members I talked with at Madina spoke clearly to this point, saying, "Religious segregation, in certain ways, has been a big problem, especially in smaller communities, smaller states, where communities are smaller and there is a lot more non-Muslim community around. Unfortunately, Muslims have a tendency to be more introverts." This is why the approach of the Madina Institute in prioritizing interfaith community engagement is so unique and important, this member emphasized, saying that "reaching out to communities around, other faiths around . . . is a big part of our vision."

For the leadership at Madina, being a religious minority means balancing community engagement and the needs of the congregation, as well. As Ms. Said puts it, "Small minority faith communities have an inherent, built-in fear that, if we work too much with others, we lose who we are. So, Imam Nawaz has also a very important role being the spiritual leader, spiritual director, of our mosque, that he prepares our community and opens their hearts for this [interfaith] work."

There is a strong focus on youth programs at the Madina Institute, which may be one reason they are able to maintain this more progressive, interfaith focus in their community engagement work. One youth volunteer I spoke with described her family becoming much more open after they started attending Madina: "Youth are more accepting and bring new ideas. That is why Madina is a more welcoming and accepting mosque. I have never seen a mosque that has fostered so many different people and religions."

A mosque fostering different religions? It may seem like an implausible idea, but at Madina, it is really happening. The mosque is named after the holy city of Madina, which was historically an interfaith city where all were welcome to practice their religions. This is the model Madina seeks to return to. And they are doing it! I heard a story of one woman who attends Madina and whose Muslim brother and Jewish sister-in-law were in town visiting and came to prayers at Madina. They felt so welcomed at the mosque that they decided to move to Little Rock from Atlanta. That is how powerful of an interfaith community Madina is creating.

And the members at Madina are embracing that vision. One member I spoke to talked about finding sanctuary in a community of faith, even when that faith looks different for different people: "Madina is really about inclusivity. We really try to be inclusive of everybody. The people who do have faith, I think it's awesome that we can all come together. Otherwise, we are dealing with the outside world and we are dealing with all these things coming in, maybe that's against our faith, but at least here, everybody knows, we are here for the same reason. We are here to worship, we are here because we believe, and we are here to love each other."

When I visited the Madina Institute on Eid al-Adha, a day celebrating the sacrifice of Abraham, I spoke with another young member of the mosque who told me about how central the interfaith values of inclusion and peace are to his own faith experience. He describes how he was motivated to interfaith work "based off of everything that's going on in the world. There's just so much interreligious violence that I wanted to do some more work on that . . . and be able to help in my community, especially seeing how there have been so many Islamophobic attacks and anti-Semitic attacks here."

This work became very personal for him a few years ago, when this young man was in high school. The principal of a local high school just outside of Little Rock posted Islamophobic comments on social media. "It hit home," he said. But when this young Muslim man and his friends heard about these hurtful public comments, they didn't demand that the principal be fired. They didn't start a petition calling for his resignation or respond by publicly shaming him on social media. Instead, they took him flowers and treats, along with an invitation to join them for Iftar, the traditional fast-breaking meal Muslims share during the holy month of Ramadan, and to learn more about Islam. The goal, he said, "was to try to stop this divisive message. . . . He's just misinformed . . . we tried to just reach out an arm and have him see the true side of Islam." These young people responded to hate with kindness and love. That is a lot to ask of teenagers, but the Madina Institute is teaching a higher way of engaging in the community with peaceful intention.

This message of peaceful action in the face of injustice was also reflected in the *khutbah*, or Friday sermon, delivered at worship services the same day of the Eid al-Adha celebration. Imam Nawaz taught about the equality in the hajj, the pilgrimage that all Muslims are required to take to Mecca once in their lifetimes. His message centered the religious as he described that "in the hajj, all pilgrims walk side by side, there is no talking about politics there, there is just asking Allah to forgive." But he also called the worshippers at Madina to action by telling them, "Wherever people are being treated unjustly, they are waiting for your contribution."

At the Madina Institute, interfaith work is not just an add-on or something nice to do every now and then. It is integral to the religious vision of the mosque and the spiritual lives of the people there. As Dr. Tariq put it, "The times when I can pinpoint where I really felt spiritually and humanistically whole and satisfied and comfortable and happy and content are really in interfaith settings." She went on to relate a specific experience she had with a local rabbi, Rabbi Block, whose exposition of the story of Jonah from the Talmud, which isn't described in much detail in the Koran, helped her understand her own religion better. "I've often learned more about my faith through other people's perspectives," she said. "That's really meaningful and important to me."

Many members of the Madina Institute were present at the eleventh annual "Love Thy Neighbor" event on September 8, 2022, hosted by the Arkansas House of Prayer and the Interfaith Center and held at St. Mark Episcopal Church. Ms. Said gave the welcome and opening remarks, where she spoke of coming together as "one people of many different faiths, who are ready to center our commonalities, cherish our differences, grateful for the diversity that lies within, and most of all, hopeful for our future together." This interfaith leadership is a hallmark of the Madina Institute's community engagement.

The theme of the interfaith "Love Thy Neighbor" event was "Sowing Seeds of Promise." Ms. Said spoke of opportunities to plant such seeds, "individually in the hearts of people and also collectively in the consciousness of our community." What is really beautiful to recognize is how the work of the Interfaith Center and the side-by-side leadership of the Madina Institute have planted those seeds and how they have begun to bear fruit in Little Rock. Ms. Said shared just a few stories of what that looks like: faith leaders coming together to be critically self-reflective about the ways their own faiths have used scripture to marginalize others; a Jewish and Christian congregation working together to care for a Muslim refugee family of fourteen; and, of course, the children from the interfaith Friendship Camp writing letters of hope to children in Syria. These stories illustrate the impact of the interfaith work that the Madina Institute is prioritizing.

The leaders at the Madina Institute will point to two major prongs of their interfaith work: the interfaith events and programs to help educate the community on one hand and the importance of an inclusive theology in the education of the members themselves on the other. But in observing the actions of the Madina Institute, one will quickly notice a third: pure service, to all members of the community, regardless of religion.

One example of this is the community mask campaign the Madina Institute started during the COVID-19 pandemic. Using donations from Muslims and non-Muslims alike, they were able to employ seamstresses who had lost their jobs due to COVID-19 in sewing masks that Madina then distributed for free to particularly vulnerable communities. These masks were distributed through an interfaith network including mosques, Latino churches, and Black churches. In a video about this campaign, Dr. Tariq quotes from the Koran, "Whoever saves a life, it is as though he had saved all mankind." And so goes the interfaith work of the Madina Institute, sending ripples of impact throughout the community.

Saint Mark Baptist Church

When you are one of the largest and best-resourced churches in the city of Little Rock, how do you decide where to put those resources? Saint Mark Baptist Church is what people often call a "megachurch." With a sprawling campus in the heart of midtown Little Rock, thousands of people attending three worship services each Sunday—with people meeting both in person and online—and an outreach ministry that helps people across the city and beyond, Saint Mark has the trust of the Black community, built and reinforced over years, and the resources to make a difference. How do they decide where to put those resources?

When I met with the leadership at Saint Mark, Pastor Lamarr Bailey pointed to a scripture in Matthew 25:40 to answer this question: when we are serving the least of these, it is like we are serving Christ. Pastor Earnest Thomas reinforced this sentiment, saying, "At any given moment, we ask ourselves, 'Who is the most vulnerable?' and the timely answer becomes our priority." The most vulnerable changes with time and circumstances, which is why Saint Mark puts different emphases on different programs over time, an approach that requires agility and adaptability. The lead pastor at Saint Mark, Pastor Phillip Pointer, talks about relying on statistical analyses and counseling together as a church leadership to make these choices, but they also make them through conversations with the community. "These are not just numbers, they're our neighbors," he says. Through it all, the guiding question of "who is the most vulnerable?" leads Saint Mark as they seek to make the best use of their resources for a city and a people in need.

Saint Mark's agility in responding to help the most vulnerable was on full display during the COVID-19 pandemic. At the onset of the pandemic in 2020, Saint Mark responded with a massive new initiative known as the Restoration Project. The goal of this project was to give small grants to families and businesses in the early days of the pandemic, before aid from the government had reached them, to fill the gap and help with critical needs. The grants ranged from $250 to help a family buy groceries or pay an electric bill to up to $4,000 to help a small business keep running. This first round of funding in 2020 was as broad as possible, reaching hundreds of families and small businesses across the community. In fact, about 85 to 90 percent of grant recipients were not members of the congregation at Saint Mark, and some of those who applied for and received grants were even from out of state. In this situation, Saint Mark was truly helping the most vulnerable—they saw a need as people were unable to work and were devastated by the pandemic but had not yet received any assistance from the government. In the interim, Saint Mark was literally the social safety net of the community.

And the members of Saint Mark responded to the need with generous giving. In 2020, the members gave more than any other year on record, with 2021 not far behind. Pastor Thomas attributes this to three things. The first is the teaching from Pastor Pointer on giving. This biblical teaching emphasizes the importance of giving to the Christian faith that the people of Saint Mark follow. Pastor Pointer preaches about how it is more blessed to give than to receive, directly referencing this principle in the teachings of Jesus Christ and also talking about how he has seen it in his own personal experience, saying, "I've seen the fruit of it. One of the greatest ways to develop as a follower of Jesus Christ is through serving people at the margins. It grows you up as a believer."

You see this attitude—about feeling blessed to be able to serve—in the volunteers at Saint Mark, such as a woman who speaks about her experience volunteering for fifteen years, including as a single mother trying to make ends meet. She recalls learning that if she gives of her time in service, God will bless her, saying, "[I just] let God use me where He wants me in the church and in the community. I got so many things that bless my life when I say, yes, I got two hours on a Saturday."

A second reason Pastor Thomas cites for the increase in giving at Saint Mark in recent years is the convenience of online giving. Saint Mark only returned to in-person worship services in March of 2022, so for two full years they operated entirely online. Because they were a large congregation at the start of the pandemic, they already had live streams of their services set up and the infrastructure for online donations in place. This put them ahead of many smaller churches that had to pivot to the online space at the pandemic's onset. The convenience of donating online meant that the average per-person donation increased and that Saint Mark's worship services were drawing people not just from Little Rock but from all over Arkansas—and even from across the country.

The third reason Pastor Thomas provides for the increase in giving during the pandemic was the sense of gratitude among the members of Saint Mark, who saw others in their community struggling and wanted to help. Again and again, the leadership of Saint Mark told me that their members see a need and respond. They hear about people who need help and then take action. Pastor Pointer says, "It is the volunteers who make it happen."

The connection between personal giving and the good that Saint Mark is able to do in the community is clear for the members of Saint Mark. During the pandemic and Project Restoration, members would hear weekly updates during virtual services. For instance, during worship services one week in May 2020, they heard, "This past week, we were able to award 18 household grants and small business grants for an additional $10,950 bringing our total so far to $127,700 for 239 grants. . . . Saint Mark family, you continue to be a conduit for God's love every time you give. Your gifts truly matter in the lives of the families we are able to reach." At worship services today, members might hear Pastor Pointer directly say that "growing in generosity allows us to do good in the community."

As the ethos of Saint Mark is to help the most vulnerable, responding to community needs takes a number of different forms. One example is a focus on helping children. On August 4–5, 2022, I was present at Saint Mark for a major back-to-school supply distribution event for the community. Saint Mark supports seven local elementary schools by providing backpacks, financial support, and food aid to families. In talking with Pastor Hersey, the outreach minister in charge of the distribution efforts, it is clear that the aid Saint Mark is giving to the schools is much more than just backpacks and crayons. The personal relationships and desire to help the most vulnerable often run deep.

The principal at Washington Elementary, for instance, is Pastor Hersey's niece; another member of Saint Mark is a nurse at one of their partner schools. When there are relationships with the partner schools that are this personal, the schools end up sharing the more significant needs that they have. For instance, Pastor Hersey described a school that asked if the church would be willing to donate washers and dryers for the school "because the need was that great for the parents there and the kids to get their clothes washed."

Volunteers at Saint Mark also provide packs of food for kids at the elementary schools to take home on the weekends, when they don't have the food from the school lunches to get them through. But it is often more than that. As Pastor Hersey says, "We think it is benefiting that child at that school; it's serving the entire family." And once again, the connection to feeding hungry schoolkids and hungry families is often personal for the volunteers and the leadership. Pastor Hersey says, "I was that kid growing up. I was that kid that had milk and no cereal, cereal and no milk, free lunch, and all of that. I understand the significance and the benefit. I was that kid at times, trying to learn and you got an empty stomach. I don't care what you say, it's hard to focus when you don't have food."

Little Rock remains a city that is divided by race, but as Pastor Hersey reminded me in one conversation, "a mom in the inner city wants the same things for her kids as a mom in west Little Rock." Saint Mark is trying to help those families in the inner city overcome the "curveballs" life has thrown at them so that their kids can have enough. When Pastor Hersey looks at the big picture work that they are doing with the outreach ministry at Saint Mark, he says, "We just give and provide hope."

Sometimes the most vulnerable people are those who have suffered from a natural disaster. As Pastor Thomas says, "When there's a tornado or storm, Saint Mark mobilizes to go and help those people because they become the most vulnerable right at that moment." Saint Mark sent busloads of people to the cities of Vilonia and Mayflower when devastating tornadoes ripped through parts of central Arkansas in April 2014; they went to help with recovery and cleanup, as well as to barbecue and fellowship. These were mostly white, rural areas of the state, making a volunteer mission from an urban, Black Protestant church particularly meaningful. "One thing about need," Pastor Hersey said, "it don't care what color you are." The people of Saint Mark just want to help those in need.

Saint Mark Baptist Church also has a very active homeless ministry that feeds an average of about forty to seventy people a day, Monday through Thursday. When I visited on a hot August day in the summer of 2022, about fifty unhoused people came by for meals, and my conversations with volunteers were punctuated by calls for additional supplies and occasionally interrupted by the bell announcing the arrival of a new volunteer at the door.

One volunteer at the homeless ministry chatted with me and shared her motivation for volunteering while we both wrapped up to-go lunches: "I like the outreach part; being able to reach out and touch, so to speak. I've had many family members who've needed the help from time to time." Another said, "Doing service like this, it keeps you humble. You realize how blessed you are." And the volunteers also make connections with one another. "It's teamwork!" one of the volunteers yells out while we are talking. "Yes!" others affirm. "You come here and you don't have a lot of drama. We don't do that. It feels like a family."

A couple of weeks after my visit with the homeless ministry at Saint Mark, when we distributed about fifty meals and ten food boxes, I received a text from Ingrid Green, who coordinates the efforts, letting me know that they "served 102 plates and passed out 56 food boxes, the highest for both to date. We believe part of the impact or reason for this is the closing of the Kroger [grocery] store on Asher. This area has become a food desert. I lived near the church growing up, so I can remember having at least 3–4 grocery stores in the neighborhood." The needs of the most vulnerable in the community around Saint Mark may be increasing, but the hearts of the congregants there are turned toward service. The five-year plan for Saint Mark includes a focus for 2023 on providing "sacrificial service to one another and the community."

Not every congregation will have the resources to engage in community service at the level of Saint Mark. But the ethos that motivates the church to seek out and help the most vulnerable in society is one that can inspire many.

Why are these the programs Saint Mark has decided to focus on? As Pastor Pointer says, "You can't be spiritual unless you're social," a statement I heard repeated by volunteers at many Saint Mark service events. The link between spirituality and helping the most vulnerable in society is clear at Saint Mark. And the church stands ready to serve wherever those needs might be.

Central Church of Christ

At a time when many congregations in the United States are losing members, Central Church of Christ is growing. In 2004, they outgrew their worship space on John Barrow Road in west central Little Rock and moved to a larger space in the heart of downtown. One of the challenges of the move is that it meant that Central couldn't really be a neighborhood church. Wade Poe, the adult ministry leader, mentioned a recent study of their membership that showed that most members live at least five miles away from the church, with many coming from ten or fifteen miles away to attend worship services in downtown Little Rock. This situation meant a new way of thinking about community for the leadership and members of Central.

Steven Hovater is the lead minister of Central Church of Christ. He and his family lived in Little Rock and had a close relationship with Central for many years before moving to Tennessee to pastor The Church of Christ at Cedar Lane and returning in 2022 to take on the role of lead minister following the retirement of longtime pastor Leon Barnes. Steven says that, because so many people travel to attend church at Central, the neighborhoods around the church became a natural place for members to want to invest in together, but he clarifies that "investment doesn't happen without intentionality."

In recent years, the leadership at Central has brought that intentionality to their relationships with the neighborhoods around their church, talking about how they have "adopted" the 72202 zip code where the church is located. As one member described it to me, "We don't have a lot of people who live downtown. So, part of that was creating community and connections for people who don't live here and people who do live here and connecting that all back to Central. That's one of the things that's exciting about this is it connects where we already are as a home base for everyone that's near and far."

Indeed, when it comes to community engagement, Central Church of Christ is investing in a myriad of ways in the community around the physical location of their church. A main focus, and unifying effort, is the Adopt-A-Block program. The program was started by the church's twenties group, made up of enthusiastic twentysomethings who wanted to get more involved in the community around the church. Working with the leadership at Central, Joanna Miller, the twenties group outreach leader, and others in the group have created a program that unifies and amplifies many of Central's community outreach efforts. At the center is Martin Luther King, Jr. Elementary School, where Joanna works as a librarian.

On the second Saturday of each month, volunteers meet at the park next to M. L. King Elementary, provide a picnic lunch, connect with people in the community, learn about any needs there, and build relationships. Some group members stay at the park, share a Bible lesson, and play with the neighborhood kids, while others walk through the neighborhood, pick up trash, and visit with and sometimes deliver food to those in need. As one volunteer said, "I want to know people outside of my church community and be involved in their lives and be invested in them."

On the Saturday that I joined their efforts, they were replanting the flower beds at the front of the school and participating in a water balloon fight. But the water balloon fight was not their idea, and to understand what is really happening in the neighborhood takes a little more context.

Joanna recalls that, as Central began their Adopt-a-Block efforts, some friends of hers who had done a similar program in another area advised her to "find the 'person of peace' in the neighborhood—the person who knows everybody . . . they'll trust you and everybody else will trust you because they trust you." In the neighborhoods where Central Church of Christ is working, this person is Shead. And on the Saturday I was attempting not to damage the flower beds at M. L. King Elementary with my poor gardening skills, Shead was organizing the water balloon fight.

Shead is a friendly woman with a wide smile that makes you immediately want to be her friend. When I met her, she was wearing at least four water guns strapped across her body and tucked into the pockets of her cargo pants. She was filling up water balloons, laughing with neighbors, and swatting away kids who were trying to steal her water guns. Joanna says, "Shead was already in the community doing everything. She would go and mow people's grass and she'll go and pick up trash—she was doing trash pickup long before we were doing trash pickup." Although the people in the twenties group from Central Church of Christ were sincere in their desire to connect with and help their neighbors, it was months before many people would come and join their park picnics or open the door for their visits and food deliveries. As a community organizer and longtime resident, Shead helped them gain some credibility, and they earned some themselves through working on houses and yards that needed revitalizing and coming back consistently.

And the volunteers from Central kept coming, every second Saturday, because they had made a long-term commitment. As one volunteer told me, "It's about showing up consistently over time. Sometimes the bigger, more event-driven outreach, where you do like one or two events a year, that's not consistent, so it doesn't build a relationship, it doesn't build trust between the community and your body of believers."

For Joanna and others, this commitment is very much a part of their faith. Joanna and her husband thought and prayed for a long time about serving a mission overseas, but the opportunity just didn't come for them. As he got involved in community nonprofit work and she took the job at M. L. King Elementary, they both felt, "Okay, well maybe we're meant to serve here right now. . . . It just felt like God's put this in front of us. . . . We are on mission here." Joanna says, "I feel very passionate about making relationships and loving people, regardless of whether or not they ever step into the church building. And a lot of them won't ever and don't want to. But the only way you are going to share Jesus with them is by going to them and talking with them."

Thus, at the heart of Central's engagement programs is a deep theological desire to build relationships, help people flourish, and share the love of God. Tammy Beck, the children's ministry leader, says that this doesn't necessarily mean "coming over here and worshipping with us," but the priority is really about "spreading God's love." Steven sees programs as the skeleton that lets you build relationships. He says, "Relationships don't happen without some venue."

Take the annual Easter egg hunt that Central hosts. Through their 72202 outreach program, they decided to move the egg hunt to the grounds of M. L. King Elementary. This shift to more of a community focus means that more neighborhood folks come out to the egg hunt and connect with the church. In 2022, the egg hunt was planned for the elementary grounds once again, but the morning of the egg hunt saw heavy rain. The organizers at the church quickly moved the event to inside the church and hid the eggs in the sanctuary. Although some were a bit dismayed by the sight of children running through the sanctuary hunting eggs, the leadership and most of the members at Central were thrilled to put the kids first and provide them with a joyful morning.

As a result of that welcoming spirit, five new families attended Easter Sunday worship services and began building relationships with the members at Central Church of Christ, many of which persist today. Tammy remarked on how beautiful it was to see how "God worked through" the Easter storm that year. Joanna and her group continue to return to the neighborhood every second Saturday. Central held a big back-to-school event at the neighborhood park in 2022. But trust builds slowly.

I met with Shead and her mentor, Suzanne, a woman with a long history of community organizing in Arkansas, who expressed no small amount of skepticism about faith-based community engagement. We met at the same park where we had thrown water balloons a few days before, in the heart of the community these women had built, to hear their thoughts on Central's efforts in their neighborhood. At the time, Central Church of Christ had been coming into their neighborhood for over a year, but "it is still a trial period" in their eyes. Shead has been working in the neighborhood for decades, and she knows that she is putting her credibility on the line when she vouches for Central. "If they did something wrong, she'd be in deep trouble," Suzanne is quick to say. "Yeah," Shead agrees, "they would mess up decades of my work." Every interaction between Central and the community is an opportunity to build or lose trust.

For instance, when a home in the neighborhood caught on fire, the church and the neighborhood stepped up with clothes and furniture for the family. One member of the congregation at Central built bunk beds for two little girls who had lost nearly everything. Those interactions built trust. While we were talking, someone from the neighborhood walked up and told us that "it's beautiful"—what Central is doing in the neighborhood—and continued, "We love it, because they bring the community together . . . and it's pure love." But Suzanne and Shead wonder if that trust will be able to weather future challenges. Suzanne asks, "What if there is a crime over here that needs a whole group of people to come and protest, or come to court, or stand up before the legislature, or transport people to the polls? If they want to be part of us, they need to be part of who we are as a neighborhood."

In speaking with leaders, volunteers, and community members, it is not clear how that kind of situation might work out. In the past, Central has been visible and vocal about issues that would likely matter to this neighborhood— marching to the capitol to pray after the murder of George Floyd, for instance. Yet Central is a very diverse congregation—economically, politically, and racially—a diversity that is increasingly rare in congregations and is valued by the members and leadership at Central. Thus, many of Central's efforts to connect with the community around their church prioritize engagement that unifies, like helping children and families and building relationships. In addition to their engagement efforts centered around the elementary school, Central also has a kid's clothing closet where parents can pick up clothes for kids who seem to keep growing out of theirs at ever-faster rates. This effort is really unique because, although there are a lot of places in the city where those in need can get gently used clothes, this is the only one I am aware of that caters specifically to kids. And, again, it is seen by the members of Central as a way to build relationships. As one volunteer told me, "There are regulars. People come and know the people who run it and have developed relationships with them."

Steven emphasizes that the theological importance of these relationships is that they "lead to acts of love, people being generous with each other, sharing wisdom, and growing." He and the other leaders at Central see their efforts in the community as planting seeds—sometimes they get to see the fruits of those efforts as people's lives are changed, they start attending church, and friendships flourish, and sometimes it may take longer for those seeds to grow, if they do at all.

This metaphor is beautifully illustrated in Shead's backyard, just three blocks south of Central Church of Christ, in the neighborhood adjacent to the M. L. King Elementary School that the church has adopted. Since 2021, Central has held its Halloween trunk-or-treat event at the elementary school, making it more of a neighborhood event than when it was in the church parking lot on a busy downtown street. In the spring of 2022, Shead approached the leadership of Central for help with planting corn in a large empty plot in her backyard. She wanted to create a corn maze for the kids to enjoy at the trunk-or-treat event that fall. Together, church members and neighbors planted seeds that would grow into something that would help bring the whole community together and bring joy to children. This is what Central's community-engagement efforts are: relationships as seeds that can help bring communities closer in fellowship and in faith.

Conclusion

Each of these four congregations are deeply and meaningfully engaged in the community, but that engagement looks very different based on theology, resources, and priorities. There is no one model for congregational community engagement. But the data clearly show that there are significant benefits when places of worship choose to engage in their local communities. Congregation leaders and members who are interested in greater community engagement should think carefully about what the best fit might be for their own congregations.

In the next chapter, we take a closer look at two community issues that have been particularly important in Little Rock: race relations and education. These two issues illustrate different ways that congregations can get involved in the community and also why congregations might choose different issues with which to engage.

Engagement in Action on Education and Race

There are an almost unlimited number of issues that congregations could choose to prioritize for their community engagement. When we asked about the community or social programs congregations provided in our 2018 LRCS survey of clergy ($n = 112$), we heard about everything from food co-ops to support for foster children to housing for cancer patients. Our project website features spotlights on community efforts as diverse as addiction recovery programs and efforts to combat human trafficking. As just one example, women from the Westover Presbyterian Church have been offering literacy classes at the Pulaski County Regional Detention Facility for years. Along with class topics like the poetry of Maya Angelou and Tupac Shakur, the students also learn grammar, punctuation, and sentence structure and have weekly vocabulary lessons. One student described the literacy classes as "a thought-provoking, mind-changing hour of empowerment." People and places of faith are creative and prolific in the ways that they serve their communities. We have been inspired by these stories and their service. But there are some issues that rise to the top as particularly important to people of faith, especially given the context of the community we live and research in—Little Rock, Arkansas.

In our 2020 LRCS survey, we asked members about the most important issues facing their communities, with a follow-up question about whether they would want their congregation to get engaged in helping to address each issue. We found that education was the most important issue to the respondents in our sample ($n = 2,293$ people from thirty-five diverse congregations)

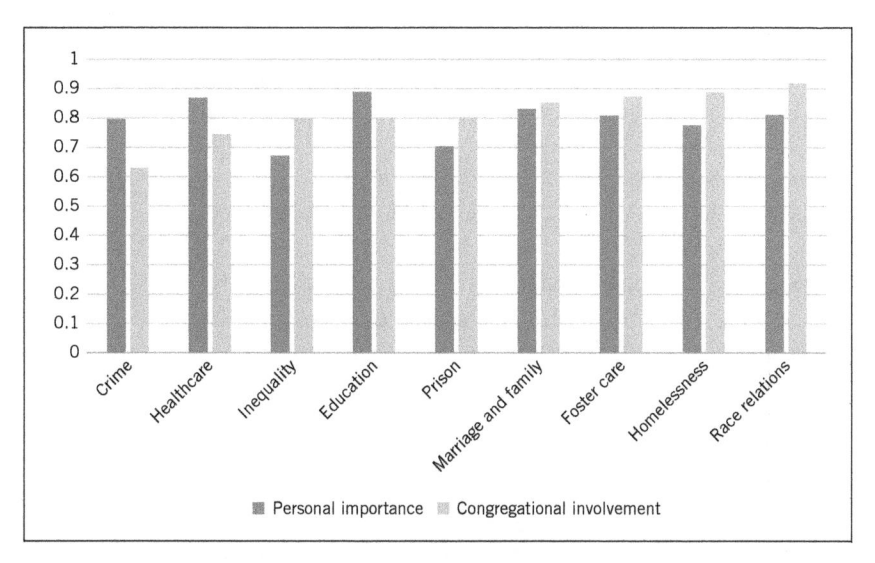

Figure 7.1 2020 LRCS Respondent Ratings of Community Issue Importance and Desire for Congregational Involvement in Addressing the Issue, Normalized on a 0 to 1 Scale

and that race relations was the issue they most wanted their congregation to get involved in helping to address. These data are presented in Figure 7.1. In this chapter, we take a closer look at these two important issues: education and race relations.

Education

The need for education support is certainly great in Little Rock. Only 23 percent of tenth graders in the Little Rock School District are at or above expected reading readiness levels (Wright 2022). The state is ranked forty-first in public education in the country (Ziegler 2022), and 71 percent of children enrolled in public schools in Pulaski County, where the city of Little Rock is located, are eligible for free or reduced school lunch (County Health Rankings, n.d.). So, it's certainly no surprise that many congregations care about and have programs to help address the issue of education. In our 2018 survey of congregation leaders (n = 112), 34 percent reported that their congregation provided education programs. And in our 2020 survey (n = 2,293), over 93 percent of members said that education was an issue that was important or very important to them.

As Chapter 5 discussed, sometimes the interests of congregations and nonprofits align on major social issues like education and they work together to address them. Although scholars have cautioned against the dangers of assuming that religious groups can step in to fill the breach when government is failing to meet citizen needs (Bane, Coffin, and Thiemann 2001), congregations and nonprofits often see it as a moral obligation to do just that. When collaboration occurs, it is possible to achieve better outcomes. We see collaboration happening in Little Rock through CityChurch Network, a 501(c)(3) organization that works to "unite the church through extraordinary prayer, trained leaders, and greater works for the good of the city" (CityChurch Network, n.d.). The organization is Christian based and made up of experienced pastors who work with local churches to enact biblically focused solutions for social problems. One area of focus is their Vital Families in Schools program.

Many congregations independently establish relationships with local schools to offer support and mentorship, but more than thirty Little Rock churches participate with CityChurch Network's structured program, each hosting a school and working with CityChurch Network's leadership team to connect students and their families to mentor families within their school's matched church. Grounded in a faith-based approach and relying on the research of scholars like Jeynes (2015), who emphasizes the importance of family involvement and faith community support for reducing the achievement gap, CityChurch Network's goal is to build relationships and genuine connections with families and their church mentors.

One example of a congregation participating in this program is St. Andrew's, which was matched up with Western Hills Elementary School. A blog post on CityChurch Network's website says that "through an annual back-to-school event, an active mentoring program, and providing volunteers for other various school events throughout the year, St. Andrew's sees these as vital opportunities to serve the families of Western Hills" (Hampton 2022). But more than the events, "the Church sees itself as a safety net providing support to the families of both the students and staff and providing for additional needs the school may have as they arise" (Hampton 2022).

In addition to the organized efforts of CityChurch Network to connect schools and churches, many congregations from diverse faith traditions are working to support education on their own. For instance, in an interview our LRCS research team did with a religious leader whose congregation has established an independent relationship with a local elementary school, this leader told us that "we do a lot of what room mothers often used to do when I was a kid. We do parties for giving things, we also do a lot of support of the teachers, and we tutor kids—that's the big thing. And we're very supportive financially of things there, too."

Beyond personal mentoring relationships and financial contributions, our research reveals that some congregations are trying to do more on the issue of education. As one leader put it, "We believe that just feeding kids or educating kids isn't enough. We have to change the policy structures that keep them from thriving. And so, we are doing a lot of work to restore local control of schools." What this religious leader is referring to with "local control" is conflicts over the Little Rock School Board and schools in the district—mostly those populated by Black students—receiving consistently failing grades and being taken over by the state (A. Harris 2019).

In Little Rock, it is impossible to understand the issue of education without looking at the history of race in the city. Historical residential segregation, combined with the geographical shift of white people to the suburbs and outlying cities around Little Rock, along with many white families opting for private schools, means that public schools in Little Rock remain largely segregated (Barth 2022; Roher 2019). White flight to outside the city of Little Rock and to private schools has been a consistent pattern since the 1957 integration crisis (Branton 1983). In 2014, almost 20 percent of all school-aged children were enrolled in one of the forty-one different private schools available to them in Pulaski County (Roher 2019). Although school segregation is subtler now than it was in 1957, Little Rock's schools are still far from integrated in the eyes of many, and the resources that majority-Black and majority-white schools receive are far from equal (Semuels 2016).

On March 8, 2023, Governor Sarah Huckabee Sanders signed the LEARNS Act into law in Arkansas, creating, among other things, "education freedom accounts" that will allow parents to use public money to enroll their children in private schools (Lenora 2023). Some fear that this may lead to greater inequality in Little Rock schools. Parents who have the time and education to navigate the school choice system will opt for private schools, and parents who have students with special needs, which private schools aren't required to accommodate as public schools are, will stay in public schools (Lenora 2023). School voucher programs across the country have not shown consistent learning gains for students (Prothero 2017), so in a state and city with a racial history like Little Rock, Arkansas, one fear is that policies like the LEARNS Act will actually exacerbate racial disparities in education (Cathey 2023; Ukanwa, Jones, and Turner 2022).

When our LRCS research team held community dialogues on the issue of education in 2021, we repeatedly heard from participants that racial segregation and poverty were major problems preventing students from attaining a quality education (Glazier 2021, 5). According to lawsuits filed in Arkansas, the disparities are stark. Public schools with the highest percentage of white students have individual computers and climbing walls, while schools whose student populations are only 2–3 percent white have rat infestations and inoperable bathrooms (Semuels 2016).

One Little Rock congregation, Saint Mark Baptist Church, has decided to invest in education assistance for vulnerable children through their Tendaji Community Development Corporation, which is a separate organization that hosts after-school programs and summer camps for kids. Tendaji, which is the Swahili word for "making things happen," is a nonprofit community-development organization that uses the Saint Mark campus during the week but is not officially part of the church. The vision for Tendaji came early in Pastor Pointer's ministry with Saint Mark. The church had raised funds to build a new and larger sanctuary, but because education is such a pressing need in the Little Rock community, Pastor Pointer wanted the money to be spent to add space for children to learn and grow.

This education program operates with a clear awareness of the history of racial disparities in education that exist in Little Rock. In addition to the after-school and summer programs, because Black children are more likely to be suspended from school than white children (Losen and Skiba 2010; Mendez and Knoff 2003), Tendaji also has a Reclaiming Scholars program for kids who have received disciplinary suspensions. They can come to the Tendaji center when they can't go to school and can keep up with their schoolwork there, and both they and their parents can receive counseling (Owens and McLanahan 2019). The Reclaiming Scholars program began in just two schools, but since 2015, it has expanded into sixteen schools. More than 180 students from the community participate in Tendaji's after-school tutoring program every year, and about 140 attend their summer camp.

Shelia Hayes, the director of the Tendaji program, was a part of the vision for the organization from the very beginning. She has an extensive history of working in education—as part of the Little Rock School District for twenty-six years and in the nonprofit sector for an additional ten—and she sees what they do at Tendaji as "enhancing the school day" for kids and "providing a service to the community." The children who participate in the program are all participating in restorative education—setting goals and learning skills to make better choices. As Director Hayes describes it, "We are taking students out of their element and bringing them to a different area. We are showing them what could be. And they come into the light."

A great example of this is Braelond Simmons, a program manager for Tendaji. Braelond's father passed away when he was six years old, and he and his siblings were raised by a single mother. He first began working with Director Hayes as a volunteer for an after-school program when he was in seventh grade, and he talks about what a difference it made for him to connect with the mentors in the program and "see people who looked like me" as a young African American man. It made him consider, for the first time, "after talking with them, and having that self-confidence, to think, 'Why not me? Why can't I go and do those same things?'" And now, as a program manager for Tendaji, Braelond is a role model for a whole new generation of kids.

Tendaji is more than just an education program. Through the growing pains of the early years of building such a far-reaching program, the staff has had their share of struggles, but Director Hayes says, "We know that this is God ordained . . . this is God's vision and we are just putting it in place. We are just acting it out. There is no other explanation for the growth that we have incurred, the number of students, the community impact. . . . There is no other way to describe it other than that this was God's mission." The connection between serving the community on the issue of education and serving God is a close one for the people working through Tendaji.

Because the issue of education is so closely tied to race in Little Rock, it was not surprising to our research team that both these issues were so near the top in terms of importance to our congregant respondents. What was surprising was just how eager people of faith in Little Rock were to see their congregations get involved in helping address the issue of race, a topic we move to in the following section.

Race Relations

As Figure 7.1 illustrates, race relations is an important issue for people of faith in Little Rock. It ranks fourth in importance, out of nine issues, with 83 percent of respondents ranking it as an important or very important issue. But, more than any other issue, race relations is the one that respondents want to see their congregation actively engaged in helping to address. In fact, 86 percent of those who received the follow-up question about whether they would like to see their congregation get involved in helping to address the issue of race relations responded yes; only 2 percent responded no.

We think this is a meaningful finding because it tells us that respondents see race as within the domain of religion. Whereas crime, for instance, might be an issue that matters to many people in Little Rock, they don't see it as an issue that their place of worship should be trying to solve. By way of comparison, 42 percent of our respondents said they wanted their congregation involved in addressing the issue of crime, less than half as many as wanted their congregation to address the issue of race relations. Although white Christian individuals and institutions in the United States in particular have often supported racist policies and doctrines (Tisby 2019), some churches today are trying to better live out their religious values through the creation of multiethnic congregations (DeYmaz 2020; DeYoung, Emerson, and Yancey 2004) and by engaging in faith-based racial justice work (Harvey 2020; Tisby 2021). These numbers reflect that desire.

In fact, religious traditions and faith leaders may be particularly well equipped to address racial injustice. With practices rooted in forgiveness and repentance, religious leaders and people of faith can appeal to those shared values and sense of higher purpose in their efforts to heal deep and devastating racial wounds, often drawing on religious texts and traditions that are widely supported by those in their faith tradition (Marsden 2012, 5). For instance, Rev. Myra Brown talks about how the true work of religion is the work of social justice, saying, "We must work tirelessly to end racism where we live. . . . We must open ourselves to others' pain, speak out against injustice, and construct the future in which we want to live" (Brown 2019, 45).

We heard similar messages from the clergy we interviewed in Little Rock, many of whom mourn the racial division and injustice in the city and see these problems as deeply religious issues. As one leader put it, "We believe [racist systems and structures] are breaking God's heart and so we are seeking to live in a different way." Another leader said, "It's our job to continue to work with, to stand up for, and to speak up for those who are marginalized." One Christian leader put it very directly, saying, "Jesus not only taught us how to be anti-racist, he lived it, he demonstrated it, and he confronted it head-on."

In the fall of 2021, the LRCS research team interviewed twenty-one clergy from diverse congregations in Little Rock on the ways that their congregations were engaging with the topic of race relations. Table 7.1 contains a list of the types of formal programs clergy mentioned to us in these interviews, categorized by the type of program. From book clubs to podcasts to sermon series, congregations in Little Rock found many ways to engage with the topic of race. Most often, these programs were focused within the congregation, but congregations also partnered with others and reached outward. They were often engaging with their members to process the current events of the day, like the murder of George Floyd and the Black Lives Matter protests, and using the tools of their faith to determine what personal or political actions to take (Glazier, Driskill, and Hanson 2022).

Through the kinds of formal programs listed in Table 7.1 and more informal outreach efforts and discussions, some congregations are trying to engage with the topic of race relations and make their places of worship more diverse and inclusive. As one religious leader told us, "We believe our church should be a reflection of our community. If we've got poor and wealthy in our community, they need to be in our church. If we have five different races in our community, we need to have five different races in our church."

When religious institutions act on the issue of race relations, it can be very meaningful for members and clergy. A Black pastor recounted a powerful moment at regional conference for their denomination when the leadership displayed a photograph of George Floyd and asked everyone to sit in silence for eight minutes and forty-six seconds (the amount of time that Officer Derek Chauvin kneeled on Floyd's neck). This pastor told us, "I was moved. . . .

TABLE 7.1 LIST OF FORMAL RACE RELATIONS EFFORTS MENTIONED BY LITTLE ROCK CLERGY IN 2021 INTERVIEWS (*N* = 21), CATEGORIZED BY TYPE
Formal program mentioned
Within congregation
Book studies
Discussion groups
Guest speakers
Hire more diverse leadership
Listen to or host podcasts
Meetings
Multiweek seminars
Research history of own church
Special sermon series
Talks around MLK Day, George Floyd, Black History Month
Watch movies
Workshops
With other congregations
Host discussions with other pastors
Joint worship services
Meet with other pastors
Partner with local organizations or congregations
Outside of congregation
Attend rallies
Issue formal statements
Outreach to diversify congregation makeup

You would think something like that might be small to some people, but to most of us, that was a major acknowledgment."

But while some congregations are eager to engage with the topic of race relations, other congregations are hesitant to talk about race. Although, as one leader put it, "racism paves the streets of Little Rock," some congregations would prefer not to talk about it at worship services. Race may be perceived as a controversial or political issue. For instance, one religious leader who has been engaged with racial justice work told us, "We've lost people. I'm trying to be honest about that. . . . We've lost people who thought, 'You have the gospel of the Jesus and you have racial justice work, but they're not the same thing.' We've lost people who felt like it wasn't the church's proper place to make policy and public pronouncements." This experience is not new for clergy in Little Rock. Historically, clergy who have spoken out on race have faced backlash. After the *Brown v. Board of Education* decision desegregated schools, few clergy were willing to speak out in favor of desegregation in Little Rock or elsewhere in the South. Those who did faced pressure from their members and their ecclesiastical leaders, in addition to physical threats (Friedland 1998).

Just like the leader who spoke of losing members as a result of racial justice work at worship services in 2020, clergy throughout the 1960s lost members and even their jobs as a result of their civil rights or anti-war activism (Friedland 1998; Gill 2011; Moon 2003). In recent years, the backlash against racial justice work at places of worship may have come about because some clergy view race in the same category as politics. They seem to categorize all of it as a distraction from religion and the true focus of their faith. We can see that approach in the language of one leader, who said, "Especially right now with the way things are going on, with the elections and the viruses . . . , around racism, and just so many other things, it's a distraction to even begin to figure it out."

Other clergy may not always see religious engagement with racial justice as sincere. As one Black leader told us, "There were several churches that wanted us to have 'swap days.' You know, I would go to the white church and preach, and the white preacher would come to our church and preach. My conception of that was they just wanted to say that they had a Black person come preach and that would be it." Our research found that although Black congregants prioritized race relations, they were less likely to say they wanted their congregation to get engaged (Glazier, Driskill, and Hanson 2022). This may be due to a sense of burnout and exhaustion from Black people having to teach white people about racial justice issues (Gorski 2019; Winters 2020). Engagement can be a lot to ask of Black congregants at the end of the day.

Other clergy expressed similar cynicism regarding the disconnect between what people say they want and what they actually enact in their lives. For instance, we heard one clergy member express this view with some frustration: "They'll say things like 'Sunday morning is the most segregated hour.' So is when you go home to your white neighborhood and your white schools. I find that entirely frustrating, and they put this burden on the church when they're not living it out."

However, our data do show that, over the years, race relations has become an increasingly important issue in the minds of the clergy of Little Rock. As Figure 7.2 shows, by the time of the 2020 LRCS clergy survey, 100 percent of the responding clergy believed race relations was an important or very important issue. This may be due in part to the timing of the 2020 clergy survey, which launched in mid-May of 2020. More than 70 percent of our responses came in after May 25, 2020, when George Floyd was murdered, making

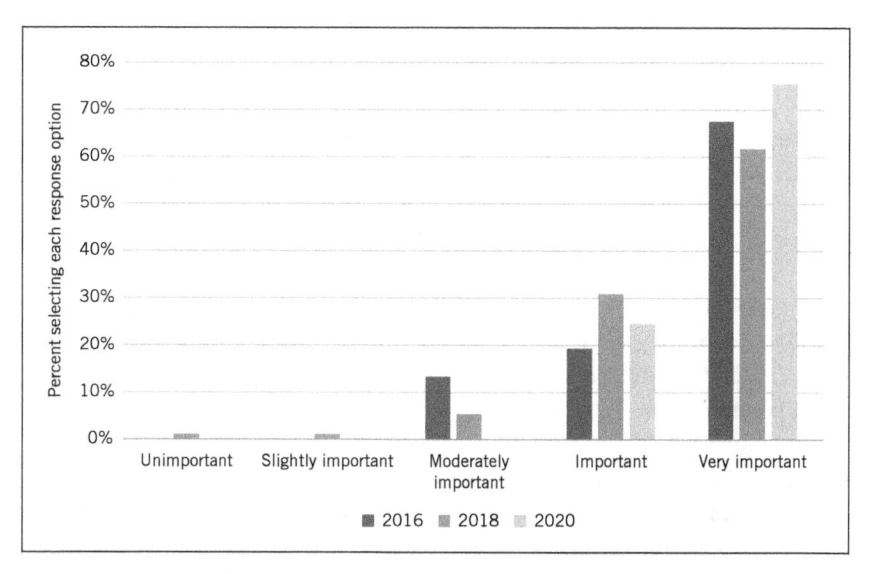

Figure 7.2 LRCS Clergy Survey Respondents' Issue Importance Ratings with Regards to Race Relations, 2016–2020
Note: 2016 clergy *n* = 83, 2018 clergy *n* = 94, 2020 clergy *n* = 57.

race relations significantly more important to clergy in 2020 (mean = 4.75 on a 1 to 5 scale) than in the other two years in our sample (mean = 4.52 on a 1 to 5 scale; difference is significant at the $p < 0.05$ level).

Engagement on the issue of race relations looks different for different congregations. As Table 7.1 illustrated, when we talked with Little Rock clergy in the summer and fall of 2021 about what they were doing on the topic of race relations, some were more focused on discussions within their own congregation about their racial past or how they could learn through things like reading groups, whereas others were trying to build relationships with congregations of other races and yet others were attending protest rallies. But engagement also looks like the deacons from Saint Mark Baptist Church out early on a Saturday morning in September 2022 with string trimmers, hedge pruners, rakes, and garbage bags cleaning up a stretch of the Twelfth Street corridor where an extensive mural has gone up since the murder of George Floyd.

The volunteers cleared weeds, cut down vines, and picked up trash so that passersby could better see the powerful images memorializing Floyd and others, honoring Black heroes, and promoting pride in Black culture. One volunteer said, "The Twelfth Street corridor is part of Saint Mark's area . . . you can see the different murals here, a lot of this came up after George Floyd and other things, so we just wanted to really make sure this part of the city has a little sparkle." Pastor Hersey, the real powerhouse behind these service efforts and the one who rallied the volunteers this Saturday morning, said, "When we come out it gives the community what I call a penicillin shot of spiritual hope. We feel good. We take pride in our community. . . . [The deacons] have sacrificed their time to be a blessing to the community, but Pastor Pointer says all the time that it's more blessed to give than to receive."

This sentiment, along with a sense of responsibility and commitment to each other, their church, and the community, was echoed by many volunteers that morning. One told me, "I just want to help the community out; it's what we do; it's our call. It's what it's all about." He went on to say that cleaning up this mural in particular shows that "the community cares. This is a great thing to do for the community." Engaging on the issue of race relations, even in a way as simple as keeping a mural clean and visible for the community, has a positive impact for the members who volunteer, the congregation, and the community.

Race relations can be a challenging community issue to engage with. Not all congregation members may be ready or eager to join in the effort. Yet, our 2020 data show that, generally speaking, race relations is an issue that members want to see their congregations engage on. Even if it may stretch a congregation, it may be worth considering. The next section directly compares which kinds of congregations might prioritize either education or race relations through the use of statistical models that predict how important each issue is to respondents.

Comparing Education and Race Relations

Both race relations and education are important issues in Little Rock. The motivations for engaging in either issue may be different. For instance, community engagement on education might focus more on changing institutions, while engagement on race relations might focus more on changing hearts, depending on people's theological and ideological perspectives. We looked at some qualitative examples of what engagement on these two issues looks like in the previous sections, but here we compare statistical models of congregant issue priorities from a pooled sample of 2016 and 2020 LRCS survey data, providing a larger and more diverse sample for analysis but limiting the number of control variables we can include in the models. Simplified versions of the results of the models predicting issue importance for both education and race relations are presented in Table 7.2, with full model results available in Table C.18 in the appendix.

There are some key similarities and differences between the variables that lead individual respondents to prioritize one issue over another. In the cases of both education and race relations, community engagement leads to the issue being ranked as more important, as does a respondent identifying as Black. A conservative political ideology tends to be associated with rating

TABLE 7.2 SIGNIFICANT VARIABLES IN MODELS OF ISSUE IMPORTANCE FOR EDUCATION AND RACE RELATIONS, USING DATA FROM LRCS CONGREGATION MEMBER SURVEYS IN 2016 AND 2020

Variable	Education		Race relations	
	Direction	Significant?	Direction	Significant?
Community engagement	Positive	Yes	Positive	Yes
Political activity	—	No	Negative	Yes
Conservative ideology	Negative	Yes	Negative	Yes
Close to congregation's ideology	—	No	Negative	Yes
Providentiality	—	No	Positive	Yes
Religiosity	—	No	Negative	Yes
Age	—	No	Positive	Yes
Female	Positive	Yes	—	No
Black or African American identity	Positive	Yes	Positive	Yes

both issues as less important. In terms of differences, women are more likely to prioritize education, but gender is not a significant predictor when it comes to race relations.

There are some surprising findings in the model of race relations. First, older respondents are more likely to say that race relations is an important issue, although this may be partly an artifact of an older sample (the average age of our respondents in this sample is around fifty-eight). Second, those who think their views are different from others at their congregation are more likely to say that race relations is an important issue. We know from previous research that political homogeneity in congregations tends to decrease political activity (Djupe and Gilbert 2009)—it seems less pressing to be active when the people in one's social circle all share the same political views— and a similar process may be at work here. When people see themselves as holding different views from the rest of the congregation, they think it's even more important to advocate for those issues that matter to them.

Finally, there are some interesting things going on with religion in the model for prioritizing race relations. Religiosity (a measure of religious behavior like prayer, scripture reading, and attendance) and providentiality (a measure of religious belief in a divinely ordained plan that people can help bring about) are pulling in opposite directions. Religiously devout people are less likely to see race relations as an important issue, but those who believe they can help carry out God's will here on earth see it as more important. Those who prioritize race relations are also less likely to be politically active, again indicating that they see this as a religious issue, or perhaps that they see the political route to change on this issue as ineffective.

Looking at these two models side by side, what emerges is a statistical picture of religious people who value diversity, are motivated by providential religious beliefs, and see themselves as ideologically out of line with others in their congregation. These are people who see themselves as going out on a limb for the issue of race relations, which they see as spiritually critical and socially relevant. We heard this in one clergy interview that referenced scripture directly: "When I read the New Testament and I read about Paul talking about Jesus breaking down the barrier between the Jewish culture and the Gentile culture—making of the two men one new man—I think that the implications for racial harmony in America are unmistakable. That's our mandate."

But for some congregations, race relations and racial justice have nothing to do with their faith. In our interviews with clergy, we actually heard some frustration with this state of affairs. As one pastor put it, "It's become so siloed, so segmented—how do we get people to start to think about the role that religion plays in the larger world again? It's like faith has to do with this aspect of my life, but when it comes to race relations, or social injustice, or economic inequality, faith has nothing to do with it. That's been such a major struggle, because it's one thing for people who don't have faith of any kind to bracket out faith . . . it's quite another for people who would say their lives are formed by faith to bracket out faith when it comes to those issues."

Education and race relations are both critical issues in Little Rock. Engagement on either issue can help the community. Deciding which issues to prioritize is a personal choice for congregation members and leaders. Using data from our 2020 survey, we can model how much members want their congregations to engage on each issue—education and race relations. The simplified results are presented in Table 7.3, and the full models are available in Table C.19 in the appendix.

Deciding to actually get involved in a community issue is very different than just saying an issue matters to you. When it comes to wanting their congregation to engage on the issue, we again see that respondents to our survey view education and race relations differently. Education seems to be more of a political issue, with individual political activity and clergy political activity both positively predicting involvement. Larger congregations and people who attend more frequently are also more likely to want their congregation to get involved in education. Given the context of the fight for local control of the Little Rock School District around the time of the 2020 survey, it makes sense that the issue of education might be politicized and large congregations with politically active clergy—many of whom spoke out on this issue—would be more willing to get involved (Miller 2019).

Interestingly, our respondents seem to view race relations as more of a religious and community issue. Here, personal political activity is not a significant predictor of engagement, while more community-engaged congregations are more likely to have members who want to get involved on the issue

TABLE 7.3 SIGNIFICANT VARIABLES IN MODELS OF ISSUE INVOLVEMENT FOR EDUCATION AND RACE RELATIONS, USING DATA FROM LRCS CONGREGATION MEMBER SURVEYS IN 2020

Variable	Education		Race relations	
	Direction	Significant?	Direction	Significant?
Community engagement	Positive	$p = 0.07$	—	No
Political activity	Positive	Yes	—	No
Conservative ideology	Negative	$p = 0.06$	Negative	Yes
Congregation's community engagement	Negative	Yes	Positive	Yes
Providentiality	—	No	Positive	Yes
Worship service attendance	Positive	Yes	—	No
Congregation's average warmth	Negative	Yes	Negative	Yes
Age	—	No	Negative	Yes
Congregation size	Positive	Yes	—	No
Clergy self-reported political activity	Positive	Yes	—	No
Ideological diversity	Positive	Yes	—	No
Black or African American identity	—	No	Negative	Yes

of race relations. One of the most interesting variables in these models is providentiality, or the religious belief that God has a plan that people can help bring about. People who want to get involved in the issue of race relations, but not education, are more likely to hold these kinds of beliefs. This may indicate that these respondents see race relations as more central to their understanding of God's plan for humanity. Serving the community by helping the local elementary school is nice, but racial harmony is essential for God's plan.

While Black or African American identity was a positive predictor of the importance of the issue of race relations, it is actually a negative predictor of wanting one's congregation to get involved in the issue of race relations. Here again, recognizing the survey context of the fall of 2020 is important. Many Black churches and Black members were and are exhausted from traumatizing events and conversations and, while they see race relations as a critical issue, may not have the energy to engage with it. Majority-white congregations may want to think carefully about the role they can play in proactively learning and acting on the issue of race relations to take some of the burden off majority-Black congregations.

Conclusion

Communities need congregations to get involved with the issues that matter to them. Often, congregations step in to "patch the social safety net" when crises happen or government services aren't available (Warren, Waring, and

Meyer 2019). At-risk schools need retired adults to read to kids, and communities struggling with racial division need the tools that faith traditions can provide to help them heal. These are just two of the many issues where congregations can make meaningful impacts in their communities.

When it comes to making a difference in their communities, some congregations view their roles as more political than others. On our LRCS surveys of clergy, we asked whether they agreed with the statement, "Political activism is an important part of my church's historical legacy and tradition." Responses are decidedly mixed, as Figure 7.3 illustrates, revealing a wide range of understanding of the relationship between religion and political activism among Little Rock clergy. However, it is important to keep in mind that political activism and community engagement are not the same thing.

Clergy are equally likely to give sermons about volunteering regardless of the church's historical legacy of engaging in politics. No matter how they view political activism and faith, all the responding clergy are equally likely to talk about community volunteering in worship services.

Congregations and clergy may be hesitant to engage on what might be viewed as divisive issues, but communities need congregations to lead—especially on difficult issues, like race relations, and issues where the need is great, like education. They have dedicated members, informed clergy who are respected community leaders, and religious tools that can help build bridges. Additionally, our LRCS data show that members *want* to see their places of worship active and engaged in the topic of race relations. When Little Rock

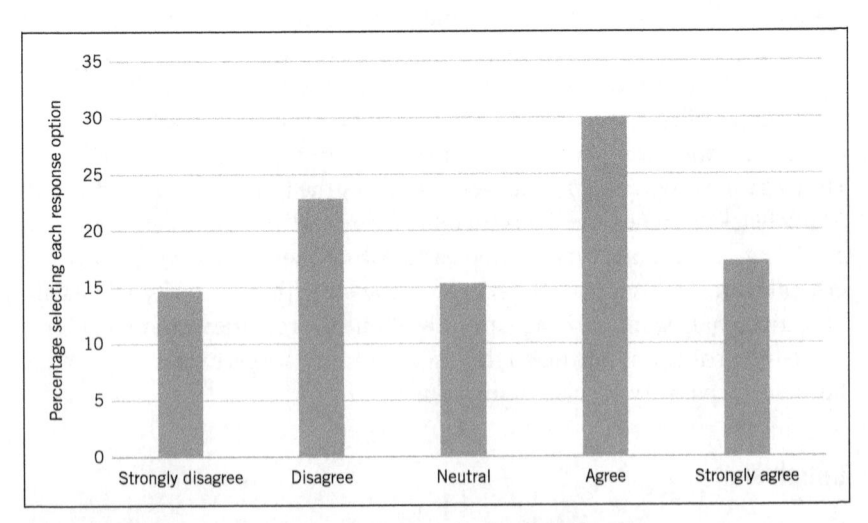

Figure 7.3 Little Rock Clergy Agreement with the Statement "Political Activism Is an Important Part of My Church's Historical Legacy and Tradition"
Note: Pooled sample, 2012–2020, $n = 307$, percentage agreement.

was facing an integration crisis in education in 1957, it was clergy who were there to escort the Little Rock Nine to Central High School (Johnson 2019). And clergy once again spoke out, wrote letters, and joined candlelight vigils in the fight to restore local control to Little Rock schools in 2019 (Miller 2019). When it comes to important community issues, people look to religious leaders and count on the good that can come when congregations get engaged in the community.

This is not always easy. As the section on race relations in particular showed, sometimes community engagement on what can be perceived as controversial issues can be challenging for congregations. But we also learned in Chapter 5 that community engagement has significant positive externalities for places of worship. Thus, engagement can create a buffer that provides the social capital and congregational warmth that make it easier to do the hard, right thing. As one leader said, "I'm convinced that the church is better positioned to deal with some of these problems and push them back even than the apparatus of government." This chapter showed how congregations are making that choice and getting involved to help improve two critical issues in Little Rock. The next chapter extends the call to act to additional issues, showing the important role congregations and clergy play as community actors and the good they can do for society and democracy.

8

Faith, Community, and the Future

Places of worship coming together can be a beautiful sight to see. In 2018, after the Tree of Life Synagogue shooting in Pittsburgh, I was privileged to be present at Temple B'nai Israel, a Jewish synagogue in Little Rock, when dozens of religious and political leaders came together with hundreds of community members to mourn and support. Each year the Interfaith Center of Arkansas hosts a "Love Thy Neighbor" event at St. Mark's Episcopal Church, which brings a diverse group of faith leaders together in a celebration of both unity and diversity in our community. At the event on September 8, 2022, Sophia Said, the director of the Interfaith Center, welcomed everyone and affirmed their mission to "reduce hatred and fear across all religions." Twice a year, faith leaders in Little Rock come together in prayer for the Victory Over Violence + One Voice Prayer Rally, which began in 2017 following the fatal shootings of two Little Rock toddlers. An interfaith and multiracial event in recognition of Juneteenth in June 2022 brought together diverse worshippers and featured speakers from both majority-Black and majority-white congregations. One white attendee remarked to their pastor as they were leaving the event, "I think that is what heaven will be like."

These moments of unity and coming together can be powerful to witness and participate in, but the feelings of community togetherness can be all too fleeting. If congregations want to be a relevant and consequential force for good in the lives of their members and in society, they need to be more consistently engaged in their communities. The key is to reap the substantial benefits associated with community engagement while minimizing the drawbacks. This can best be done by focusing on the community aspects of engagement and minimizing explicitly partisan politics.

The Benefits and Drawbacks of Community Engagement

The benefits of community engagement have been clearly outlined in previous chapters of this book. Here, they are summarized, with supportive quotes from interviews with Little Rock clergy to illustrate how religious leaders view their applicability in practice. The drawbacks of community engagement are then described, together with similar qualitative data from clergy, to illustrate the challenges that may accompany such efforts. Despite the challenges congregations may face with community-engagement programs, the LRCS data indicate such programs are worth the investment.

The Benefits of Community Engagement for Members

As described in Chapter 3, there are many benefits of community engagement that members themselves reap. Some of these come directly from being a part of a community-engaged congregation, but some of these benefits could come to any person who was engaged in their community, whether religious or not. Statistically speaking, people who are more engaged in their communities, hear community-oriented sermons at their place of worship, and provide service outside their congregations have higher life satisfaction, feel closer to God, feel more loved by God, have better physical health, and have higher levels of political efficacy (these benefits are summarized in Table 3.3 in Chapter 3).

The clergy we talked with over the years through the LRCS have repeatedly shared with us the benefits of community engagement they see flowing to the individuals in their congregations, usually focusing on the spiritual benefits. Sometimes clergy explain this as almost a quid pro quo. In speaking about members engaging in community service, one leader put it this way: "If they show themselves faithful, God will show himself faithful. You will be surprised the resources that will go your way when you do the right thing." But most of the time, religious leaders speak about bringing members into the process of engaging and serving as a gradual progression that grows their faith. Take, for instance, this description from a leader:

> People have a sense of "I want to do some good." And then that motivates them sometimes to volunteer a little bit. Then, as they engage in the practice of their faith more, then that turns from just a kind of common humanity to a response to God at work in their life and to the very clear call of Jesus in the Gospels to serve others, to love

your neighbor. As Jesus talks about, he is constantly expanding the notion of who neighbor is, and in the gospel, he's always pushing people beyond, through their initial thoughts about [who their] neighbor would be, and clearly is pushing it to everybody. And so that's something that we're constantly looking at, and as people grow in their faith, it expands that notion of "who is everybody?"

Another religious leader similarly sees engagement as a higher level of faith development, saying, "As our people are getting more deeply connected with Christ, then they're searching for that way to find a place, an outlet, to exhibit their faith and to live out their faith."

Religious leaders and members alike see serving as a spiritual experience that brings the love of God and closeness with divinity that we saw in the statistical data into people's lives in a meaningful way. One leader explained it like this: "The way our congregation relates to Jesus most is through an incarnational view that this is God in the flesh. And so, when we want to encounter God, we go to the flesh and engage in relationships, and in relieving of people suffering."

Another leader who sees spiritual growth happening through service put it this way: "If you are going to have spiritual development within the church, then there has to be a connection [between faith and community]. Within the churches, a connection is good for your fellow man. . . . That's how you grow." Similarly, another leader said, "One of the greatest ways to develop as a follower of Jesus Christ is through serving people." Clearly, religious leaders see engagement as a path to spiritual development and growth. Their views here support what we have seen in the data in previous chapters.

The Benefits of Community Engagement for Congregations

When congregations and their members get engaged in the community, there are a number of benefits that flow to the place of worship—both directly and indirectly. Higher levels of community engagement are associated with greater service to the congregation, which is associated with more frequent attendance, more generous giving, and stronger feelings of warmth and connection to the congregation. The complex statistical relationships among engagement and congregational benefits are mapped in Chapter 4 and displayed graphically in Figure 4.3. Members who are engaged in the community feel a greater sense of spiritual peace and well-being and are generally more religious, both outcomes that tend to benefit congregations.

When we talked with religious leaders, we found that they often extolled the benefits of community engagement for their congregations, both on religious and practical grounds. For instance, one leader connected community engagement directly to the problem of declining membership identified in Chapter 1, saying, "You see that a lot of churches are declining in membership; primarily I think we're declining because the people don't see us in the communities as much as they should."

Other religious leaders similarly spoke about community engagement as important to the identity and survival of congregations. One said, "So, I think community engagement, in many ways, is not something a church does; it springs from who that church is," and another cautioned, "It's a dangerous thing for a congregation to be so internally focused."

The clergy we spoke with also readily identified a key benefit of congregational community engagement: the fellowship and warmth it generates among their members. Serving together helps build friendships and creates relationships that don't easily happen through other means. As one leader put it, "People enjoy helping others, they enjoy sharing their resources, the things that they have. They have been blessed and gifted by God, and they enjoy just meeting other people."

Interestingly, this sense of warmth and fellowship seems to happen even when the individuals themselves aren't necessarily engaged in the service efforts of the congregation. They seem to identify with the culture of service at their place of worship even if their own efforts don't directly contribute. They feel engaged when their congregation is engaged. In speaking about the members at his congregation, one leader put it this way: "They would see themselves as being very active because their church in general is doing that, even though they aren't directly active in that work." Through the community gathering in classes and Sunday School, the members are learning of the work and feel connected to it, even if they don't personally show up to the neighborhood cleanup next Saturday.

Thus, just hearing about the congregation's community-engagement efforts draws the congregation together, but actually serving together creates an even stronger sense of warmth and connection. One lay leader who had served on many committees organizing service projects and community outreach efforts for decades said of her place of worship, "It is a warm and giving congregation. Some of my best lifelong friendships have developed at this church." In speaking of the community-engagement efforts of his congregation, one leader put it this way: "People actually prefer the more tangible ways, I think, because they could see it. It's a visual in the congregation. And it's just been well received. What we do normally is have a worship service that is centered around that issue, and we laid it all out to say, 'This is what we do in this congregation.'" Service and engagement become the culture of the congregation, and people begin to connect with each other and identify with that culture. Such a process strengthens a congregation because the members will feel more connected to their place of worship—and thus attend, serve, and give more there.

The Benefits of Community Engagement for Society and Democracy

When congregations are deciding which community projects to give their time and resources to, they may not be considering how their efforts will strengthen political efficacy and democracy, but the data presented in Chapter 5 demonstrate that they do. The benefits of engagement that flow to the community are much more than just the direct social services that people in need receive, although those are certainly valued. While the data in Chapter 5 focused both on how the individual political efficacy and political activity benefits of engagement aggregate up to benefit communities *and* on the direct services that benefit communities, most clergy are focused on the latter.

Clergy are primarily concerned with a religious imperative to give selfless service to people in need. As one leader succinctly put it, "We're not here to serve ourselves, we're here to serve others." Some leaders more directly connected their efforts with God's will, in a providential sense, and saw themselves as doing what God would have done. Take, for instance, the leader who said, "God would have us to be involved in community . . . especially reaching out to people around us, like the homeless of Little Rock, the people who are hurting, and stuff like that."

A lay leader at another congregation similarly saw the hand of God in the community-engaged work that the congregation was doing, saying, "God was able to intertwine our desire to be involved in the community, to have our church be a presence, a place for people to go when they did have struggles." Another leader, in speaking about how their congregation selected the community projects they engaged with, said, "We are always paying attention and watching what is happening in our world, in our culture, and trying to find ways to plug into how the church needs to be the voice out there." In this quote we again see the sense that there is a religious imperative for the church to be engaged and "out there."

In our conversations with clergy, this imperative almost always came down to caring for those who need it. They were almost never thinking about politics, the incidental civic skills their members were learning through organizing community projects, or the positive impact they were having on efficacy. Statistically, we know that these are benefits of community engagement that accrue to society and democracy as a whole, but they are not on the radar of religious leaders. If they mention politics in the context of community engagement, it is usually to note how service transcends political barriers, as with this quote from a religious leader: "This particular church, whatever side of the political spectrum people find themselves, just really believes that it is deeply part of being a faithful and loving person to care for those whom society has pushed to the side—whoever that is." Despite this beautiful and hopeful statement, that unity doesn't always last. We begin exploring the drawbacks of community engagement next, starting with the times when it can be perceived as political or divisive.

The Drawbacks of Community Engagement:
Being Perceived as Political or Divisive

While the optimists among us might want to think that community engagement is objectively positive and all members would happily agree to support and even participate in community-engagement efforts at their congregations, reality does not always fit that optimistic ideal. Sometimes there are disagreements over which issues to prioritize or, even before the decision to engage is made, fear that engaging will be perceived as political or divisive. In Chapter 7, we saw data from the 2020 LRCS that demonstrated that race relations was the issue that members most wanted their place of worship to get involved in helping to address in their community. Yet some clergy are hesitant to engage on the topic of race because it is seen as controversial. One leader told us, when we asked about race in the fall of 2021, "I've been very intentional not to say anything about injustice." This leader talked about trying to build one-on-one relationships first before broaching race as a topic because it was so difficult to address. With media controversy over CRT (critical race theory), what might begin as a simple conversation or social media post can turn into a political firestorm (Wingfield 2021). No wonder clergy and congregants might be hesitant to engage.

In Chapter 5, we saw just how beneficial it can be for a congregation to have an ideologically diverse membership. Not only does it encourage service to the congregation, but it also boosts political efficacy. But maintaining that ideological diversity can be challenging. Congregation members set and transmit social norms to one another, which leads to a tendency to align political views (Mangum 2008; Stroope and Baker 2014). Additionally, the ideological self-sorting that is increasingly common in the United States makes people less likely to put themselves into contact with those they disagree with politically (Bishop 2009; Mekouar 2022). When congregations are able to achieve some amount of ideological diversity, they may be very hesitant to risk it on a community-engagement project that could be perceived as being divisive. As one leader told us, "We are about a half liberal, half conservative congregation who sees that we can disagree about issues and still pray and serve together. From my perspective, that's pretty amazing in today's society."

However, when a congregation has a lot of members with different political views, just the logistics of deciding on a project can be challenging. One leader described their congregation as a "big tent church" and went on to say, "So our biggest barrier just might be managing the differences in our congregation." Another leader was hesitant about getting involved in a neighborhood issue he viewed as more political, saying, "There's a part of me that thinks there would be a strong segment [of the congregation] that would want to carefully maintain the church's nonpartisanship."

For many clergy, the problem of potentially dividing their congregation over a community issue may be more than just intellectual. Research shows that if leaders speak in worship services on political topics that their members don't agree with, they see a measurable decline in offerings (Calfano 2010; Calfano, Oldmixon, and Gray 2014). But if they can get people serving together, most ideological differences will fade away. Volunteering and serving the community together will build social capital (D. Campbell 2013)—both in a generalized sense and in terms of bonds among congregation members. Ultimately, congregations will reap the benefits of ideologically diverse congregations engaging together and serving that we saw in Chapter 5. As one leader said about their own congregation, "It's a pretty interesting mix of conservatives and liberals, so Republicans and Democrats, that just show up to work together."

The key to getting people to "just show up to work together" across ideological lines may be to focus on the community and religious aspects of engagement while minimizing those areas that might be seen as political. For instance, one congregation leader put it this way: "We do not use, and we do not think it appropriate to use, the word 'political' to describe social justice advocacy and community engagement. When we engage in issue advocacy, we are advocating for the values of our faith." Almost across the board, clergy talk about serving and engaging as ways of living out their faith. With this frame front and center, political concerns can take a back seat and will be less of a drawback for community-engagement efforts.

The Drawbacks of Community Engagement: Members Are Hesitant

As discussed in Chapter 1, many congregations are facing demographic challenges. Their members tend to be on the older side, and their numbers are dwindling. In Little Rock and other communities, neighborhood demographics may have shifted over the years, as well, so that the church some members attended since they were children is situated in a neighborhood they no longer recognize. For older and smaller congregations, these changes may feel disconcerting. Instead of engaging with the community, they may instead respond by retreating from it (Davidson 1986; Gibson 1961). One pastor, who had only been leading his congregation for a few months, told me that when he arrived, "They locked the doors on Sunday mornings once service started and if they didn't know you were coming, you didn't get into the church. They were scared of their community; they were scared of their neighborhood." Unfortunately, this is one of the congregations that did not make it through the challenges of the pandemic and had to close its doors for good.

Other congregations are facing similar changes but are trying to adapt to the shifts happening around them. One leader told us that this can make community engagement challenging, as the members of the church may not be like the community around the church, saying, "We're there in the community, but we're not necessarily *like* our community. [The church] was started thirty-five years ago when Southwest Little Rock was just a different community. And so, we are just wrestling with that as a congregation—how the culture has changed."

Especially when there is a mismatch between the demographics of the congregation and the demographics of the community they are serving, members may be hesitant to get engaged because they are worried that their motives may be questioned. At times, we heard from community activists that majority-white congregations coming into majority-Black neighborhoods for community service and relationship building is really about "white saviorism." This is where partnerships could be particularly helpful. One activist put it very directly, saying, "If they really wanted to make relationships over here, we've got three churches in this neighborhood; you would go to those pastors and say, 'Our church has got money, y'all don't have shit. Let's see what we can do for you.'"

As we saw in Chapter 5, collaboration is sometimes easier said than done. There remain many barriers to collaboration, and members may be hesitant to work with people from different faith traditions or different racial or socioeconomic backgrounds. One fear, when it comes to partnering on community engagement with other congregations in particular, was articulated by a community activist who said, "Whether they intend it or not, it seems like they are scavenging for members." For many congregations, in a time of dwindling church attendance and tight budgets, they may be concerned about outreach efforts that could put them into contact with what could be perceived as competitor congregations.

The Drawbacks of Community Engagement: Belief That Faith Should Take Precedent

Another concern that may arise around the issue of limited resources is the idea that matters of faith should take precedence over community engagement. We heard this concern from multiple religious leaders who expressed the belief that engagement was a distraction from their more central work. One leader put it this way (a comment that was actually written in all caps on a clergy survey): "We preach the gospel to the community. We are not involved in social and community affairs." Another leader put it somewhat softer but made the same essential point, emphasizing the theological foundations of this focus:

> We would say without hesitation that we're more concerned about someone's spiritual health than their physical well-being. That may sound harsh, but you've got to realize where we're coming from. We believe that someone who is lost and dies lost that they're separated from God forever. That's our belief; that's the biblical belief. Well, if that's true, which we believe that that's true, then our focus can never be more material than spiritual.

When we conducted interviews with clergy in 2018, we explicitly asked about this relationship between the spiritual and material, showing them the spectrum in Figure 8.1 and asking, "In talking with places of worship in Little Rock, we find that most congregations fall somewhere along this spectrum, where one end represents a total focus on spiritual concerns, without paying much attention to physical or material problems, and the other end represents a complete focus on physical concerns without paying much attention to spiritual problems, and the center point represents an equal focus on both the spiritual and the physical. Where would you put your congregation?" We conducted sixty-four interviews, and the average number where congregation leaders placed themselves was 2.8 (standard deviation = 0.64). The most common response was 3 ($n = 32$). But there were eleven clergy who opted out of our scale altogether. These leaders told us that they saw no difference between the spiritual and the material and that placing them at opposite ends of the spectrum didn't make sense. The congregations led by these clergy

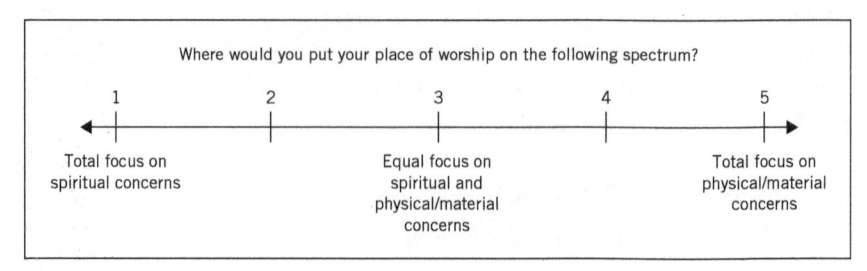

Figure 8.1 Spectrum of Spiritual to Material Concerns; Question Asked in 2018 LRCS Clergy Interviews

were significantly more likely to be engaged in the community (Glazier and Street 2020).

This is likely because these clergy see material service as meeting spiritual needs. As one leader who looked at Figure 8.1 said, "Those things are completely interwoven, and I think that the healthiest manifestation of the church is one that is able to bring those two things together in a way that is not just complimentary, but understands that they were never really different things at all." Another pastor, when presented with the spiritual-material spectrum, said, "You're not going to like this. There's no divergence. If spiritual doesn't manifest itself in material, it's worthless, but if the material has no soul, then it's worthless. There is no difference."

But perhaps most pertinent to the people who would argue that faith should take precedence, we also heard from many clergy who told us that you don't have to sacrifice religion and evangelism to have community engagement. One leader put it in very practical terms this way: "Whenever people are hungry, then they won't listen to anything you have to say. Or when they think they're gonna get deported, they're not listening to anything you have to say. And so, evangelism becomes more than just putting a tract in somebody's hand for us." Building relationships through service also leads to more sincere opportunities for evangelism, some clergy told us. One described it this way: "The people who we served in the youth program or daycare or substance abuse or housing normally were people who would join the church. So, that was mission *and* evangelism." Because of this connection between spiritual and material, evangelism and service, the people who were converted to the church went on to serve and convert others: "They had a commitment to the church because the church served them—other than having them read scriptures. They served them and helped develop them to become disciples to serve others who might be going through some of the same issues."

We often heard clergy talking about people living their faith through action; they would connect spiritual and material through making a practical difference with their faith. As one leader said, "We can't consider ourselves spiritual if we're not concerned about the social needs of the community." Theological priorities are up to the people and leaders of each congregation, but for most religious traditions, caring for those in need and serving each other are principles of faith. One leader put it this way, "Our hope is that as people are . . . deepening in their faith, there's something inside of them that says, 'What does this mean for me? What do I do with the faith that I have? What do I do with the love that I've received, and where and how do I give that love away?'" Individuals, religious leaders, and statistical data have repeatedly illustrated that faith grows through community engagement. Serving others is a great way to strengthen a religious community, grow an individual's religious faith, and share that faith with others.

What Comes First? Congregational or Member Engagement?

Imagine for a moment that you are a religious leader and, after weighing the benefits and drawbacks, you decide that community engagement is the best path forward for your congregation. Does your institution drive the service orientation of your congregation, or do the members? What comes first, congregational or member engagement? It can be hard to pull the two apart, and they are likely mutually reinforcing. In our 2020 congregation survey, individual community engagement and the congregational average of community engagement are only correlated at 0.25. So, one is not determining the other, but they do seem to have a positive relationship.

One path would be to have member engagement drive service. People who want to be engaged would then join the congregation because that is what matters to them. As one leader of a very community-engaged congregation put it, "I think congregations attract likeminded people. I mean . . . if I'm going to do our church, then I got to be a doer."

Another path would be to prioritize engagement as a congregation and persuade the members who are already there to get on board. It may only take a few key members of the congregation promoting engagement work to help develop a culture of engagement. As one leader said, "When you're around people who care about something, you're going to care about it, too. . . . When you're surrounded by people who value serving others more than they value personal enrichment or whatever, it rubs off."

But it likely doesn't have to be just one path or the other. In the very same congregation, members can join for the service *and* the service culture can draw people who are already members into engagement. Consider a congregation like Second Presbyterian Church in Little Rock, which has a long-standing reputation for being a church that prioritizes community engagement. I spoke with a number of lay leaders and volunteers at Second Pres. For some of them, they came to the church precisely for that engagement. One told me that she learned about the church through their work with Habitat for Humanity: "I was looking for a church that was accepting of many different viewpoints. And did things. I wanted a church that wasn't just all talk. . . . I was really attracted by the service aspect of Second Pres." Another said something similar: "One of the things, when I was considering coming to Second, is clearly there's such a long, long history of commitment to outreach into the community. . . . That was something that clearly was of interest to me and helped me make a decision." But for others, the service came later. One member told me that she had been a Presbyterian all her life and that when she moved to Little Rock she was "invited to Second by friends, and then I fell in love with the service here."

With these multiple and reciprocal paths, as exemplified by Second Presbyterian Church, members both drive engagement and are drawn further into engagement by the culture of the congregation, which they help create, through a positive feedback loop. Additionally, members can both provide service and benefit from service as part of these reciprocal processes.

The story of a single person, Troy Hunter, illustrates how this reciprocity works in practice. Troy's experience shows how members can both contribute to and benefit from congregational community engagement, the two can reinforce one another, and the impact of both can have far-reaching effects. In 2021, Troy was heading to the store to pick up some groceries for his family. On his way, he saw a woman holding a sign that said that she was hungry. When Troy got to the store, his shopping list was forgotten, replaced with sandwich supplies, snack cakes, and chips that he wanted to get for this hungry woman and other people in need. But by the time he got back to the intersection where she had been standing, the woman was gone. Finding himself newly laden with food supplies, Troy wasn't sure what to do. As Troy tells it, he and his family had recently started viewing online services at Saint Mark Baptist Church and had heard "Pastor Pointer talking about giving." With that message "sitting on my spirit," as Troy puts it, a cousin suggested he get in touch with the church, who might be better able to distribute the food he had bought to those in need.

When Troy got in touch with the outreach ministry at Saint Mark, he found that they were—right at that very moment—packing sack lunches with supplies nearly identical to the ones he had purchased. He headed over with his contribution to add to the meals and was greeted by a welcoming staff member, who was not only happy to have the help but also prayed with Troy, who was going through some of his own challenges.

Now, one thing that is essential to know about Troy is that he loves food and loves to cook. On the day that he walked into Saint Mark hoping to provide sandwiches to people in need, Troy had been wanting to go to culinary school for five years, but he had been thwarted by challenges with financial aid. As his relationships with staff and volunteers at Saint Mark's outreach ministry grew, he began cooking for the unhoused population that would come for lunch four days a week. And he also shared his dream of going to culinary school. They were able to make some calls and help remove the roadblocks to his schooling. Troy recounts, "God was helping open those doors for me. . . . I went there with the intent to help and to offer my expertise in cooking, but it went from that to being introduced to this lady at the culinary school who helped me, in turn, resolve my financial aid issue, and then I became a student, and then I was even more driven to use my skill set to help the outreach."

Troy continues to volunteer with Saint Mark's homeless ministry, cooking a hot meal for upward of fifty people every Monday. The other volunteers will sometimes tease him good-naturedly because he cooks such great meals—they all want to volunteer on Mondays! Even though the population they are serving is unhoused, Troy seasons the food purposefully, plates it beautifully, and garnishes it with parsley. He says, "Everybody deserves a good meal, a tasty meal, something that makes you feel wholesome." For Troy, it is personal. He says, "I know and understand how it feels to need a meal or how it feels to need someone to give you a helping hand." He also sees service as "part of my duty as a growing Christian." Cooking is a way to give back that is spiritual for him. Troy says that cooking and sharing food in service is "just a part of me now. It's very spiritual and very connected to God."

Troy recently finished his second semester of culinary school, and, in addition to cooking with Saint Mark's outreach ministry on Mondays, he also works as a culinary assistant at a high-end steak house in Little Rock. He never again saw the woman from the intersection holding the sign that she was hungry. He says that she was almost like an angel because she started this journey he has been on—a journey that has led him into greater service, a career path he is passionate about, more active church membership, and a growing faith that is deeply meaningful to him. Troy is both a giver and a receiver of service in this story—and because of his continued service, people in need of a wholesome meal in Little Rock find themselves treated with a dignity and kindness they might not have expected. His experience exemplifies how community engagement can create a positive reinforcement loop.

A Call to Action for Clergy

Clergy are respected congregational leaders and community members (Djupe and Calfano 2009). Their congregants are willing to listen to them on a wide range of issues, from health care to family planning to immigration (Anshel and Smith 2014; Azmat 2011; Wallsten and Nteta 2016). They are often well educated and well spoken and tend to have thought through moral issues and established a clear worldview (Beatty and Walter 1989; Crawford and Olson 2001; Guth et al. 1997). Thus, clergy are "particularly effective opinion leaders" (Wald and Calhoun-Brown 2010, 115); they can take a social or community issue and show people why it is religiously relevant. When religious leaders talk about a topic during worship services—perhaps a community issue that many in the congregation hadn't considered before—they provide congregants with a religious lens through which to see the issue (Djupe and Gilbert 2003; Schwadel 2005; Smidt 2004, 2003).

When it comes to the community leadership potential of clergy, credibility matters (Lupia and McCubbins 1998). Generally speaking, clergy have less credibility when they communicate political rather than religious messages (Djupe and Calfano 2009; Kohut et al. 2000), so it is important for clergy to frame engagement in community rather than political terms. When they can connect community-engagement efforts to religious values, they are likely to have the greatest impact and the greatest professional credibility (Olson 2009, 375). Clergy can build bridges between religious beliefs and social and political reality, helping congregation members connect the two and see the relevance of their faith for community engagement (Glazier 2015).

However, returning to the drawbacks of community engagement, clergy can lose their legitimacy if they are seen as inappropriately political (Olson 2009), so once again, ensuring that the community aspects of engagement are emphasized, and not the political, might be key to maintaining support. But even with these frames in hand, the influence of clergy is limited by the characteristics of the people receiving their messages (Djupe and Gilbert 2009; Huckfeldt and Sprague 1995; Leege 1985). For instance, no matter what clergy say, some members may project their own views onto those messages (Krosnick 1989; Krosnick et al. 1993), interpret the messages through a lens of confirmation bias (Dickinson 2020; Munro et al. 2002), or get defensive when taking in new information (Chaiken, Giner-Sorolla, and Chen 1996).

Despite these limitations, clergy are still often the best leaders for congregational community engagement. If places of worship are going to become more engaged in their communities, the impetus for that engagement is likely going to need to come from clergy. And many clergy are already talking to their congregations about community engagement. Consider the following statistics, drawn from various iterations of the LRCS's survey of clergy:

- Across four iterations of our clergy survey—2012, 2016, 2018, and 2020—including a total of 299 respondents, 59 percent of clergy said that they gave sermons urging their congregants to vote.
- In 2012 and 2016, we asked if they gave sermons taking a stand on a political issue and if they gave sermons taking a stand on a moral issue ($n = 145$).
  - A total of 51 percent of the respondents from these two years said they took a stand on a political issue.
  - Nearly 90 percent said they took a stand on a moral issue.
- In 2016 ($n = 84$), we asked how frequently clergy spoke to their congregations about the following topics:
  - The importance of political participation (very frequently or sometimes = 59 percent).
  - The need for members to volunteer in the community (very frequently or sometimes = 84 percent).
  - Social problems facing the community (very frequently or sometimes = 95 percent).

What these data reveal is that clergy are very willing to—and regularly do—talk to their congregations about moral and community issues. They are less likely to talk about political issues or urge political participation, but doing so is still the majority behavior among our sample. Advocating for engagement is not a big reach for clergy.

Again, clergy are excellent advocates for congregational community engagement not only because they are literally leading congregations but because most people trust their religious leaders (Djupe and Calfano 2009; Wald and Calhoun-Brown 2010). Fewer than 8 percent of the respondents from our 2020 LRCS survey of congregation members said they would agree or strongly agree with the statement, "I find it difficult to approach religious leaders in this congregation." These quantitative data show that the vast majority of people find their congregation leader accessible. Qualitative data collected by the LRCS also reflect a high level of respect and trust for religious leaders.

In 2016, respondents were provided with space to leave open-ended remarks, with the prompt: "Please use this space to tell us what you like best about your place of worship, or anything else you want us to know." About one-third of congregants gave some response here (453/1,475, or 30.7 percent). These responses were coded by the LRCS study director according to a codebook available in Appendix D under "Codebook for General Open-Ended Comments, 2016 LRCS Congregation Member Survey," with 20 percent of responses randomly recoded to ensure reliability (percent agreement = 98.5, Krippendorf's alpha = 0.93).[1] The coded responses are displayed graphically in Figure 8.2.

Of the 453 people who left some open-ended comment, 86, or about 19 percent, mentioned their clergy in this space. These remarks were overwhelmingly positive and showed the positive influence clergy have on their congregants. For instance, one person wrote, "It feels like a family. My pastor is easily approachable," and another wrote, "Our Pastor is a leader who makes us understand that we have a responsibility to our community in order for us all to be the best."

Of these comments, only three included anything negative about clergy. One was about the Catholic Church and the clergy abuse scandal ("It is unfortunate that priests who over stepped boundaries were not prosecuted as

---

1. This simple codebook tracked the presence or absence (through binary 0/1 coding) of four variables: whether the clergy was mentioned (percent agreement = 97.4, Krippendorf's alpha = 0.86), whether the spiritual benefits or congregational warmth of the place of worship were mentioned (percent agreement = 97.4, Krippendorf's alpha = 0.94), whether community engagement was mentioned (percent agreement = 98.9, Krippendorf's alpha = 0.94), and whether politics were mentioned (percent agreement = 100, Krippendorf's alpha = 1.0). More detail on the codebook is available in Appendix D under "Codebook for General Open-Ended Comments, 2016 LRCS Congregation Member Survey."

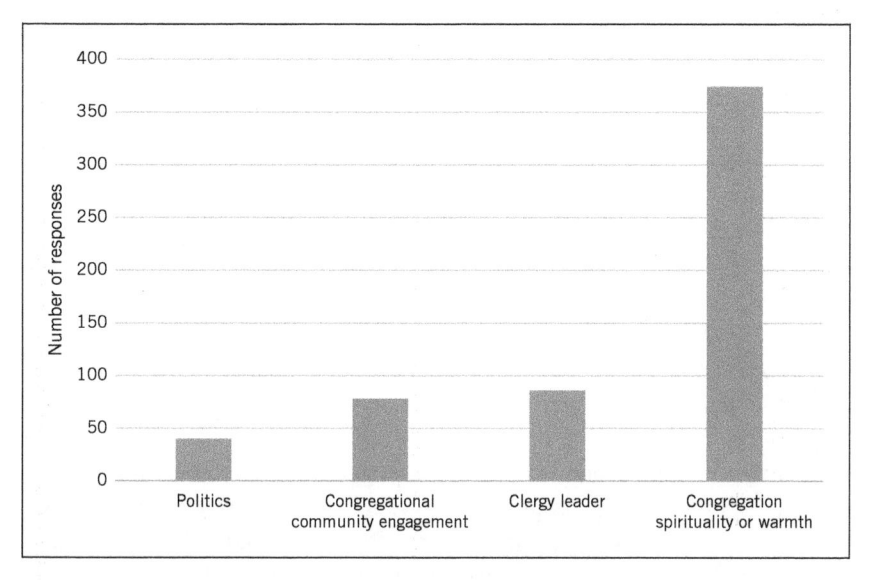

Figure 8.2 Open-Ended Responses to the Prompt "Please Use This Space to Tell Us What You Like Best about Your Place of Worship, or Anything Else You Want Us to Know" on the 2016 LRCS Congregant Survey, Coded by Category, *n* = 453
Note: Some respondents left open-ended comments that were coded into more than one category.

they should have been equal to any other committing crimes against children and that this will/may forever change the credibility of the Catholic Church"), and one was about a leader in a previous congregation who mixed religion and politics ("I have been to a church where pastor said how to vote and I didn't go back"). Only one comment was a negative comment about a leader at a congregation the person was currently attending ("The current leadership is a problem for the church"). Thinking back to the declining attendance data presented in Chapter 1, one thing we can infer is that not many people will continue to attend a congregation where they don't like the leader. Instead, most people are incredibly positive toward their clergy, marking them as important figures with key potential for spiritual, community, and social leadership. As one person put it, "I have talked to the pastor on a personal matter. He is always available. He pushes and encourages and prays over us to do our best toward God." Another wrote about an even broader vision from their clergy, saying, "I think our clergy . . . are trying to lead us to see our spirituality as something that motivates us to work in the world, to make life better for all people."

The vast majority of respondents wrote about the spiritual benefits of their congregation, including the warmth, relationships, and inclusiveness they feel there. More than 82 percent (374 of the 453 respondents) mentioned something about the spirituality or warmth of their congregation, saying things like "Our worship services are inspiring" and "We are family and I thank God for our pastor." We can see just how critical this sense of connection is to some respondents through statements like this one: "We first generation immigrants have nowhere to find family except our worship place. They are my parents, brothers, sisters, sons, daughters, etc. We are family." Sometimes, a leader's teaching was directly linked to helping create that spiritually nourishing and connected environment, as in this comment: "I love my pastor. He is involved in helping with the community. He is a great teacher." This is also echoed in this comment: "I feel that my church is a very important part of my life. Our pastor is very caring and concerned. I cannot imagine it not being in my life."

People also mentioned the community engagement of their place of worship in response to the prompt to tell us what they like best about where they worship. Seventy-eight respondents, or a little more than 17 percent of the people who left open-ended remarks, said something about community engagement, leaving comments like "It encourages the worshipper to be helpful and positive and give back to the community" and "It's a great congregation that truly focuses on service." Another respondent wrote, "I love the involvement of my church in the community and our world."

And, just like the clergy we have heard from throughout the book, these members sometimes identified links between spirituality and community engagement. We can see this in comments like this one: "My church family tries things at local and global levels. It doesn't always work, but we are trying. We try to help others (and ourselves) better know and follow Christ. Often physical needs must be met by tending to spiritual needs." Another respondent wrote, "This body of believers is committed to loving God and loving others outside of these walls and that is exactly what God has called us all to do as His people." One person said that what they liked best about their congregation was "its feet on the ground in the community meeting needs of our neighbors."

Perhaps here again we are seeing the influence of clergy on their members as they link service and spirituality in action and in sermons and those links are reflected back in the comments on the surveys. For instance, one respondent to these anonymous surveys wrote, "A church can't be spiritual without being social!" This is a phrase I heard repeatedly from Pastor Pointer of Saint Mark Baptist Church both in sermons and in personal conversation.

So far, the data have shown that clergy frequently talk about social problems and volunteer opportunities in their community when they deliver sermons and that their members view them quite positively as leaders whom they can turn to, who create congregational cultures of warmth and service, and whose teachings they internalize. Additionally, in our interviews with clergy—out in the community, at events, in coffee shops, and over Zoom—we have heard from them how important they see community engagement to their roles as religious leaders. The call to action for faith leaders to deepen the community engagement of their congregations doesn't just come from the research of the LRCS—it comes from faith leaders themselves.

Take, for instance, the associate pastor from a Black Protestant congregation who joined her members at a polling location during the 2022 election, explicitly recognizing this responsibility by saying, "You can't just tell people what to do. You have to lead them. That's the whole point of being a leader, and if you know what is right and you do what is right, then you can have people follow you or you can encourage them to do the right thing as well."

We heard a similar message from a leader of a multiethnic church who saw a responsibility for religious leaders in helping to unify a divided people, saying, "An increasingly diverse and painful society is no longer finding credible the message of God's love for all people as preached from segregated pulpits and pews on Sunday mornings." For this leader, the answer was clear: get to work outside the walls of the church. The leader continued, "And so, this is true with most humans, but especially with the generations that are younger, that they want to see a lot less talking, and a lot more walking and working together as one beyond distinctions that otherwise keep us apart."

When we talk with religious leaders about how they might see faith and engagement connected, we often hear them reference stories from sacred texts; in the American South, this is often the Bible. Many clergy explicitly look to the life of Jesus for guidance, asking, "What does Jesus do? He calls the disciples close to him and then forms them by being engaged and active in the community. And so, as leaders, that's our role, that's our vocation, is to call people close to God, in part by being actively engaged in God's activity in the world." Another leader put it this way: "We are called by God to make a difference. When you look at the Bible, when you find Jesus, he's in the community, he's not in a church, he's in the community. And so we are called to be in the community." One final quote shows once more how clergy directly make the connection between community engagement and the life of Jesus: "In my own sort of leadership, I'm always encouraging us to get out beyond the walls and touch the world. Because I mean, I think scripturally that's just, that's what Jesus is about."

Clergy have many responsibilities and can feel pulled in multiple directions. They are responsible to their congregants, their own moral views, and their religious tradition and the governance structure therein (Campbell and Pettigrew 1959b). But in their classic study of how clergy responded to the racial crisis surrounding integration in Little Rock in 1957, Campbell and Pettigrew (1959a) found that clergy are strategic actors. They work hard to balance these tensions and are aware of the consequences of elevating personal morals that may conflict with the views of their congregants. This is one reason why some clergy remained silent during the integration crisis. But if they have support for engagement from their congregation, their peers, or their leadership, taking action is easier. A replication of Campbell and Pettigrew's study in Boston, more than twenty-five years later, found that having support from friends in clergy and church hierarchy was associated with higher levels of clergy social activism during Boston's own integration crisis (Thomas 1985). While clergy are critical leaders for community engagement, they can't be expected to do it alone.

When clergy spoke with our research team about community engagement, they often described seeing their members eager to "make a practical difference with their faith." Providing them with opportunities to do so and showing them the real-world applications of their religious beliefs are roles that clergy can play. Community engagement is good for individuals, places of worship, and societies. This call to action is targeted to clergy because they are most directly in positions of authority and responsibility where they can make a difference in terms of engagement, but as they do so, the benefits will be apparent to those around them. Community engagement can measurably improve outcomes at all three levels. The fruits of their efforts may just mean that they won't have to do community engagement alone for long.

Conclusion

As we have seen since the opening chapter, congregations today are facing many challenges—from declining membership to aging attendees to diminishing relevance. But community engagement is a way to address these pressing challenges and reignite faith, revitalize congregations, and heal divided communities. Getting engaged in the community has great benefits for people and places of worship—and it can do a lot of good for people in need in a congregation's own neighborhood, as well as for society as a whole. But how can congregations get started? Finding or selecting a project might feel overwhelming, and resources might seem scarce. While starting a community-engagement project will take an investment of time and resources, it is an investment that the data clearly show will pay off with spiritual benefits for members and congregational benefits for a place of worship.

In thinking about community engagement, congregations can start small. Numerically smaller congregations with fewer resources may want to form partnerships or encourage individual members to connect with organizations that are particularly meaningful to them. One leader told us that "because we are a small congregation and our resources are limited, we encourage folks to go out into the community and find those organizations or help them make that connection. We've got a number of folks that volunteer at Children's Hospital making cards and a variety of things like that. We have some folks that volunteer with Habitat for Humanity. Some folks that volunteer with VIPS, the Volunteers in Public Schools." Most communities have dozens or hundreds of nonprofit organizations who would be thrilled to have volunteers. Hosting a volunteer fair, perhaps with other congregations, could be a good way to present opportunities to members.

As neighborhoods change and demographics shift, staying connected to the community around a place of worship might require more intention, but this is another important form of community engagement. A religious leader at one commuter congregation talked about efforts to do just that at his church: "Even though they don't live there, they're purposefully going to connect and buy from businesses in Southwest Little Rock, and they were encouraging our members to do the same. Like on Sunday. Instead of going to my usual west Little Rock club lunch, what if we pick restaurants in our community, and local business leaders that we could support and uplift and, you know, be proud of?"

In choosing how to get engaged in the community, every congregation has to figure out what works best for them. As one leader put it, "No church, no organization, can say yes to everything. And so you have to discern where your congregation's resources and passions are. I think, just like people have gifts, congregations have gifts." As congregations work to figure out what those gifts are, they would be wise to heed the words of a leader who told us that congregations seeking greater community engagement don't have to start from scratch. Instead, he advised, "you find out where God is moving and then you join in."

Although Chapter 5 demonstrated that there are barriers to collaborative community engagement, collaboration is one way to share the burdens and resources associated with engagement. The leadership at St. James United Methodist Church, for instance, told us about their partnership with the Church of Jesus Christ of Latter-day Saints as part of the Family Promise program to provide temporary housing for unhoused families: "We partner with the Latter-day Saints, because we had the facility to house these families. They had the volunteers, but not necessarily a space to have them. So, we partner with them, which has been a great, great relationship."

In getting started, it really helps to have a champion in the congregation who will spearhead the efforts. I walked away from an interview with one lay leader who serves just such a role in her congregation thinking about how it's all the personal connections and individual motivation that get the work done. As another lay leader told me, "Where we can go deeper, have work we put more emphasis on, it tends to be because, in the ministry groups, you've got those champions for their causes." When one congregation was trying to decide where to direct their engagement efforts, they picked a project where they had connections in the community and a champion in the congregation, telling me, "It made sense. It was the most attainable. We had the will and the manpower. Okay, let's start here and see where it goes."

Little Rock is only one city. With a population of around 200,000 and about 350 congregations in the city limits (U.S. Census Bureau 2021), there is about one place of worship for every 571 people, one of the higher ratios in America (Speiser 2015). What the data and stories of Little Rock and its congregations represent are ways that religion and community engagement can meet to improve life for the city's residents, whether they be people of faith or not. The benefits of community engagement reach far beyond the people and places of faith studied by the researchers of the LRCS. While the qualitative and quantitative data presented here can illustrate the benefits of community engagement, to really see its effects, one needs to get out there and start serving.

List of Resources Available in the Appendixes

APPENDIX A: VARIABLE QUESTION WORDING

Table A.1 2020 Ideology Variables
Table A.2 2020 Engagement Variables
Table A.3 2020 Religion Variables
Table A.4 2020 Political Variables
Table A.5 Control Variables
Table A.6 Variables from 2020 Clergy Survey

APPENDIX B: SUMMARY INFORMATION

Table B.1 Academic Papers Published Using LRCS Data
Table B.2 Community Reports Published by the Little Rock Congregations Study
Table B.3 Important Stories from the Little Rock Congregations Study Website
List of All Student Researchers Who Have Contributed to the Little Rock Congregations
    Study, Alphabetical by First Name (n = 202)

APPENDIX C: MODELS AND MODEL CONSTRUCTION

Note on Statistical Model Construction
Table C.1 OLS Regression Model of Community Engagement
Table C.2 Ordered Logit Model of Feeling God's Love
Table C.3 Ordered Logit Model of Feeling Closer to God Today Than a Year Ago
Table C.4 OLS Regression Model of Life Satisfaction
Table C.5 Ordered Logit Model of Physical Health
Table C.6 Ordered Logit Model of Mental Health
Table C.7 OLS Regression Models of Political Efficacy

APPENDIX D: CODEBOOKS

Appendixes

APPENDIX A: VARIABLE QUESTION WORDING

TABLE A.1 2020 IDEOLOGY VARIABLES

2020 ideology variables	Level measured at	Question wording	Summary statistics
Personal ideology	Individual	Many people use the terms liberal, moderate, and conservative to recognize different political opinions. On a scale from 0 to 6, where 0 is the most liberal position and 6 the most conservative, where would you rank yourself when you think of your general political views?	Range: 0 to 6 Mean: 3.35 SD: 1.91
Ideological closeness to others in the congregation	Individual	How would you compare your views with other congregation members' on political issues? Respondents were presented with a sliding scale from 0 to 6 with the options: Mine more liberal = 0, About the same = 3, Mine more conservative = 6. Recoded so that responses that are more similar are coded higher.	Range: 0 to 3 Mean: 1.69 SD: 0.88
Average ideological standard deviation of the congregation	Congregation	The standard deviation of the statistical average of personal ideology of all respondents in a congregation.	Range: 0 to 0.42 Mean: 0.09 SD: 0.06

(*continued*)

TABLE A.1 2020 IDEOLOGY VARIABLES *(continued)*			
2020 ideology variables	Level measured at	Question wording	Summary statistics
Clergy perception of the political division of the congregation	Congregation	Asked of clergy; the same score assigned to all congregation members: Would you say that your congregation is politically united (members agree on political issues)? 1 = Very politically united, 2 = Somewhat politically united, 3 = Neither united or divided, 4 = Somewhat politically divided, 5 = Very politically divided	Range: 1 to 5 Mean: 3.15 SD: 1.14

TABLE A.2 2020 ENGAGEMENT VARIABLES			
2020 engagement variables	Level measured at	Question wording	Summary statistics
Community engagement scale	Individual	Summary measure of Likert agreement (1 to 5) with the following six statements: 1. I do things to make the community a better place. 2. I am aware of the important needs in the community. 3. I rarely talk with my friends and/or family about community problems (reversed). 4. Becoming involved in political or social issues is a good way to improve the community. 5. Government is too complicated for me to understand (reversed). 6. I believe that I can personally make a difference in my community.	Range: Originally scaled from 6 to 30, rescaled from 0 to 1 Mean: 0.728 SD: 0.121
Community action	Individual	First three questions of the community engagement scale.	Range: Originally scaled from 3 to 15, rescaled from 0 to 1 Mean: 0.621 SD: 0.124

(continued)

TABLE A.2 2020 ENGAGEMENT VARIABLES (*continued*)			
2020 engagement variables	Level measured at	Question wording	Summary statistics
Political efficacy	Individual	Last three questions of the community engagement scale.	Range: Originally scaled from 3 to 15, rescaled from 0 to 1 Mean: 0.732 SD: 0.151
Community sermons	Individual	How often do the worship service messages by your religious leader: 1. Encourage you to serve or volunteer in the community? 2. Encourage you to help those less fortunate in your own community? 1 = Never, 2 = Seldom, 3 = Sometimes, 4 = Often, 5 = Always	Range: 2 to 10 Mean: 7.29 SD: 1.72
Participate in a community group at their place of worship	Individual	Thinking about your activity during "normal" times, that is, not during a pandemic, do you regularly take part in any activities of this congregation that reach out to the wider community (for instance, visitation, evangelism, outreach, community service, advocacy)? Please check all that apply. Respondent was then presented with a variety of options. This variable represents those who checked the box corresponding to the option: "Yes, in community service or advocacy activities of this congregation."	Range: 0 to 1 Mean: 0.302 SD: 0.46
Service outside the congregation	Individual	In the past month, how many hours of unpaid service have you given outside your place of worship? 1 = Zero, 2 = One to five, 3 = Six to ten, 4 = Eleven to fourteen, 5 = Fifteen or more	Range: 1 to 5 Mean: 1.92 SD: 1.16
Average community engagement scale for the congregation	Congregation	The average of all the community engagement scales for respondents in the congregation. The score is the same for all members of a congregation.	Range: 18.225 to 27.06 Mean: 23.40 SD: 0.970

TABLE A.3 2020 RELIGION VARIABLES

2020 religion variables	Level measured at	Question wording	Summary statistics
Religiosity (prayer and scripture reading)	Individual	Combination of two religiosity questions, one measuring prayer and one measuring scripture reading: About how often do you spend time alone praying outside of religious services? 1 = Never, 2 = Only on certain occasions, 3 = Once a week or less, 4 = A few times a week, 5 = Once a day, 6 = Multiple times a day Outside of attending religious services, about how often do you spend time alone reading the Bible, Koran, Torah, or other sacred texts? 1 = Never, 2 = Occasionally, 3 = Two to three times a month, 4 = About once a week, 5 = A few times a week, 6 = Daily	Range: 2 to 12 Mean: 8.62 SD: 2.76
Worship service attendance	Individual	How often do you attend religious services? 1 = Never, 2 = Occasionally, 3 = About once a month, 4 = Two to three times a month, 5 = Every week, 6 = Multiple times a week	Range: 1 to 6 Mean: 4.64 SD: 1.18
Providentiality	Individual	Combination of two questions: Would you say your religion provides some guidance in your day-to-day life, quite a bit of guidance, or a great deal of guidance in your day-to-day life? 2 = Some guidance, 3 = Quite a bit of guidance, 4 = A great deal of guidance, 1 = Religion isn't that important to me Please mark how much you agree or disagree with the following statement: God has a plan and I have a part to play in it. 5 = Strongly agree, 4 = Agree, 3 = Neither agree nor disagree, 2 = Disagree, 1 = Strongly disagree	Range: 2 to 9 Mean: 7.95 SD: 1.34

Congregational warmth	Individual	A combined measure of agreement with four statements about the respondent's congregation. Please mark how much you agree or disagree with the following statements about your congregation: • My congregation feels like family to me. • My congregation meets my spiritual needs. • I feel like an outsider in my congregation (reversed). • I would be prepared to invite friends or relatives to a worship service here. 5 = Strongly agree, 4 = Agree, 3 = Neither agree nor disagree, 2 = Disagree, 1 = Strongly disagree	Range: Originally scaled from 4 to 20, rescaled from 0 to 1 Mean: 0.792 SD: 0.186
Congregational social capital	Individual	A combined measure of agreement with three statements about the respondent's congregation. 5 = Strongly agree, 4 = Agree, 3 = Neither agree nor disagree, 2 = Disagree, 1 = Strongly disagree Please mark how much you agree or disagree with the following statements about your congregation: • My congregation feels like family to me. • I feel like an outsider in my congregation (reversed). • I would be prepared to invite friends or relatives to a worship service here.	Range: Originally scaled from 3 to 15, rescaled from 0 to 1 Mean: 0.785 SD: 0.194
Average congregational warmth	Congregation	The average of all of the congregational warmth scores for respondents in the congregation. The score is the same for all members of a congregation.	Range: 14.65 to 19 Mean: 16.66 SD: 0.77
Service to the congregation	Individual	In the past month, how many hours of unpaid service have you given to your place of worship? 1 = Zero, 2 = One to Five, 3 = Six to Ten, 4 = Eleven to Fourteen, 5 = Fifteen or More	Range: 1 to 5 Mean: 1.93 SD: 1.16

(continued)

TABLE A.3 2020 RELIGION VARIABLES (*continued*)

2020 religion variables	Level measured at	Question wording	Summary statistics
Sermon content	Individual	How often do the worship service messages by your religious leader: • Focus on the importance of marriage and family? • Focus on advocacy or social action? • Encourage you to serve or volunteer in the community? • Encourage you to help those less fortunate in your own community? • Encourage you to help those less fortunate around the world? • Focus on personal spiritual growth? • Urge you to register to vote? 1 = Never, 2 = Seldom, 3 = Sometimes, 4 = Often, 5 = Always	Range for each measure: 1 to 5 **Marriage and family** Mean: 3.45 SD: 1.01 **Social action** Mean: 3.31 SD: 1.04 **Volunteer** Mean: 3.47 SD: 0.99 **Help community** Mean: 3.82 SD: 0.87 **Help world** Mean: 3.75 SD: 0.90 **Spiritual growth** Mean: 4.12 SD: 0.82 **Vote** Mean: 2.52 SD: 1.34

TABLE A.4 2020 POLITICAL VARIABLES			
2020 political variables	Level measured at	Question wording	Summary statistics
Political activity	Individual	Summary of the frequency of participation in seven political activities. In the past year, have you: • Tried to persuade someone to vote? • Donated money to a political candidate or campaign? • Signed a petition? • Participated in a local political or community group? • Participated in a national political group? • Contacted public officials on a political or social issue? • Posted or shared something political through social media (like Facebook or Twitter)? 1 = No, 2 = Yes, once or twice, 3 = Yes, a few times, 4 = Yes, many times	Range: 0 to 21 Mean: 5.29 SD: 4.78
Clergy political activity	Congregation	Summary of the clergy member's frequency of participation in seven political activities. In the past year, have you: • Tried to persuade someone to vote? • Donated money to a political candidate or campaign? • Signed a petition? • Participated in a local political or community group? • Participated in a national political group? • Contacted public officials on a political or social issue? • Posted or shared something political through social media (like Facebook or Twitter)? 1 = No, 2 = Yes, once or twice, 3 = Yes, a few times, 4 = Yes, many times	Range: 0 to 21 Mean: 4.53 SD: 5.57

(*continued*)

TABLE A.4 2020 POLITICAL VARIABLES (*continued*)

2020 political variables	Level measured at	Question wording	Summary statistics
Political sermons	Individual	Summary measure of the reported frequency of hearing two kinds of political sermons: How often do the worship service messages by your religious leader: • Focus on advocacy or social action? • Urge you to register to vote? 1 = Never, 2 = Seldom, 3 = Sometimes, 4 = Often, 5 = Always	Range: 2 to 10 Mean: 5.82 SD: 2.00
Congregation election activity	Congregation	Summary measure of the congregation's involvement in the following five election-related activities: During elections, some places of worship provide materials to help members make important choices. For the 2020 election, will you, • Make voter guides available? • Hold a candidate forum for candidates for any level of political office? • Hold any meetings to discuss important issues in the election? • Be involved in a voter registration drive? • Be involved in getting out the vote? 1 = Yes, 0 = No	Range: 0 to 4 Mean: 1.02 SD: 1.01

TABLE A.5 CONTROL VARIABLES

Control variables	Level measured at	Question wording	Summary statistics
Education	Individual	What is the highest year in school/degree you have achieved? 1 = Less than high school, 2 = High school graduate, 3 = Some college, 4 = College graduate, 5 = Postgraduate	Range: 1 to 5 Mean: 4.10 SD: 0.95
Income	Individual	By your best estimate, what was your total household income last year, before taxes? 1 = $10,000 or less, 2 = $10,001 to $20,000, 3 = $20,001 to $35,000, 4 = $35,001 to $50,000, 5 = $50,001 to $100,000, 6 = $100,001 to $150,000, 7 = more than $150,000	Range: 1 to 7 Mean: 5.26 SD: 1.38
Gender	Individual	What is your gender? 1 = Female, 0 = Male (The survey provided nonbinary and other response options, but they were selected by 0.003% of respondents and are excluded for the purposes of these analyses.)	$N = 1,490$ Percent of the total sample that identifies as female = 64.80%
Age	Individual	Respondents were asked: In what year were you born? That number was then subtracted from 2020 (the year of the survey) to calculate age.	Range: 19 to 89 Mean: 60.44 SD: 15.85
Black racial identity	Individual	Respondent selected "Black or African American" in response to the question: What is your race/ethnicity?	$N = 247$ Percent of the total sample = 10.77%

TABLE A.6 VARIABLES FROM 2020 CLERGY SURVEY

Variable	Question wording	Summary statistics
Total attendance (congregation size)	What is the estimated total attendance at all of your worship services over a typical week (assuming the coronavirus pandemic is not typical)?	Range: 12 to 2,300 Mean: 270.14 SD: 412.35
Years the leader has been with the congregation	How many years have you served this congregation? 1 = Less than one year, 2 = One to five years, 3 = Six to ten years, 4 = Eleven to fifteen years, 5 = More than fifteen years	Range: 1 to 5 Mean: 2.72 SD: 1.23
Number of community programs the congregation provides	What kinds of direct social/community services does your congregation provide? (Respondents can check boxes associated with a list of thirteen programs, including a box for other where they can list any programs not available in the provided list.)	Range: 0 to 9 Mean: 3.46 SD: 2.37

(continued)

TABLE A.6 VARIABLES FROM 2020 CLERGY SURVEY (*continued*)		
Variable	Question wording	Summary statistics
Congregation hosts a group to organize volunteer work	Within the past twelve months, have there been any groups or meetings at your congregation specifically focused on the following purposes? • To organize or encourage people to do volunteer work. 1 = Yes, 0 = No	Range: 0 to 1 Mean: 0.81 SD: 0.39

APPENDIX B: SUMMARY INFORMATION

TABLE B.1 ACADEMIC PAPERS PUBLISHED USING LRCS DATA

Authors	Title	Journal	Year published
Leach, Kirk, Gerald Driskill, and Rebecca A. Glazier	"African American Pastors: Navigating Dialectics in the Collaborative Process"	*Journal of Applied Communication Research*	2023
Glazier, Rebecca A., and Morgan Paige Topping	"Using Social Media to Advance Community-Based Research"	*PS: Political Science and Politics*	2021
Glazier, Rebecca A., and Warigia Bowman	"Teaching through Community-Based Research: Undergraduate and Graduate Collaboration on the Little Rock Congregations Study."	*Journal of Political Science Education*	2021
Glazier, Rebecca A., and Emilie Street	"When Spiritual and Material Meet: Explaining Congregational Engagement in the Local Community."	*Interdisciplinary Journal of Research on Religion*	2020
Glazier, Rebecca A.	"The Differential Impact of Religion on Political Activity and Community Engagement."	*Review of Religious Research*	2020
Glazier, Rebecca A., Gerald Driskill, and Kirk Leach.	"Connecting with Community and Facilitating Learning through the Little Rock Congregations Study."	*Metropolitan Universities*	2020
Glazier, Rebecca A.	"Acting for God? Types and Motivations of Clergy Political Activity."	*Politics and Religion*	2018
Glazier, Rebecca A.	"Providentiality: A New Measure of Religious Belief."	*Interdisciplinary Journal of Research on Religion*	2017
Glazier, Rebecca A.	"Bridging Religion and Politics: The Impact of Providential Religious Beliefs on Political Activity"	*Politics and Religion*	2015

Title of report	Date published	Report link	Focus of report
TABLE B.2 COMMUNITY REPORTS PUBLISHED BY THE LITTLE ROCK CONGREGATIONS STUDY			
2022 Little Rock Race and Faith Summit	November 2, 2022	https://ualr.edu/lrcs/files/2022/11/Race-and-Faith -Summit-Packet-with-QR-code.pdf	Resources for congregations doing faith-based racial justice and reconciliation work.
2021 Little Rock Congregations Study Community Dialogues	April 1, 2021	https://ualr.edu/lrcs/files/2021/04/2021-LRCS -Dialogue-Summary-Final.pdf	Summary of community focus groups on issues that matter most to congregations.
2020 Little Rock Congregations Study Executive Report	January 21, 2020	https://ualr.edu/lrcs/files/2021/01/2020-LRCS -Executive-Report-Final.pdf	Findings of the 2020 survey of Little Rock congregations.
2019 Little Rock Congregations Study Executive Report on Nonprofits in Little Rock	December 11, 2019	https://ualr.edu/lrcs/files/2019/12/2019-LRCS -Nonprofits-Report.pdf	Research on collaboration between nonprofit organizations and congregations.
2019 Little Rock Religious Leaders Summit	April 11, 2019	https://ualr.edu/lrcs/files/2019/04/Religious-Leaders -Summit-Summary-Report-Optimized.pdf	Results of discussions among religious leaders about issues facing the community.
2018 Little Rock Congregations Study Executive Report on Congregation and Nonprofit Collaboration	April 11, 2019	https://ualr.edu/lrcs/files/2019/04/2018-Little -Rock-Congregations-Study-Executive-Report -Final-Compressed.pdf	Investigates how and when nonprofit cooperation with congregations occurs.
2016 Little Rock Congregations Study	April 13, 2017	https://ualr.edu/lrcs/files/2017/11/2016-Little -Rock-Congregations-Study-Executive-Report.pdf	Findings of the 2016 survey of Little Rock congregations.
2012 Little Rock Congregations Study Report	Fall 2012	https://ualr.edu/lrcs/files/2019/01/2012 -Congregation-Study-Report-Glazier.pdf	Findings of the 2012 survey of Little Rock congregations.

TABLE B.3 IMPORTANT STORIES FROM THE LITTLE ROCK CONGREGATIONS STUDY WEBSITE			
Story title	Date	Summary	Link
"Race and Faith Resources"	November 2, 2022	A report on the 2022 Little Rock Race and Faith Summit and the release of the race and faith resources created by the LRCS research team.	https://ualr.edu/lrcs/2022/11/02/race-and-faith-resources/
"Congregation Resources"	September 22, 2020	A page filled with downloadable resources for congregations who participated in the 2020 LRCS, including timelines, social media posts, FAQs, and a video.	https://ualr.edu/lrcs/2022/11/02/race-and-faith-resources/
"A Time to Listen"	July 21, 2020	Rebecca Glazier invites participants to complete surveys indicating what issues they would like the LRCS to focus on, and racial divisions are one of the largest talking points requested.	https://ualr.edu/lrcs/2020/07/31/a-time-to-listen/
"Understanding Faith and Race through the Data of the Little Rock Congregations Study"	June 3, 2020	In 2020, no responding clergy thought that race relations was anything less than important, and 86% thought Little Rock has a racial division problem.	https://ualr.edu/lrcs/2020/06/03/understanding-faith-and-race-through-the-data-of-the-lrcs/
"Religious and Community Leaders Share Words of Support for the Little Rock Congregations Study"	May 27, 2020	Statements of support for the 2020 LRCS data collection from fourteen different religious, nonprofit, and community leaders.	https://ualr.edu/lrcs/2020/05/27/religious-and-community-leaders-share-words-of-support-for-the-little-rock-congregations-study/
"Congregation B'nai Israel's Engagement to Make the Little Rock Community Better"	April 27, 2020	Student researchers in an International Religious Freedom class wrote about how religious minorities assist the community by providing social services. This student-authored article specifically talks about Congregation B'nai Israel and the aid they provide to the community.	https://ualr.edu/lrcs/2020/04/27/congregation-bnai-israel/
"Uniting Religious Communities in Little Rock: The City Church Network"	February 5, 2020	Leaders of the CityChurch Network provide training and encourage citywide worship and prayer experiences, including hosting a semiannual citywide One Voice concert.	https://ualr.edu/lrcs/2020/02/05/city-church-network/
"Mapping Little Rock's Congregations"	January 12, 2019	The LRCS research team created a map of congregations and categorized the congregations by religious tradition, year founded, and racial majority in that congregation.	https://ualr.edu/lrcs/2019/01/12/mapping-little-rocks-congregations/
"Uniting Greater Little Rock: Making Connections at City Connections"	November 13, 2019	City Connections is a faith-based organization that offers the community many public services and helps connect community members with volunteer opportunities.	https://ualr.edu/lrcs/2019/11/13/city-connections/

List of All Student Researchers Who Have Contributed to the Little Rock Congregations Study, Alphabetical by First Name (n = 202)

Alanna Tatum, Alicia Dorn, Allie M. Woodville, Allison Gwinup, Amanda Cady, Amie Alexander, Amy Stewart, Anabel H. Logan, Anabella Barnett, Andrew Trevino, Anet C. Rosas Labrada, Angela Logue, Anika R. Partlow-Loyall, Anna C. Doss, Anna Gayle Griffiths, Anna P. Aguilar, Arielle Metcalf, Armando Arellano, Ashley Ollison, Austin Soulsby, B. Tessie Ebenja, Benjamin C. Bowers, Blake E. Christy, Brady N. Cross, Brandon Trevino, Brian Gregory, Brian Howard, Brittney Dennis, Caitlin Campbell, Camille Watson, Candice Randall, Carli E. Steelman, Caroline Dunlap, Carolyn Wilkerson, Catherine A. Hickman, Catherine Campos, Cedric A. Egbers, Chad Hunter, Charlana Benefiel, Charles B. Handford, Charles Kaylah, Chelsea Miller, Chris W. Kilburn, Christopher Gardner, Chuck G. Savage, Colby Qualls, Connor Donovan, Courtney R. Sheets, Crystal Mercer, Daisy Vasquez Guevara, Dani Franz, Daniel Hickey, Darlynton Adegor, David Lewis, Demas Soliman, Dewayne Green, DJ Williams, Dominic Lasorsa, Don Bright, Dorothea Greulich, Eli Sievert, Elissa Cook, Emilie Street, Emily Loker, Emily Smith, Eric Pardoe, Erica Torrence, Essence Thomas, Eva Hansen, Evan Hicks, Faith Thomas, Fiona Sloan, Hamza Arshad, Hannah Bahn, Isaac Thomas, J. William Hall, Jack Schlotter, Jackson Bittner, Jacob Chisom, Jacob Rateliff, Jade McCain, Jalen Stevenson, James Furlong, Jasmine Pugh, Jason Jackson, Jason Lochmann, Jennifer Barrett, Jennifer Rivera, Jeremiah Sniffin, Jessica Olson, Johnny Margaret, Jonathan L. Nwosu, Jordan Wallis, Joshua K. Miller, Joshua Snyder, Joshua Thomsen, Joshua Williams, Josie E. Keathley, Kaitlyn Callahan, Kalidash Adhikari, Kammi Ward, Kate Deegan, Katelyn V. Sims, Kathy Beynon, Kayla Maxwell, Kaylyn Hager, Kenneth Bittencourt, Kierra Williams, Kirsten Elliott, Kwami Abdul-Bey, Kyle Smith, Kyle Winters, Lamar Townsend, Landon DeKay, Laura McClellan, Laura Ruiz Astorga, Layne Coleman, Leah Santos, Liz Reich, Logan Mosley, Louis R. Houser, Lucy Kagan, Madeleine Chaisson, Madeline Burke, Madison Rodgers, Maggie Mencer, Maria Zarate, Mariam S. Bouzihay, Marisha Twillie, Maroo Hansa, Marsha Scullark, Matthew D. Maguire, Matthew McGregor, Megan Jackson, Megan Kurten, Megan Parrish, Michael Shinn Ptak, Miriam Dominguez, Mollie Henneger, Molly Edwards, Morgan Paige Topping, Natalie Ramm, Nathan Davis, Naty Doris, Nick Stevens, Nicolaas Harrington, Nicole D. Ursin, Nora Bouzihay, Odette Cooh, Olga Calderon, Oluwaseun Olaniyi, Othenia M. Dowell, Owen Haynes, Paige S. Sallis, Paola Cavallari, Paxton Richardson, Precious Sims, Rashad Roberts, Rasim Shah, Ravyn Towns, Rebecca Agyei, Rebecca Bailey, Reggie Ballard, Richard Jones, Robert Cole, Robert M. Harrison, Ross Owyoung, Sabah Ismail, Sai Charan Machavarapu, Samson L. Gottshall, Sara Windsor, Sarah Neal, Savannah Gann, Shadeed O. Dawkins, Shalondra Martin, Shannan M. Stewart, Shem Ngwira, Sophia M. Barnes, Sri Ramya Kandimalla, Stacy Cox, Steven Kwizera, Susanna Creed, Taylor Donnerson, Taylor Romeeka, Thaddeus Smith, Thatch Jordon, Thurman Green, Ti'Anna Dedmon, Tiffany Meeks, Tony Nickerson, Travis Taylor, Ty Collins, Tyler Batson, Tyler Stewart, Veronica Aldridge, Vinay Raj, Violet Gresham, Yasmin Basilio, Yvonne Rodriguez, Zach Huffman, Zachary Hale, Zachary L. Priest, and Zartashia Javid.

APPENDIX C: MODELS AND MODEL CONSTRUCTION

Note on Statistical Model Construction
The full statistical models are presented in the tables that follow in Appendix C and not in the full text of the book so that the findings are as accessible as possible to the reader and the statistical details don't interrupt the flow of the book. For the more statistical-

minded readers, the full model results are presented in the following tables and discussed briefly here. The specifics of each model depend on many factors, including which survey iteration is under examination, which dependent variable is being evaluated, and so on. Each time the results of a model are presented in the text, the source of the data, the type of model used, and the appendix table where the full results can be found are named.

The largest and most commonly used dataset in the book is the 2020 LRCS survey of congregation members. The baseline model for this dataset includes twenty-four variables, all of which are named and described in the variable tables in Appendix A. The variables in the baseline model are as follows: five community engagement measures (community engagement, hearing community sermons, membership in a congregational community group, service outside of the congregation, and the congregation average of community engagement), two individual political measures (political activity and ideology), five congregation-level political measures (ideological closeness to the congregation, clergy political activity, congregation election activity, congregation ideological diversity, and clergy perceived ideological division), three religion measures (religiosity, providentiality, and worship service attendance), four congregation measures (congregation size, individual perception of congregation warmth, congregation average of congregation warmth, and service to the congregation), and five demographic controls (age, gender, education, income, and Black or African American identity).

When statistical models deviate from this baseline model, they do so for a specific purpose. Sometimes this purpose is discussed in the text. For instance, in Chapter 3, the community engagement variable is broken down into its component questions and political efficacy is treated as both a dependent and independent variable. But sometimes the minutiae of model construction are not particularly relevant to the main argument in the text. In those cases, it will be discussed in notes following the models themselves here in the appendixes. For instance, in the model of the extent to which respondents feel God's love, presented in Table C.2, the providentiality variable in excluded from the model, as God's love and providential beliefs are theoretically similar and correlated at 0.51.

TABLE C.1 OLS REGRESSION MODEL OF COMMUNITY ENGAGEMENT				
Variable	Coefficient	Robust standard error	T-score	P-value
Political sermons	−0.002	0.002	−0.950	0.348
Political activity	0.007***	0.001	5.230	0.000
Community sermons	0.014***	0.002	5.830	0.000
Member of community group	0.017*	0.008	2.100	0.044
Providentiality	0.007	0.004	1.860	0.073
Education	0.013*	0.006	2.280	0.030
Income	0.004	0.003	1.450	0.156
Age	0.000	0.000	0.450	0.657
Female	−0.026*	0.012	−2.210	0.034
Worship service attendance	0.005	0.004	1.350	0.187
Religiosity (scripture reading and prayer)	0.004**	0.001	3.460	0.002
Conservative ideology	−0.012***	0.003	−4.430	0.000
Close to congregation's ideology	−0.006	0.005	−1.310	0.201
Black or African American identity	0.008	0.019	0.440	0.663
Congregation warmth	0.050	0.039	1.300	0.203
Service to congregation	−0.003	0.004	−0.610	0.544
Service outside of congregation	0.020***	0.003	5.980	0.000
Congregation average congregational warmth	−0.008	0.010	−0.850	0.401
Congregation average community engagement	0.006	0.005	1.100	0.281
Congregation average attendance	0.000	0.000	−1.070	0.293
Clergy political activity	−0.001	0.001	−1.570	0.127
Congregation election activity	−0.002	0.005	−0.410	0.687
Congregation ideological diversity	−0.024	0.070	−0.340	0.736
Clergy-perceived ideological division	−0.005	0.006	−0.910	0.369
Constant	0.446***	0.175	2.550	0.016
$N = 1,023$				
$R^2 = 0.365$				
Note: Standard errors are clustered by thirty-five congregations.				
* $p < 0.05$, ** $p < 0.01$, *** $p < 0.001$				

TABLE C.2 ORDERED LOGIT MODEL OF FEELING GOD'S LOVE

Variable	Coefficient	Robust standard error	Z-score	P-value
Community engagement	0.069*	0.035	1.99	0.047
Political activity	−0.020	0.019	−1.01	0.312
Community sermons	0.136	0.075	1.81	0.071
Member of community group	−0.019	0.163	−0.12	0.906
Education	0.027	0.125	0.22	0.827
Income	0.053	0.099	0.53	0.594
Age	0.003	0.011	0.29	0.774
Female	0.372*	0.188	1.98	0.048
Worship service attendance	−0.101	0.105	−0.96	0.338
Religiosity (scripture reading and prayer)	0.239***	0.043	5.56	0.000
Conservative ideology	0.087	0.052	1.68	0.092
Close to congregation's ideology	−0.182*	0.085	−2.13	0.033
Black or African American identity	0.682*	0.342	2	0.046
Congregation warmth	0.139***	0.027	5.15	0.000
Service to congregation	0.032	0.066	0.48	0.632
Service outside of congregation	−0.014	0.056	−0.25	0.804
Congregation average congregational warmth	0.322*	0.167	1.93	0.054
Congregation average community engagement	−0.260**	0.098	−2.66	0.008
Congregation average attendance	0.000	0.000	−0.32	0.748
Clergy political activity	0.010	0.016	0.61	0.541
Congregation election activity	0.111	0.106	1.05	0.294
Congregation ideological diversity	−1.149	2.090	−0.55	0.583
Clergy-perceived ideological division	0.263***	0.082	3.2	0.001
cut1	1.494	3.901		
cut2	3.300	3.717		
cut3	3.861	3.721		
cut4	4.519	3.692		
cut5	6.486	3.686		
cut6	8.274	3.655		
$N = 1,021$				
Pseudo $R^2 = 0.094$				

Note: The ordered logit model of God's love presented here includes all the variables of the baseline model described in Appendix C except for the measure of providential beliefs. The providentiality variable is excluded from the model because feeling God's love and holding providential beliefs are theoretically similar and are also correlated at 0.51.
* $p < 0.05$, ** $p < 0.01$, *** $p < 0.001$

TABLE C.3 ORDERED LOGIT MODEL OF FEELING CLOSER TO GOD TODAY THAN A YEAR AGO

Variable	Coefficient	Robust standard error	Z-score	P-value
Community engagement	−0.742	0.795	−0.930	0.351
Political activity	0.004	0.015	0.250	0.799
Community sermons	0.130*	0.063	2.070	0.039
Member of community group	−0.189	0.168	−1.120	0.261
Education	−0.291***	0.082	−3.550	0.000
Income	−0.048	0.065	−0.740	0.456
Age	−0.002	0.005	−0.320	0.746
Female	−0.079	0.140	−0.560	0.576
Worship service attendance	0.127*	0.064	1.980	0.048
Religiosity (scripture reading and prayer)	0.284***	0.039	7.220	0.000
Conservative ideology	0.066	0.054	1.220	0.223
Close to congregation's ideology	−0.029	0.079	−0.370	0.712
Black or African American identity	1.299***	0.383	3.390	0.001
Congregation warmth	0.989	0.545	1.810	0.070
Service to congregation	−0.020	0.069	−0.290	0.772
Service outside of congregation	0.131***	0.053	2.450	0.014
Congregation average congregational warmth	−0.177	0.144	−1.230	0.217
Congregation average community engagement	0.021	0.116	0.180	0.857
Congregation average attendance	0.000	0.000	0.160	0.872
Clergy political activity	0.025	0.018	1.400	0.161
Congregation election activity	0.144	0.130	1.100	0.269
Congregation ideological diversity	−2.244	1.851	−1.210	0.225
Clergy-perceived ideological division	0.094	0.103	0.910	0.360
cut1	−4.491	3.500		
cut2	−1.926	3.338		
cut3	0.891	3.340		
cut4	2.378	3.330		
$N = 1,031$				
Pseudo $R^2 = 0.11$				

Note: The ordered logit model of feeling closer to God presented here includes all the variables of the baseline model described in Appendix C except for the measure of providential beliefs. The providentiality variable is excluded from the model because feeling closer to God and holding providential beliefs are theoretically similar and are also correlated at 0.27.
* $p < 0.05$, ** $p < 0.01$, *** $p < 0.001$

TABLE C.4 OLS REGRESSION MODEL OF LIFE SATISFACTION

Variable	Coefficient	Robust standard error	T-score	P-value
Community engagement	9.973*	4.991	2.000	0.054
Political activity	−0.061	0.139	−0.440	0.662
Community sermons	−1.406**	0.415	−3.390	0.002
Member of community group	−1.086	1.414	−0.770	0.448
Providentiality	3.317**	1.004	3.310	0.002
Education	0.233	0.834	0.280	0.781
Income	1.792*	0.743	2.410	0.022
Age	0.082	0.047	1.770	0.087
Female	−4.493**	1.366	−3.290	0.002
Worship service attendance	−0.510	0.799	−0.640	0.528
Religiosity (scripture reading and prayer)	0.143	0.267	0.540	0.595
Conservative ideology	0.397	0.330	1.200	0.238
Close to congregation's ideology	−0.483	0.853	−0.570	0.576
Black or African American identity	9.457**	3.718	2.540	0.016
Congregation warmth	14.564***	3.430	4.250	0.000
Service to congregation	−0.007	0.515	−0.010	0.989
Service outside of congregation	−0.181	0.946	−0.190	0.850
Congregation average congregational warmth	0.140	0.969	0.140	0.886
Congregation average community engagement	−0.482	0.578	−0.830	0.410
Congregation average attendance	−0.001	0.001	−0.980	0.335
Clergy political activity	−0.232	0.185	−1.260	0.218
Congregation election activity	−0.330	0.575	−0.570	0.570
Congregation ideological diversity	−38.079*	18.302	−2.080	0.046
Clergy-perceived ideological division	−1.746***	0.486	−3.590	0.001
Constant	57.780***	20.120	2.870	0.007
$N = 1,034$				
$R^2 = 0.213$				

Note: Standard errors are clustered by thirty-five congregations.
* $p < 0.05$, ** $p < 0.01$, *** $p < 0.001$

Variable	Coefficient	Robust standard error	Z-score	P-value
TABLE C.5 ORDERED LOGIT MODEL OF PHYSICAL HEALTH				
Community engagement	−0.093	0.976	−0.100	0.924
Political activity	−0.045	0.024	−1.920	0.055
Community sermons	−0.114*	0.055	−2.090	0.037
Member of community group	−0.037	0.163	−0.230	0.818
Providentiality	−0.019	0.111	−0.180	0.860
Education	0.045	0.168	0.270	0.790
Income	0.223**	0.071	3.130	0.002
Age	−0.007	0.007	−1.040	0.300
Female	−0.373	0.210	−1.780	0.076
Worship service attendance	0.122	0.075	1.620	0.106
Religiosity (scripture reading and prayer)	0.044	0.045	0.970	0.331
Conservative ideology	−0.135	0.072	−1.860	0.063
Close to congregation's ideology	0.021	0.094	0.220	0.827
Black or African American identity	−0.070	0.406	−0.170	0.863
Congregation warmth	0.890	0.684	1.300	0.193
Service to congregation	−0.166**	0.057	−2.920	0.003
Service outside of congregation	0.339***	0.096	3.550	0.000
Congregation average congregational warmth	−0.252**	0.101	−2.500	0.012
Congregation average community engagement	0.030	0.079	0.380	0.702
Congregation average attendance	0.000	0.000	0.730	0.466
Clergy political activity	0.033*	0.017	1.960	0.050
Congregation election activity	−0.048	0.098	−0.490	0.625
Congregation ideological diversity	−1.031	1.213	−0.850	0.395
Clergy-perceived ideological division	−0.001	0.072	−0.020	0.987
cut1	−5.903	2.332		
cut2	−5.651	2.340		
cut3	−4.946	2.268		
cut4	−3.971	2.260		
cut5	−2.585	2.275		
$N = 1,042$				
Pseudo $R^2 = 0.05$				

Note: Standard errors are clustered by thirty-five congregations.
* $p < 0.05$, ** $p < 0.01$, *** $p < 0.001$

TABLE C.6 ORDERED LOGIT MODEL OF MENTAL HEALTH				
Variable	Coefficient	Robust standard error	Z-score	P-value
Community engagement	−0.367	0.762	−0.480	0.630
Political activity	−0.027	0.024	−1.150	0.249
Community sermons	−0.102	0.055	−1.840	0.065
Member of community group	−0.049	0.177	−0.280	0.780
Providentiality	0.195	0.115	1.700	0.089
Education	−0.025	0.140	−0.180	0.859
Income	0.232***	0.056	4.130	0.000
Age	0.029***	0.007	4.400	0.000
Female	−1.051***	0.205	−5.130	0.000
Worship service attendance	−0.081	0.113	−0.720	0.475
Religiosity (scripture reading and prayer)	0.025	0.046	0.550	0.584
Conservative ideology	0.090	0.047	1.910	0.056
Close to congregation's ideology	−0.087	0.106	−0.820	0.411
Black or African American identity	0.580	0.457	1.270	0.204
Congregation warmth	2.553***	0.451	5.660	0.000
Service to congregation	0.110	0.082	1.340	0.179
Service outside of congregation	0.095	0.101	0.940	0.350
Congregation average congregational warmth	−0.157	0.115	−1.360	0.173
Congregation average community engagement	0.023	0.091	0.250	0.804
Congregation average attendance	0.000	0.000	−0.230	0.817
Clergy political activity	−0.015	0.012	−1.230	0.218
Congregation election activity	0.026	0.126	0.210	0.834
Congregation ideological diversity	−2.869	1.744	−1.650	0.100
Clergy-perceived ideological division	−0.003	0.051	−0.070	0.948
cut1	−1.931	2.561		
cut2	−1.541	2.568		
cut3	−0.620	2.556		
cut4	0.943	2.510		
cut5	2.886	2.497		
N = 1,043				
Pseudo R^2 = 0.10				

Note: Standard errors are clustered by thirty-five congregations.
* $p < 0.05$, ** $p < 0.01$, *** $p < 0.001$

TABLE C.7 OLS REGRESSION MODELS OF POLITICAL EFFICACY

Variable	Coefficient	Robust standard error	T-score	P-value	Coefficient	Robust standard error	T-score	P-value
Political sermons	0.004	0.004	0.930	0.361	0.003	0.004	0.870	0.393
Political activity	0.007***	0.001	7.510	0.000	0.007***	0.001	7.320	0.000
Community sermons	−0.003	0.004	−0.670	0.507	−0.002	0.004	−0.560	0.583
Community activity	0.023***	0.003	6.440	0.000	0.023***	0.004	6.440	0.000
Member of community group	−0.010	0.010	−1.010	0.320	−0.010	0.010	−0.990	0.331
Providentiality	0.007	0.008	0.930	0.359	0.007	0.008	0.910	0.369
Education	0.012	0.010	1.130	0.268	0.012	0.011	1.100	0.279
Income	0.005	0.003	1.530	0.135	0.005	0.003	1.510	0.141
Age	0.000	0.000	−1.100	0.281	0.000	0.000	−1.110	0.277
Female	−0.038***	0.010	−3.830	0.001	−0.039***	0.010	−3.930	0.000
Worship service attendance	0.000	0.005	−0.070	0.948	0.000	0.005	−0.080	0.938
Religiosity (scripture reading and prayer)	0.005**	0.002	3.040	0.005	0.005**	0.002	2.980	0.006
Conservative ideology	−0.013***	0.003	−5.060	0.000	−0.014***	0.003	−4.920	0.000
Close to congregation's ideology	−0.007	0.006	−1.070	0.293	−0.007	0.006	−1.050	0.303
Black or African American identity	0.000	0.021	0.010	0.991	−0.003	0.020	−0.160	0.877
Congregation warmth	0.077*	0.028	2.730	0.010	0.077*	0.028	2.720	0.011
Service to congregation	−0.014*	0.005	−2.700	0.011	−0.014*	0.005	−2.630	0.013

(continued)

TABLE C.7 OLS REGRESSION MODELS OF POLITICAL EFFICACY (*continued*)

Variable	Coefficient	Robust standard error	T-score	P-value	Coefficient	Robust standard error	T-score	P-value
Service outside of congregation	0.016***	0.003	4.690	0.000	0.016***	0.003	4.690	0.000
Congregation average congregational warmth	0.002	0.010	0.200	0.843	0.003	0.009	0.310	0.758
Congregation average community engagement	−0.008	0.008	−0.990	0.327	−0.008	0.007	−1.100	0.278
Congregation average attendance	0.000	0.000	−0.660	0.514	—	—	—	—
Clergy political activity	−0.002	0.001	−1.560	0.128	−0.001	0.001	−1.500	0.144
Congregation election activity	0.002	0.006	0.370	0.717	0.001	0.006	0.180	0.861
Congregation ideological diversity	0.077	0.098	0.780	0.441	0.122*	0.063	1.950	0.060
Clergy-perceived ideological division	−0.008	0.006	−1.400	0.172	−0.009	0.006	−1.490	0.146
Constant	0.476**	0.188	2.530	0.016	0.468**	0.191	2.450	0.020
$N = 1,053$								
R^2	0.35				0.35			

Note: Standard errors are clustered by thirty-five congregations. Because of a strong negative correlation between ideological diversity and congregation size (−0.73), Table C.7 contains statistical models that both include congregation size and exclude it. The borderline significant finding for the positive influence of ideological diversity on political efficacy discussed in Chapter 5 ($p = 0.06$) is only present when the variable for congregation average attendance is excluded from the model.

* $p < 0.05$, ** $p < 0.01$, *** $p < 0.001$

TABLE C.8 ORDERED LOGIT MODEL OF WORSHIP SERVICE ATTENDANCE

Variable	Coefficient	Robust standard error	Z-score	P-value
Community engagement	1.035	0.927	1.120	0.264
Political activity	−0.032	0.026	−1.230	0.220
Political sermons	−0.077	0.048	−1.610	0.107
Community sermons	0.147*	0.067	2.190	0.029
Member of community group	0.243	0.146	1.660	0.097
Providentiality	0.011	0.099	0.110	0.915
Education	−0.241	0.134	−1.790	0.073
Income	−0.055	0.064	−0.860	0.388
Age	0.002	0.007	0.380	0.706
Female	−0.191	0.340	−0.560	0.573
Religiosity (scripture reading and prayer)	0.266***	0.081	3.300	0.001
Conservative ideology	0.064	0.049	1.300	0.192
Close to congregation's ideology	0.120	0.067	1.800	0.073
Black or African American identity	0.095	0.311	0.310	0.759
Congregation warmth	1.069	0.928	1.150	0.249
Service to congregation	0.349***	0.060	5.810	0.000
Service outside of congregation	−0.053	0.105	−0.510	0.613
Congregation average attendance (size)	−0.029	0.127	−0.230	0.820
Congregation average community engagement	0.000	0.000	0.190	0.853
Clergy political activity	−0.018	0.021	−0.870	0.386
Congregation election activity	0.119	0.151	0.790	0.432
Congregation ideological diversity	−1.323	1.625	−0.810	0.416
Clergy-perceived ideological division	−0.032	0.149	−0.210	0.832
cut1	−1.354	3.296		
cut2	0.357	3.411		
cut3	0.697	3.376		
cut4	1.848	3.336		
cut5	5.509	3.354		
$N = 1,023$				
Pseudo $R^2 = 0.114$				

Note: Standard errors are clustered by thirty-five congregations.
* $p < 0.05$, ** $p < 0.01$, *** $p < 0.001$

TABLE C.9 ORDERED LOGIT MODEL OF WORSHIP SERVICE ATTENDANCE INCREASING, THIRTY-FIVE CONGREGATIONS THAT PARTICIPATED IN THE FULL 2020 LRCS

Variable	Coefficient	Standard error
Total attendance (congregation size)	−0.00076	−0.88
Years the leader has been with the congregation	−0.328	−0.85
Number of community programs the congregation provides	0.431*	−2.02
Congregation hosts a group to organize volunteer work	3.2*	−1.95
cut1	0.798	−0.57
cut2	3.842*	−2.44
$N = 35$		
Pseudo $R^2 = 0.207$		
* $p < 0.05$, ** $p < 0.01$, *** $p < 0.001$		

TABLE C.10 ORDERED LOGIT MODEL OF WORSHIP SERVICE ATTENDANCE INCREASING, SIXTY-THREE CONGREGATIONS THAT RESPONDED TO 2020 LRCS SURVEY OF CLERGY

Variable	Coefficient	Standard error
Total attendance (congregation size)	−0.0006	−0.82
Years the leader has been with the congregation	0.00256	−0.01
Number of community programs the congregation provides	0.316*	−2.14
Congregation hosts a group to organize volunteer work	1.56*	−1.94
cut1	−0.334	−0.34
cut2	2.493*	−2.36
$N = 55$		
Pseudo $R^2 = 0.0106$		
* $p < 0.05$, ** $p < 0.01$, *** $p < 0.001$		

TABLE C.11 ORDERED LOGIT MODEL OF CONGREGATIONAL GIVING				
Variable	Coefficient	Robust standard error	Z-score	P-value
Community engagement	−0.365	1.237	−0.290	0.768
Political activity	−0.038	0.025	−1.520	0.128
Community sermons	0.069	0.049	1.410	0.158
Member of community group	0.243	0.184	1.320	0.187
Providentiality	0.059	0.082	0.720	0.473
Education	−0.015	0.121	−0.120	0.901
Income	0.209**	0.069	3.050	0.002
Age	0.012*	0.006	1.940	0.052
Female	0.067	0.262	0.260	0.798
Worship service attendance	0.425**	0.158	2.680	0.007
Religiosity (scripture reading and prayer)	0.182***	0.041	4.410	0.000
Conservative ideology	0.084	0.081	1.040	0.299
Close to congregation's ideology	0.008	0.087	0.090	0.929
Black or African American identity	0.602	0.675	0.890	0.372
Congregation warmth	0.667	1.061	0.630	0.530
Service to congregation	0.229**	0.072	3.160	0.002
Service outside of congregation	−0.082	0.054	−1.510	0.132
Congregation average community engagement	−0.162	0.248	−0.650	0.513
Congregation average congregational warmth	−0.001	0.000	−1.740	0.082
Average attendance	0.051	0.354	0.140	0.886
Clergy political activity	0.010	0.028	0.340	0.736
Congregation election activity	0.016	0.253	0.060	0.949
Congregation ideological diversity	−0.040	3.223	−0.010	0.990
Clergy-perceived ideological division	0.163	0.197	0.830	0.409
cut1	−0.259	5.518		
cut2	1.149	5.314		
cut3	3.113	5.240		
cut4	5.002	5.188		
N = 1,041				
Pseudo R^2 = 0.133				

Note: Standard errors are clustered by thirty-five congregations.
* $p < 0.05$, ** $p < 0.01$, *** $p < 0.001$

TABLE C.12 OLS REGRESSION MODEL OF CONGREGATIONAL WARMTH				
Variable	Coefficient	Robust standard error	T-score	P-value
Community engagement	0.142	0.103	1.380	0.178
Political activity	0.003	0.003	1.200	0.237
Community sermons	0.029***	0.006	4.630	0.000
Member of community group	0.062***	0.015	4.180	0.000
Providentiality	0.023***	0.006	3.960	0.000
Education	−0.023**	0.008	−2.670	0.012
Income	0.003	0.005	0.570	0.575
Age	0.001	0.001	0.980	0.333
Female	−0.040**	0.018	−2.270	0.030
Worship service attendance	0.016	0.011	1.500	0.144
Religiosity (scripture reading and prayer)	−0.006	0.004	−1.540	0.134
Conservative ideology	−0.002	0.005	−0.320	0.752
Close to congregation's ideology	0.014**	0.006	2.270	0.030
Black or African American identity	0.036	0.034	1.050	0.301
Service to congregation	−0.002	0.012	−0.170	0.867
Service outside of congregation	−0.025**	0.009	−2.820	0.008
Congregation average community engagement	−0.014	0.011	−1.260	0.215
Congregation average congregational warmth	0.053**	0.016	3.240	0.003
Average attendance	0.000	0.000	1.090	0.282
Clergy political activity	0.005**	0.002	2.780	0.009
Congregation election activity	0.001	0.011	0.070	0.944
Congregation ideological diversity	−0.034	0.140	−0.240	0.810
Clergy-perceived ideological division	0.006	0.012	0.510	0.611
Constant	−0.282	0.307	−0.920	0.365
$N = 1,043$				
$R^2 = 0.291$				

Note: Standard errors are clustered by thirty-five congregations.
* $p < 0.05$, ** $p < 0.01$, *** $p < 0.001$

TABLE C.13 ORDERED LOGIT MODELS OF SERVICE INSIDE AND OUTSIDE OF CONGREGATIONS								
	Service to congregations				Service outside of congregations			
Variable	Coefficient	Robust standard error	Z-score	P-value	Coefficient	Robust standard error	Z-score	P-value
Community engagement	0.089	0.868	0.100	0.918	4.765***	0.707	6.740	0.000
Political sermons	−0.151**	0.068	−2.230	0.026	−0.057	0.049	−1.150	0.249
Political activity	0.029	0.029	1.010	0.313	0.021	0.022	0.920	0.356
Community sermons	0.099	0.087	1.140	0.254	0.168**	0.057	2.950	0.003
Member of community group	0.847**	0.274	3.090	0.002	0.465**	0.155	3.000	0.003
Providentiality	0.142*	0.055	2.580	0.010	−0.029	0.116	−0.250	0.805
Education	0.080	0.111	0.720	0.471	−0.031	0.078	−0.390	0.695
Income	0.098	0.065	1.510	0.132	0.138*	0.068	2.020	0.044
Age	0.004	0.005	0.790	0.431	0.003	0.006	0.550	0.580
Female	−0.139	0.172	−0.810	0.417	−0.084	0.135	−0.620	0.534
Worship service attendance	0.378***	0.076	4.980	0.000	−0.075	0.109	−0.690	0.489
Religiosity (scripture reading and prayer)	0.036	0.032	1.130	0.260	0.093*	0.042	2.230	0.026
Congregational giving	0.246**	0.096	2.550	0.011	−0.097	0.073	−1.330	0.184
Conservative ideology	−0.069	0.060	−1.140	0.255	0.056	0.047	1.200	0.230
Close to congregation's ideology	0.154	0.085	1.820	0.069	−0.020	0.114	−0.170	0.862
Black or African American identity	−0.339	0.484	−0.700	0.484	1.064**	0.385	2.770	0.006
Congregation warmth	0.143	0.971	0.150	0.883	−1.554**	0.632	−2.460	0.014
Service to congregation					0.284***	0.080	3.540	0.000
Service outside of congregation	0.257**	0.092	2.790	0.005				
Congregation average congregational warmth	−0.050	0.220	−0.230	0.819	−0.306**	0.103	−2.980	0.003

(continued)

TABLE C.13 ORDERED LOGIT MODELS OF SERVICE INSIDE AND OUTSIDE OF CONGREGATIONS (*continued*)

Variable	Service to congregations				Service outside of congregations			
	Coefficient	Robust standard error	Z-score	P-value	Coefficient	Robust standard error	Z-score	P-value
Congregation average community engagement	−0.057	0.165	−0.350	0.729	0.153	0.117	1.310	0.190
Average attendance	0.000	0.000	−1.760	0.078	0.000	0.000	0.030	0.973
Clergy political activity	−0.047*	0.023	−2.010	0.045	0.026	0.015	1.780	0.075
Congregation election activity	−0.110	0.151	−0.730	0.467	−0.174	0.106	−1.630	0.102
Congregation ideological diversity	4.112*	2.014	2.040	0.041	−2.021	1.793	−1.130	0.260
Clergy-perceived ideological division	−0.196	0.173	−1.130	0.257	−0.061	0.114	−0.540	0.591
cut1	2.942	3.803			−3.757	2.931		
cut2	4.975	3.845			2.325	2.437		
cut3	5.903	3.796			4.144	2.441		
cut4	6.732	3.806			5.229	2.489		
cut 5	0.089	0.868			5.712	2.518		
	$N = 1{,}022$				$N = 1{,}022$			
	Pseudo $R^2 = 0.138$				Pseudo $R^2 = 0.096$			

Note: Standard errors are clustered by thirty-five congregations. The ordered logit models of service both to and outside of congregations presented here include all the variables of the baseline model described in Appendix C and also include the variable for congregational giving. There is some literature that indicates that members may substitute financial giving for service hours, so including congregational giving is theoretically warranted here (Drollinger 2010; Feldman 2010; Voorintholt 2022). When it comes to service to the congregation, it appears that giving serves to create a stronger connection to the congregation and encourage service, rather than substitute for it.

$* \ p < 0.05, \ ** \ p < 0.01, \ *** \ p < 0.001$

TABLE C.14 OLS REGRESSION MODEL OF RELIGIOSITY				
Variable	Coefficient	Robust standard error	T-score	P-value
Community engagement	1.854**	0.615	3.020	0.005
Political activity	0.006	0.027	0.220	0.829
Community sermons	−0.067	0.066	−1.000	0.323
Member of community group	0.386*	0.189	2.040	0.050
Providentiality	0.810***	0.087	9.340	0.000
Education	−0.230	0.159	−1.440	0.158
Income	−0.071	0.065	−1.090	0.282
Age	0.007	0.008	0.910	0.371
Female	0.149	0.273	0.550	0.589
Worship service attendance	0.423**	0.150	2.810	0.008
Congregational giving	0.420***	0.115	3.640	0.001
Conservative ideology	0.138*	0.065	2.110	0.043
Close to congregation's ideology	−0.104	0.128	−0.810	0.422
Black or African American identity	0.848**	0.283	2.990	0.005
Congregation warmth	−1.293	0.730	−1.770	0.086
Service to congregation	0.076	0.072	1.050	0.302
Service outside of congregation	0.137	0.082	1.680	0.103
Congregation average congregational warmth	−0.401**	0.126	−3.180	0.003
Congregation average community engagement	−0.006	0.122	−0.050	0.959
Clergy political activity	0.000	0.000	−1.960	0.059
Congregation election activity	−0.017	0.023	−0.750	0.459
Congregation ideological diversity	0.040	0.134	0.290	0.770
Clergy-perceived ideological division	−3.894*	1.700	−2.290	0.029
Constant	0.279*	0.135	2.070	0.046
N = 1,041				
R^2 = 0.427				

Note: Standard errors are clustered by thirty-five congregations. The regression model of religiosity presented here includes all the variables of the baseline model described in Appendix C and also includes the variable for congregational giving. Giving financially to one's congregation is likely to be a strong predictor of other, private religious behaviors, and the fact that community engagement variables remain significant with the inclusion of congregational giving and other religion variables is an indicator of their predictive power.

* $p < 0.05$, ** $p < 0.01$, *** $p < 0.001$

TABLE C.15 OLS REGRESSION MODEL OF SPIRITUAL PEACE AND WELL-BEING

Variable	Coefficient	Robust standard error	T-score	P-value
Community engagement	0.246	0.446	0.550	0.585
Political activity	−0.022	0.012	−1.910	0.065
Community sermons	0.036	0.028	1.290	0.207
Member of community group	−0.104	0.115	−0.900	0.374
Education	−0.057	0.060	−0.950	0.351
Income	0.050	0.038	1.300	0.204
Age	0.006	0.003	1.960	0.058
Female	−0.154	0.135	−1.150	0.260
Worship service attendance	−0.029	0.082	−0.360	0.723
Religiosity	0.132***	0.025	5.310	0.000
Conservative ideology	0.059	0.030	1.950	0.060
Close to congregation's ideology	−0.020	0.060	−0.330	0.741
Black or African American identity	0.368*	0.168	2.190	0.036
Congregation warmth	0.918	0.555	1.650	0.108
Service to congregation	0.002	0.037	0.050	0.961
Service outside of congregation	0.092*	0.042	2.230	0.033
Congregation average congregational warmth	0.002	0.057	0.030	0.976
Congregation average community engagement	−0.052	0.052	−1.010	0.322
Average attendance	0.000*	0.000	−2.060	0.048
Clergy political activity	−0.019*	0.008	−2.250	0.031
Congregation election activity	0.087	0.065	1.340	0.189
Congregation ideological diversity	−0.806	0.995	−0.810	0.423
Clergy-perceived ideological division	0.009	0.044	0.200	0.842
Constant	3.915*	1.837	2.130	0.041
$N = 1,042$				
$R^2 = 0.201$				

Note: Standard errors are clustered by thirty-five congregations. The regression model of spiritual peace presented here includes all the variables of the baseline model described in Appendix C except for the measure of providential beliefs. The providentiality variable is excluded from the model because feeling a sense of spiritual peace and well-being and holding providential beliefs are theoretically similar and are also correlated at 0.45.

* $p < 0.05$, ** $p < 0.01$, *** $p < 0.001$

TABLE C.16 OLS REGRESSION MODEL OF CONGREGATIONAL SOCIAL CAPITAL

Variable	Coefficient	Robust standard error	T-score	P-value
Political activity	0.003	0.003	1.070	0.292
Political sermons	0.006	0.006	0.920	0.363
Community engagement	0.170	0.103	1.650	0.108
Community sermons	0.021	0.005	4.480	0.000
Member of community group	0.071	0.013	5.480	0.000
Providentiality	0.023	0.006	3.630	0.001
Education	−0.024	0.009	−2.800	0.009
Income	0.006	0.006	1.070	0.292
Age	0.000	0.001	0.530	0.600
Female	−0.042	0.018	−2.300	0.028
Worship service attendance	0.016	0.010	1.550	0.132
Religiosity (scripture reading and prayer)	−0.007	0.004	−1.810	0.079
Conservative ideology	−0.001	0.005	−0.270	0.785
Close to congregation's ideology	0.014	0.008	1.850	0.074
Black or African American identity	0.039	0.037	1.040	0.304
Service to congregation	−0.005	0.014	−0.340	0.733
Service outside of congregation	−0.024	0.009	−2.550	0.016
Congregation average congregational warmth	0.058	0.016	3.540	0.001
Congregation average community engagement	−0.013	0.014	−0.910	0.372
Congregation size	0.000	0.000	0.870	0.389
Clergy political activity	0.004	0.002	1.990	0.055
Congregation election activity	−0.003	0.012	−0.250	0.807
Congregation ideological diversity	0.033	0.173	0.190	0.851
Clergy-perceived ideological division	0.002	0.014	0.110	0.915
Constant	−0.371	0.314	−1.180	0.246
$N = 1{,}036$				
$R^2 = 0.275$				

Note: Standard errors are clustered by thirty-five congregations.
* $p < 0.05$, ** $p < 0.01$, *** $p < 0.001$

TABLE C.17 POISSON MODEL OF POLITICAL ACTIVITY				
Variable	Coefficient	Robust standard error	Z-score	P-value
Political sermons	0.023	0.022	1.050	0.292
Community engagement	1.952***	0.350	5.570	0.000
Community sermons	0.003	0.032	0.100	0.917
Member of community group	0.056	0.087	0.650	0.517
Providentiality	−0.068*	0.028	−2.390	0.017
Education	0.128***	0.035	3.700	0.000
Income	−0.014	0.026	−0.550	0.582
Age	0.002	0.002	1.270	0.204
Female	0.056	0.093	0.600	0.548
Worship service attendance	−0.041	0.041	−1.010	0.311
Religiosity (scripture reading and prayer)	0.003	0.018	0.160	0.871
Conservative ideology	−0.068	0.040	−1.730	0.083
Close to congregation's ideology	−0.127*	0.052	−2.460	0.014
Black or African American identity	−0.114	0.145	−0.790	0.432
Congregational warmth	0.307	0.300	1.020	0.306
Service to congregation	0.049	0.044	1.120	0.262
Service outside of congregation	0.023	0.032	0.710	0.475
Congregation average congregational warmth	0.044	0.039	1.130	0.260
Congregation average community engagement	0.060	0.042	1.450	0.146
Congregation size	0.000	0.000	1.620	0.105
Clergy political activity	−0.004	0.005	−0.700	0.485
Congregation election activity	0.039	0.035	1.130	0.260
Congregation ideological diversity	0.723	0.426	1.700	0.089
Clergy-perceived ideological division	−0.056	0.044	−1.270	0.203
Constant	−2.083*	0.913	−2.280	0.022
N = 1,023				

Note: Standard errors are clustered by thirty-five congregations. Because the political activity variable is a count variable, asking congregants how frequently they engaged in particular political behaviors in the previous year, we used a Poisson regression model with clustered standard errors as the most appropriate modeling strategy.
* $p < 0.05$, ** $p < 0.01$, *** $p < 0.001$

TABLE C.18 ORDERED LOGIT MODELS OF THE IMPORTANCE OF EDUCATION AND RACE RELATIONS								
	Race relations				Education			
Variable	Coefficient	Robust standard error	Z-score	P-value	Coefficient	Robust standard error	Z-score	P-value
Year	0.001	0.041	0.030	0.974	−0.081	0.046	−1.760	0.078
Year respondent was born	−0.015	0.004	−3.900	0.000	−0.005	0.004	−1.320	0.187
Male	−0.137	0.116	−1.180	0.239	−0.239	0.124	−1.920	0.054
Income	−0.073	0.045	−1.620	0.106	−0.038	0.049	−0.760	0.446
Education	−0.109	0.076	−1.430	0.151	−0.038	0.083	−0.460	0.643
Black or African American identity	1.265	0.205	6.180	0.000	1.186	0.245	4.830	0.000
Conservative ideology	−1.869	0.274	−6.810	0.000	−0.667	0.303	−2.210	0.027
Close to congregation's ideology	−1.049	0.305	−3.440	0.001	−0.446	0.343	−1.300	0.193
Political sermons	0.061	0.073	0.840	0.401	0.127	0.081	1.560	0.118
Community engagement	0.146	0.022	6.720	0.000	0.130	0.024	5.500	0.000
Providentiality	0.114	0.049	2.340	0.020	−0.034	0.057	−0.600	0.549
Religiosity	−0.083	0.023	−3.670	0.000	−0.036	0.025	−1.450	0.148
Political activity	−0.082	0.028	−2.900	0.004	0.004	0.031	0.120	0.902
cut1	−29.751	83.936			−178.353	93.590		
cut2	−28.487	83.934			−176.655	93.587		
cut3	−27.141	83.931			−175.186	93.586		
cut4	−25.276	83.929			−173.117	93.584		
cut 5					−165.087	93.573		
Pseudo R^2	0.127				0.078			
	$N = 1,253$				$N = 1,257$			

* $p < 0.05$, ** $p < 0.01$, *** $p < 0.001$

Variable	Coefficient	Robust standard error	Z-score	P-value	Coefficient	Robust standard error	Z-score	P-value
	Race relations				Education			
Community engagement	−0.007	0.089	−0.070	0.941	0.085	0.047	1.800	0.071
Political sermons	−0.067	0.145	−0.460	0.642	0.006	0.113	0.050	0.959
Political activity	0.068	0.045	1.520	0.129	0.085*	0.039	2.200	0.028
Community sermons	0.077	0.178	0.430	0.667	0.172	0.103	1.680	0.093
Member of community group	−0.007	0.363	−0.020	0.984	0.043	0.407	0.100	0.917
Providentiality	0.509***	0.139	3.670	0.000	−0.111	0.106	−1.060	0.291
Education	−0.239	0.247	−0.970	0.332	0.072	0.201	0.360	0.721
Income	−0.167	0.170	−0.980	0.327	−0.068	0.079	−0.860	0.389
Age	−0.025*	0.011	−2.200	0.028	−0.008	0.007	−1.150	0.249
Female	−0.598	0.450	−1.330	0.184	0.097	0.270	0.360	0.720
Worship service attendance	−0.003	0.289	−0.010	0.991	0.331*	0.143	2.310	0.021
Religiosity	0.062	0.086	0.720	0.473	−0.049	0.054	−0.900	0.367
Conservative ideology	−0.566***	0.090	−6.310	0.000	−0.134	0.072	−1.850	0.064
Close to congregation's ideology	0.120	0.282	0.430	0.670	0.067	0.163	0.410	0.681
Black or African American identity	−1.759*	0.799	−2.200	0.028	−0.256	0.630	−0.410	0.684
Congregation warmth	−0.140	0.149	−0.940	0.346	0.003	0.055	0.050	0.956

TABLE C.19 ORDERED LOGIT MODELS OF DESIRE FOR CONGREGATIONAL INVOLVEMENT IN EDUCATION AND RACE RELATIONS

Service to congregation	0.050	0.186	0.270	0.788	−0.020	0.119	−0.170	0.867
Service outside of congregation	−0.116	0.183	−0.640	0.524	−0.220	0.126	−1.740	0.081
Congregation average congregational warmth	−0.658	0.340	−1.940	0.053	−0.531*	0.213	−2.500	0.012
Congregation average community engagement	0.804*	0.346	2.320	0.020	−0.668*	0.302	−2.210	0.027
Average attendance	0.000	0.000	1.080	0.281	0.001***	0.000	3.630	0.000
Clergy political activity	0.027	0.042	0.660	0.509	0.159***	0.032	4.960	0.000
Congregation election activity	−0.365	0.284	−1.280	0.199	0.022	0.196	0.110	0.911
Congregation ideological diversity	4.037	3.091	1.310	0.192	6.859*	3.090	2.220	0.026
Clergy-perceived ideological division	0.135	0.243	0.550	0.580	−0.147	0.128	−1.150	0.252
Congregation welcoming to other races	−0.231	0.240	−0.960	0.337	—	—	—	—
cut1	0.877	7.739			−22.418	6.724		
cut2	3.594	7.765			−20.721	6.725		
Pseudo R^2	0.23				0.153			
	$N = 478$				$N = 662$			

Note: Standard errors are clustered by thirty-five congregations.

* $p < 0.05$, ** $p < 0.01$, *** $p < 0.001$

APPENDIX D: CODEBOOKS

*Open-Ended Worship Service Attendance Codebook, 2020 LRCS Survey of
Congregation Members*

Codebook designed for coding open-ended responses to the 2020 LRCS Congregant
Survey:
"What is the main reason why you are attending more often now?"
"What is the main reason why you are attending less often now?"

- Give up to three codes per open-ended response
- Put each code in a new column in the spreadsheet (More1, More2, More3, or Less1, Less2, Less3)

Reasons for attending more now

20: spiritual reason; e.g., wanting to grow, wanting to be close to God
codes here should also include theological reasons; e.g., sermons are welcoming, theology feels right to me
30: personal social reason; e.g., made a new friend, resolved a conflict
31: institutional social reason; e.g., liked the new group the congregation started
32: politically-motivated social reason; e.g., connecting with people I agree with politically, seeing social justice issues as more important
Note: codes 30–32 were aggregated to a single social reason code for the purposes of analysis
40: ease of access; it is easier to view services from home
50: specific COVID institutional reason; e.g., place of worship has made services more accessible because of COVID, so I am able to attend more, view and participate online
51: specific COVID personal reason; e.g., realizing how important faith is now because of COVID
Note: codes 50 and 51 were aggregated to a single specific COVID code for the purposes of analysis
52: COVID general (they just wrote "COVID" or "pandemic")
99: other; not able to code, doesn't fit into one of these categories, doesn't make sense

Reasons for attending less now

60: spiritual reason; e.g., don't believe any more, having a crisis of faith
codes here should include theological reasons; sermons are too hard, theology is too traditional, theology is too progressive
70: personal social reason; e.g., fight with a friend, personal conflict
71: institutional social reason; e.g., too many cliques, don't like the groups, falling out with the pastor
72: politically motivated social reasons; it's too political and charged; I'm uncomfortable with the politics
Note: codes 70–72 were aggregated to a single social reason code for the purposes of analysis
80: difficulty of access; it is hard to get access to services online
90: COVID institutional reason; e.g., the church has stopped holding services
91: COVID personal reason; e.g., don't like virtual services, don't think it's safe to attend, too busy
Note: codes 90 and 91 were aggregated to a single specific COVID code for the purposes of analysis

92: COVID general (they just wrote "COVID" or "pandemic")
99: other; not able to code, doesn't fit into one of these categories, doesn't make sense

TABLE D.1 CODEBOOK FOR OPEN-ENDED RESPONSES OF CONGREGATION PRIORITIES, 2020 LRCS CONGREGATION MEMBER SURVEY

Code	Description
General	
10	Priorities were equal; hard to choose between them
11	Church is going great, church does all of this
20	General unity, community building, gathering, growing, helping (not specific to congregation or to community outside of congregation)
Congregation related	
31	Closer connection, support (among the church family)
32	Religious specific (Bible study, spiritual growth, Zion community, liturgical music)
33	Congregational governance/leadership
34	COVID specific
Social/cultural issues in congregation	
40	Want to avoid social/cultural issues
41	Want to engage social/cultural issues
42	More welcoming and inclusive, in general; following codes are specific:
43	Race
44	LGBTQ
45	Families/children
46	Socioeconomically
47	Abilities
49	Other congregation work (people should convert to my religion, congregation)
External to the congregation	
51	Closer connection, community involvement
52	Advocacy, helping, unity, in general; following codes are specific:
53	Race
54	LGBTQ
55	Children/schools/youth (generic education coded here)
56	Homeless/poor
57	Sick
58	Addicted
60	Evangelizing, sharing truth, foreign missions
69	Other community work (supporting the arts, nature)
99	Generic other (drag and drop function wasn't working, I can't answer until the pandemic is over)

*Codebook for General Open-Ended Comments, 2016 LRCS
Congregation Member Survey*

Prompt: "Please use this space to tell us what you like best about your place of worship, or anything else you want us to know."

Response *N* = 453

Each response receives a binary code for each of following four variables:
Mentions clergy leader (include mention of the sermon or the preaching)

Yes = 1
No = 0

Mentions community engagement

Yes = 1
No = 0

Mentions something about politics (include social justice)

Yes = 1
No = 0

Mentions something about how they are spiritually fed or grow at the congregation (include sense of belonging or congregational warmth or inclusiveness)

Yes = 1
No = 0

References

Abdullah, Halimah. 2012. "'Other-ness': What Obama and Romney Have in Common on Religion, Race." *CNN*, last modified May 23, 2012. https://www.cnn.com/2012/05/22/politics/obama-romney-race-religion-other/index.html.

Abramowitz, Alan I., and Jennifer McCoy. 2019. "United States: Racial Resentment, Negative Partisanship, and Polarization in Trump's America." *Annals of the American Academy of Political and Social Science* 681 (1): 137–156.

Abramowitz, Alan I., and Steven Webster. 2016. "The Rise of Negative Partisanship and the Nationalization of U.S. Elections in the 21st Century." *Electoral Studies* 41:12–22. Available at https://doi.org/10.1016/j.electstud.2015.11.001.

Abramson, Paul R., and John H. Aldrich. 1982. "The Decline of Electoral Participation in America." *American Political Science Review* 76 (3): 502–521.

Aknin, Lara B., and Ashley V. Whillans. 2021. "Helping and Happiness: A Review and Guide for Public Policy." *Social Issues and Policy Review* 15 (1): 3–34. Available at https://doi.org/10.1111/sipr.12069.

Almond, Gabriel A., and Sidney Verba. 1963. *The Civic Culture: Political Attitudes and Democracy in Five Nations.* Princeton, NJ: Princeton University Press.

Altheimer, Irshad. 2022. "Does Islam Encourage Civic Engagement?" Soul Revival Foundation. Last modified July 17, 2022. Available at https://aboutislam.net/shariah/shariah-and-humanity/shariah-and-life/islam-and-civic-engagement/.

Amato, Paul R., and Stacy J. Rogers. 1997. "A Longitudinal Study of Marital Problems and Subsequent Divorce." *Journal of Marriage and Family* 59 (3): 612–624. Available at https://doi.org/10.2307/353949.

Ammerman, Nancy T. 1997a. *Congregation and Community.* New Brunswick, NJ: Rutgers University Press.

———. 1997b. "Organized Religion in a Voluntaristic Society." *Sociology of Religion* 58 (3): 203–215.

———. 2001. "Doing Good in American Communities: Congregations and Service Organizations Working Together." Hartford, CT: Hartford Institute for Religion Research, Hartford Seminary.

———. 2005. *Pillars of Faith: American Congregations and Their Partners*. Berkeley, CA: University of California Press.

Anderson, Erin, and Sandy D. Jap. 2005. "The Dark Side of Close Relationships." *MIT Sloan Management Review* 46 (3): 75.

Andreasen, Alan R. 1996. "Profits for Nonprofits: Find a Corporate Partner." *Harvard Business Review* 74 (6): 47–50, 55–59.

Andrews, Rhys, and David Turner. 2006. "Modelling the Impact of Community Engagement on Local Democracy." *Local Economy* 21 (4): 378–390. Available at https://doi.org/10.1080/02690940600951956.

Anshel, Mark H., and Mitchell Smith. 2014. "The Role of Religious Leaders in Promoting Healthy Habits in Religious Institutions." *Journal of Religion and Health* 53 (4): 1046–1059.

Aronson, Janet Krasner, Leonard Saxe, Charles Kadushin, Matthew Boxer, and Matthew A. Brookner. 2019. "A New Approach to Understanding Contemporary Jewish Engagement." *Contemporary Jewry* 39 (1): 91–113. Available at https://doi.org/10.1007/s12397-018-9271-8.

Association of Religion Data Archives. 2010. *Pulaski County, Arkansas—County Membership Report*. Association of Religion Data Archives. Available at https://thearda.com/us-religion/census/congregational-membership.

Azmat, Syed Khurram. 2011. "Mobilizing Male Opinion Leaders' Support for Family Planning to Improve Maternal Health: A Theory-Based Qualitative Study from Pakistan." *Journal of Multidisciplinary Healthcare* 4:421–431.

Bakker, Janel Kragt. 2013. *Sister Churches: American Congregations and Their Partners Abroad*. Oxford: Oxford University Press.

Bane, Mary Jo, Brent Coffin, and Ronald Thiemann, eds. 2001. *Who Will Provide? The Changing Role of Religion in American Social Welfare*. New York: Taylor & Francis.

Barna Group. 2020. "One in Three Practicing Christians Has Stopped Attending Church during COVID-19." In *Barna: State of the Church*. July 8, 2020. Available at https://www.barna.com/research/new-sunday-morning-part-2/.

———. 2022. "Pastors Share Top Reasons They've Considered Quitting Ministry in the Past Year." April 27, 2022. Available at https://www.barna.com/research/pastors-quitting-ministry/.

Barnes, Sandra Lynn. 2005. "Black Church Culture and Community Action." *Social Forces* 84 (2): 967–994. Available at https://doi.org/10.1353/sof.2006.0003.

———. 2011. "Black Megachurches: Social Gospel Usage and Community Empowerment." *Journal of African American Studies* 15 (2): 177–198. Available at https://doi.org/10.1007/s12111-010-9148-8.

Barth, Jay. 2022. "White Flight." Central Arkansas Library System Encyclopedia of Arkansas. Last modified April 5, 2022. Available at https://encyclopediaofarkansas.net/entries/white-flight-4917/.

Bass, Ryan. 2023. "EF3 Tornado Leaves Parts of Little Rock in Shambles." *NewsNation*, last modified April 4, 2023. Available at https://www.newsnationnow.com/weather/little-rock-arkansas-tornado/.

Baugh, Amanda J. 2016. *God and the Green Divide: Religious Environmentalism in Black and White*. Berkeley: University of California Press.

Beatty, Kathleen Murphy, and Oliver Walter. 1989. "A Group Theory of Religion and Politics: The Clergy as Group Leaders." *Western Political Quarterly* 42 (1): 129–146.

Bellah, Robert N., Richard Madsen, William M. Sullivan, Ann Swidler, and Steven M. Tipton. 2007. *Habits of the Heart, with a New Preface: Individualism and Commitment in American Life*. Berkeley: University of California Press.

Beyerlein, Kraig, and Mark Chaves. 2003. "The Political Activities of Religious Congregations in the United States." *Journal for the Scientific Study of Religion* 42 (2): 229–246. Available at https://doi.org/10.2307/1387839.

Beyerlein, Kraig, and John R. Hipp. 2006. "From Pews to Participation: The Effect of Congregation Activity and Context on Bridging Civic Engagement." *Social Problems* 53 (1): 97–117. Available at https://doi.org/10.1525/sp.2006.53.1.97.

Bishop, Bill. 2009. *The Big Sort: Why the Clustering of Like-Minded America Is Tearing Us Apart*. New York: Houghton Mifflin Harcourt.

Bomhoff, Eduard J., and Audrey Kim Lan Siah. 2019. "The Relationship between Income, Religiosity and Health: Their Effects on Life Satisfaction." *Personality and Individual Differences* 144:168–173. Available at https://doi.org/10.1016/j.paid.2019.03.008.

Bowles, Samuel, and Herbert Gintis. 2002. "Social Capital and Community Governance." *Economic Journal* 112 (483): F419–F436. Available at https://doi.org/10.1111/1468-0297.00077.

Bracic, Ana. 2018. "For Better Science: The Benefits of Community Engagement in Research." *PS: Political Science and Politics* 51 (3): 550–553. Available at https://doi.org/10.1017/S1049096518000446.

Brady, Henry E., Sidney Verba, and Kay Lehman Schlozman. 1995. "Beyond SES: A Resource Model of Political Participation." *American Political Science Review* 89 (2): 271–294.

Branton, Wiley A. 1983. "Little Rock Revisited: Desegregation to Resegregation." *Journal of Negro Education* 52 (3): 250–269. Available at https://doi.org/10.2307/2294663.

Brauer, Simon. 2018. "The Surprising Predictable Decline of Religion in the United States." *Journal for the Scientific Study of Religion* 57 (4): 654–675. Available at https://doi.org/10.1111/jssr.12551.

Brown, Jacob R., and Ryan D. Enos. 2021. "The Measurement of Partisan Sorting for 180 Million Voters." *Nature Human Behaviour* 5 (8): 998–1008. Available at https://doi.org/10.1038/s41562-021-01066-z.

Brown, Myra. 2019. "A Love That Does Justice." *Contexts* 18 (3): 42–49. Available at https://doi.org/10.1177/1536504219864958.

Brown, R. Khari, and Ronald E. Brown. 2003. "Faith and Works: Church-Based Social Capital Resources and African American Political Activism." *Social Forces* 82 (2): 617–641.

Bryson, John M., Barbara C. Crosby, and Melissa Middleton Stone. 2006. "The Design and Implementation of Cross-Sector Collaborations: Propositions from the Literature." *Public Administration Review* 66 (s1): 44–55.

Burdick, Brent H. 2018. "The Status of the Church in North America." *Review and Expositor* 115 (2): 200–213.

Burge, Ryan P. 2021. *The Nones: Where They Came From, Who They Are, and Where They Are Going*. Minneapolis, MN: Fortress Press.

Burwell, Rebecca, Edwin I. Hernandez, Milagros Pena, Jeffrey Roy Smith, and David Sikkink. 2010. *The Chicago Latino Congregations Study (CLCS): Methodological Consid-*

erations. South Bend, IN: University of Notre Dame Institute for Latino Studies, Center for the Study of Latino Religion.

Calfano, Brian Robert. 2010. "Prophetic at Any Price? Clergy Political Behavior and Utility Maximization." *Social Science Quarterly* 91 (3): 649–668. Available at https://doi.org/10.1111/j.1540-6237.2010.00712.x.

Calfano, Brian Robert, Elizabeth A. Oldmixon, and Mark Gray. 2014. "Strategically Prophetic Priests: An Analysis of Competing Principal Influence on Clergy Political Action." *Review of Religious Research* 56 (1): 1–21.

Calhoun-Brown, Allison. 1996. "African American Churches and Political Mobilization: The Psychological Impact of Organizational Resources." *Journal of Politics* 58 (4): 935–953.

———. 1998. "While Marching to Zion: Otherworldliness and Racial Empowerment in the Black Community." *Journal for the Scientific Study of Religion* 37 (3): 427–439. Available at https://doi.org/10.2307/1388050.

Campbell, Angus, Gerald Gurin, and Warren E. Miller. 1954. *The Voter Decides.* Evanston, WY: Row, Peterson.

Campbell, Anthony David. 2021. "Clergy Perceptions of Mental Illness and Confronting Stigma in Congregations." *Religions* 12 (12): 1110.

Campbell, David E. 2013. "Social Capital and Service Learning." *PS: Political Science and Politics* 33 (3): 641–646. Available at https://doi.org/10.2307/420872.

Campbell, Ernest Queener, and Thomas F. Pettigrew. 1959a. *Christians in Racial Crisis: A Study of Little Rock's Ministry.* Washington, DC: Public Affairs Press.

———. 1959b. "Racial and Moral Crisis: The Role of Little Rock Ministers." *American Journal of Sociology* 64 (5): 509–516.

Campbell, Marci Kramish, Marlyn Allicock Hudson, Ken Resnicow, Natasha Blakeney, Amy Paxton, and Monica Baskin. 2007. "Church-based Health Promotion Interventions: Evidence and Lessons Learned." *Annual Review of Public Health* 28:213–234.

Cassel, Carol A. 1999. "Voluntary Associations, Churches, and Social Participation Theories of Turnout." *Social Science Quarterly* 80 (3): 504–517.

Cathey, Libby. 2023. "Sarah Huckabee Sanders Signs Sweeping Education Bill, to Praise and Protests." *ABC News,* last modified March 8, 2023. Available at https://abcnews.go.com/Politics/sarah-huckabee-sanders-signs-sweeping-education-bill-praise/story?id=97708033.

Cavendish, James C. 2000. "Church-Based Community Activism: A Comparison of Black and White Catholic Congregations." *Journal for the Scientific Study of Religion* 39 (3): 371–384.

Chaiken, Shelly, Roger Giner-Sorolla, and Serena Chen. 1996. "Beyond Accuracy: Defense and Impression Motives in Heuristic and Systematic Information Processing." In *The Psychology of Action: Linking Cognition and Motivation to Behavior,* edited by Peter M. Gollwitzer and John A. Bargh, 553–578. New York: Guilford.

Chaves, Mark. 2004. *Congregations in America.* Cambridge, MA: Harvard University Press.

Chaves, Mark, and Lynn M. Higgins. 1992. "Comparing the Community Involvement of Black and White Congregations." *Journal for the Scientific Study of Religion* 31 (4): 425–440.

Chaves, Mark, Mary Ellen Konieczny, Kraig Beyerlein, and Emily Barman. 1999. "The National Congregations Study: Background, Methods, and Selected Results." *Journal for the Scientific Study of Religion* 38 (4): 458–476.

Chaves, Mark, Joseph Roso, Anna Holleman, and Mary Hawkins. 2021. *National Congregations Study: Waves I–IV Summary Tables*. Durham, NC: Duke University Department of Sociology.

Chaves, Mark, and William Tsitsos. 2001. "Congregations and Social Services: What They Do, How They Do It, and with Whom." *Nonprofit and Voluntary Sector Quarterly* 30 (4): 660–683.

Chaves, Mark, and Bob Wineburg. 2010. "Did the Faith-Based Initiative Change Congregations?" *Nonprofit and Voluntary Sector Quarterly* 39 (2): 343–355. Available at https://doi.org/10.1177/0899764009333955.

CityChurch Network. n.d. "About Us." Accessed December 6, 2022. Available at https://citychurchar.org/about-us/.

Claridge, T. 2004. "Social Capital and Natural Resource Management: An Important Role for Social Capital?" Unpublished Ph.D. diss., University of Queensland.

Clerkin, Richard M., and Kirsten A. Grønbjerg. 2007. "The Capacities and Challenges of Faith-Based Human Service Organizations." *Public Administration Review* 67 (1): 115–126. Available at https://doi.org/10.1111/j.1540-6210.2006.00701.x.

Clopton, Aaron Walter, and Bryan L. Finch. 2011. "Re-conceptualizing Social Anchors in Community Development: Utilizing Social Anchor Theory to Create Social Capital's Third Dimension." *Community Development* 42 (1): 70–83.

Cnaan, Ram A., Stephanie C. Boddie, Femida Handy, Gaynor Yancey, and Richard Schneider. 2002. *The Invisible Caring Hand: American Congregations and the Provision of Welfare*. New York: New York University Press.

Cnaan, Ram A., Stephanie C. Boddie, and Gaynor I. Yancey. 2003. "Bowling Alone but Serving Together: The Congregational Norm of Community Involvement." In *Religion as Social Capital: Producing the Common Good*, edited by Corwin E. Smidt, 19–31. Waco, TX: Baylor University Press.

Cnaan, Ram A., and Daniel W. Curtis. 2013. "Religious Congregations as Voluntary Associations: An Overview." *Nonprofit and Voluntary Sector Quarterly* 42 (1): 7–33. Available at https://doi.org/10.1177/0899764012460730.

Cnaan, Ram A., Jill W. Sinha, and Charlene C. McGrew. 2004a. "Congregations as Social Service Providers." *Administration in Social Work* 28 (3–4): 47–68. Available at https://doi.org/10.1300/J147v28n03_03.

———. 2004b. "Congregations as Social Service Providers: Services, Capacity, Culture, and Organizational Behavior." *Administration in Social Work* 28 (3–4): 47–68.

Colon-Otero, Gerado, Monica Albertie, Judith Rodriquez, Garik Nicholson, Irina Kolomeyer, Alvaro Moreno-Aspita, Mary Lesperance, and Edith A Perez. 2014. "A Church-Based, Spanish-Language Community Education Breast Health Program Increases Awareness and Utilization of Breast Diagnostic Services among Hispanics." *Journal of Higher Education Outreach and Engagement* 18 (1): 43–60.

Cooper, Anthony-Paul, Ilkka Jormanainen, Annastasia Shipepe, and Erkki Sutinen. 2021. "Faith Communities Online: Christian Churches' Reactions to the COVID-19 Outbreak." *International Journal of Web Based Communities* 17 (2): 99–119. Available at https://doi.org/10.1504/ijwbc.2021.114453.

Corporation for National and Community Service. 2007. *The Health Benefits of Volunteering: A Review of Recent Research*. Purdue University, Corporation for National and Community Service, Office of Research and Policy Development.

Costello, Jennifer, Krystal Hays, and Ana M. Gamez. 2021. "Using Mental Health First Aid to Promote Mental Health in Churches." *Journal of Spirituality in Mental Health* 23 (4): 381–392. Available at https://doi.org/10.1080/19349637.2020.1771234.

Costello, Jennifer, Mandy Smith, Marni Straine, and Daphne Thomas. 2022. "Love Your Neighbor Collaborative: A MultiSector Collaborative to Target Health Disparities for Vulnerable Populations." *Social Work and Christianity* 49 (3): 229–240.

County Health Rankings. n.d. "Children Eligible for Free or Reduced Price Lunch in Arkansas." University of Wisconsin Population Health Institute, School of Medicine and Public Health. Accessed December 6, 2022. Available at https://www.countyhealth rankings.org/explore-health-rankings/arkansas?year=2022&measure=Children+El igible+for+Free+or+Reduced+Price+Lunch*.

Cox, Daniel A. 2022. "Generation Z and the Future of Faith in America." Survey Center on American Life. March 24, 2022. Available at https://www.americansurveycenter .org/research/generation-z-future-of-faith/#_edn10.

Cox, Daniel A., Jacqueline Clemence, and Eleanor O'Neil. 2019. *The Decline of Religion in American Family Life: Findings from the November 2019 American Perspectives Survey.* Washington, DC: American Enterprise Institute.

Coyne, Michael D., D. Betsy McCoach, Susan Loftus, Richard Zipoli Jr., Maureen Ruby, Yvel C. Crevecoeur, and Sharon Kapp. 2010. "Direct and Extended Vocabulary Instruction in Kindergarten: Investigating Transfer Effects." *Journal of Research on Educational Effectiveness* 3 (2): 93–120.

Crawford, Sue E. S., and Laura R. Olson. 2001. *Christian Clergy in American Politics.* Baltimore, MD: Johns Hopkins University Press.

Cronshaw, Darren. 2020. "Exploring Local Church Praxis of Public Theology." *International Journal of Public Theology* 14 (1): 68–96. Available at https://doi.org/10.1163/15 697320-12341601.

Dada, Debbie, Joseph Nguemo Djiometio, SarahAnn M. McFadden, Jemal Demeke, David Vlahov, Leo Wilton, Mengzu Wang, et al. 2022. "Strategies That Promote Equity in COVID-19 Vaccine Uptake for Black Communities: A Review." *Journal of Urban Health* 99 (1): 15–27. Available at https://doi.org/10.1007/s11524-021-00594-3.

Damon, Will, Cody Callon, Lee Wiebe, Will Small, Thomas Kerr, and Ryan McNeil. 2017. "Community-Based Participatory Research in a Heavily Researched Inner City Neighbourhood: Perspectives of People Who Use Drugs on Their Experiences as Peer Researchers." *Social Science and Medicine* 176:85–92. Available at https://doi.org/10.1016 /j.socscimed.2017.01.027.

Davern, Michael, Rene Bautista, Jeremy Freese, Stephen L. Morgan, and Tom W. Smith. 2021. General Social Survey 2021 Cross-Section (machine-readable data file). 1 datafile (68,846 cases) and 1 codebook (506 pages). Principal investigator, Michael Davern; co-principal investigators, Rene Bautista, Jeremy Freese, Stephen L. Morgan, and Tom W. Smith. NORC ed. Chicago.

Davidson, James D. 1986. "Captive Congregations: Why Local Churches Don't Pursue Equality." In *The Political Role of Religion in the United States*, edited by Stephen D. Johnson and Joseph B. Tamney, 239–261. London: Routledge.

DeFilippis, James. 2008. "Community Control and Development." In *The Community Development Reader*, edited by James DeFilippis and S. Saegert, 28–35. New York: Routledge.

Dekker, Paul, and Eric M. Uslaner. 2003. Introduction to *Social Capital and Participation in Everyday Life*, edited by Eric M. Uslaner, 1–8. London: Routledge.

De Las Nueces, Denise, Karen Hacker, Ann DiGirolamo, and LeRoi S. Hicks. 2012. "A Systematic Review of Community-Based Participatory Research to Enhance Clinical Trials in Racial and Ethnic Minority Groups." *Health Services Research* 47 (3pt2): 1363–1386. Available at https://doi.org/10.1111/j.1475-6773.2012.01386.x.

de Tocqueville, Alexis. 1969. *Democracy in America*. Edited by J. P. Mayer and Max Lerner. New translation by George Lawrence. New York: Doubleday, Anchor Books.

DeYmaz, Mark. 2020. *Building a Healthy Multi-ethnic Church: Mandate, Commitments, and Practices of a Diverse Congregation*. Minneapolis, MN: Fortress Press.

DeYoung, Curtiss Paul, Michael O. Emerson, and George Yancey. 2004. *United by Faith: The Multiracial Congregation as an Answer to the Problem of Race*. New York: Oxford University Press.

Dickinson, David L. 2020. "Deliberation Enhances the Confirmation Bias: An Examination of Politics and Religion." IZA Discussion Paper No. 13241. Available at https://ssrn.com/abstract=3602417 or http://dx.doi.org/10.2139/ssrn.3602417.

Dirksen, Carolyn. 2020. "Community Engagement for Student Faith Development: Service-Learning in the Pentecostal Tradition." *Christian Higher Education* 19 (1–2): 78–90. Available at https://doi.org/10.1080/15363759.2019.1689198.

Djupe, Paul A. 2019. "Do People Really Want Religion Out of Politics?" *Religion in Public* (blog). November 18, 2019. Available at https://religioninpublic.blog/2019/11/18/do-people-really-want-religion-out-of-politics/.

Djupe, Paul A., and Brian R. Calfano. 2009. "Justification Not by Faith Alone: Clergy Generating Trust and Certainty by Revealing Thought." *Politics and Religion* 2 (1): 1–30.

Djupe, Paul A., and Christopher P. Gilbert. 2003. *The Prophetic Pulpit: Clergy, Churches, and Communities in American Politics*. Lanham, MD: Rowman & Littlefield.

———. 2006. "The Resourceful Believer: Generating Civic Skills in Church." *Journal of Politics* 68 (1): 116–127.

———. 2009. *The Political Influence of Churches*. New York: Cambridge University Press.

Djupe, Paul A., and Gregory W. Gwiasda. 2010. "Evangelizing the Environment: Decision Process Effects in Political Persuasion." *Journal for the Scientific Study of Religion* 49 (1): 73–86. Available at https://doi.org/10.1111/j.1468-5906.2009.01493.x.

Djupe, Paul A., and Jacob R. Neiheisel. 2012. "How Religious Communities Affect Political Participation among Latinos." *Social Science Quarterly* 93 (2): 333–355.

Djupe, Paul A., Jacob R. Neiheisel, and Anand E. Sokhey. 2018. "Reconsidering the Role of Politics in Leaving Religion: The Importance of Affiliation." *American Journal of Political Science* 62 (1): 161–175. Available at https://doi.org/10.1111/ajps.12308.

Dougherty, Kevin D., and Kimberly R. Huyser. 2008. "Racially Diverse Congregations: Organizational Identity and the Accommodation of Differences." *Journal for the Scientific Study of Religion* 47 (1): 23–44. Available at https://doi.org/10.1111/j.1468-5906.2008.00390.x.

Drescher, Elizabeth. 2016. *Choosing Our Religion: The Spiritual Lives of America's Nones*. Oxford, United Kingdom: Oxford University Press.

Driskell, Robyn L., Elizabeth Embry, and Larry Lyon. 2008. "Faith and Politics: The Influence of Religious Beliefs on Political Participation." *Social Science Quarterly* 89 (2): 294–314. Available at https://doi.org/10.1111/j.1540-6237.2008.00533.x.

Driskell, Robyn L., Larry Lyon, and Elizabeth Embry. 2008. "Civic Engagement and Religious Activities: Examining the Influence of Religious Tradition and Participation." *Sociological Spectrum* 28 (5): 578–601. Available at https://doi.org/10.1080/02732170802206229.

Drollinger, Tanya. 2010. "A Theoretical Examination of Giving and Volunteering Utilizing Resource Exchange Theory." *Journal of Nonprofit and Public Sector Marketing* 22 (1): 55–66. Available at https://doi.org/10.1080/10495140903190416.

Earls, Aaron. 2021. "Average U.S. Pastor and Churchgoer Grow Older." Lifeway Christian Resources. November 1, 2021. Available at https://research.lifeway.com/2021/11/01/americas-pastors-and-churchgoers-are-getting-older/.

Ebaugh, Helen Rose, and Paula F. Pipes. 2001. "Immigrant Congregations as Social Service Providers: Are They Safety Nets for Welfare Reform?" In *Religion and Social Policy*, edited by Paula D. Nesbitt, 95–110. Lanham, MD: Rowman & Littlefield.

Ebaugh, Helen Rose, Paula F. Pipes, Janet Saltzman Chafetz, and Martha Daniels. 2003. "Where's the Religion? Distinguishing Faith-Based from Secular Social Service Agencies." *Journal for the Scientific Study of Religion* 42 (3): 411–426. Available at https://doi.org/10.1111/1468-5906.00191.

Einolf, Christopher J. 2011. "The Link between Religion and Helping Others: The Role of Values, Ideas, and Language." *Sociology of Religion* 72 (4): 435–455. Available at https://doi.org/10.1093/socrel/srr017.

Ellison, Christopher G., and Linda K. George. 1994. "Religious Involvement, Social Ties, and Social Support in a Southeastern Community." *Journal for the Scientific Study of Religion* 33 (1): 46–61. Available at https://doi.org/10.2307/1386636.

Fackenheim, Emil L. 1970. *God's Presence in History: Jewish Affirmations and Philosophical Reflections*. New York: J. Aronson.

Fairweather, Daryl. 2021. "Redfin Predicts a More Balanced Housing Market in 2022." Redfin News. November 18, 2021. Available at https://www.redfin.com/news/housing-market-predictions-2022/.

Feldman, Naomi E. 2010. "Time Is Money: Choosing between Charitable Activities." *American Economic Journal: Economic Policy* 2 (1): 103–130.

Finifter, Ada W. 2014. "The Friendship Group as a Protective Environment for Political Deviants." *American Political Science Review* 68 (2): 607–625. Available at https://doi.org/10.2307/1959508.

Finkel, Steven E. 1985. "Reciprocal Effects of Participation and Political Efficacy: A Panel Analysis." *American Journal of Political Science* 29 (4): 891–913. Available at https://doi.org/10.2307/2111186.

Frémeaux, Sandrine. 2020. "A Common Good Perspective on Diversity." *Business Ethics Quarterly* 30 (2): 200–228.

Friedland, Michael B. 1998. *Lift Up Your Voice Like a Trumpet: White Clergy and the Civil Rights and Antiwar Movements, 1954–1973*. Chapel Hill: University of North Carolina Press.

Fukuyama, Francis. 2001. "Social Capital, Civil Society and Development." *Third World Quarterly* 22 (1): 7–20.

Fulton, Brad R. 2016. "Trends in Addressing Social Needs: A Longitudinal Study of Congregation-Based Service Provision and Political Participation." *Religions* 7 (5): 51.

Gates, Carrie. 2022. "'On the Brink of a New Civil War': New National Survey Highlights Fragility of American Democracy, Stark Partisan Divides." University of Notre Dame. November 3, 2022. Available at https://www.newswise.com/articles/on-the-brink-of-a-new-civil-war-new-national-survey-highlights-fragility-of-american-democracy-stark-partisan-divides.

Gazley, Beth, Brad R. Fulton, Wesley Mlsna Zebrowski, and David P. King. 2022. "Giving and Going: US Congregational Participation in Disaster Response." *Nonprofit Management and Leadership* 33 (1): 157–178. Available at https://doi.org/10.1002/nml.21503.

Gibson, Winter. 1961. *The Suburban Captivity of the Churches: An Analysis of Protestant Responsibility in the Expanding Metropolis*. Garden City, NY: Doubleday.

Giles, Kate, Dee Dyas, and Becky Payne. 2021. *Churches, COVID-19, and Communities: Experiences, Needs and Supporting Recovery.* Centre for the Study of Christianity and Culture, York, United Kingdom: University of York.

Gill, Jill. 2011. *Embattled Ecumenism: The National Council of Churches, the Vietnam War, and the Trials of the Protestant Left.* DeKalb: Northern Illinois University Press.

Gimpel, James G., Nathan Lovin, Bryant Moy, and Andrew Reeves. 2020. "The Urban–Rural Gulf in American Political Behavior." *Political Behavior* 42 (4): 1343–1368.

Glazier, Rebecca A. 2015. "Bridging Religion and Politics: The Impact of Providential Religious Beliefs on Political Activity." *Politics and Religion* 8 (3): 458–487. Available at https://doi.org/10.1017/S1755048315000139.

———. 2018. "Acting for God? Types and Motivations of Clergy Political Activity." *Politics and Religion* 11 (4): 760–797.

———. 2019a. "The Differential Impact of Religion on Political Activity and Community Engagement." *Review of Religious Research* 62:1–26. Available at https://doi.org/10.1007/s13644-019-00388-9.

———. 2019b. *Opportunities for Collaboration: An Executive Report of Results from the 2019 Little Rock Congregations Study Survey of Nonprofit Organizations.* Little Rock: University of Arkansas at Little Rock.

———. 2021. *2021 Little Rock Congregations Study Facilitated Dialogue Series.* Little Rock: University of Arkansas at Little Rock and the Clinton School of Public Service.

Glazier, Rebecca A., and Warigia M. Bowman. 2021. "Teaching through Community-Based Research: Undergraduate and Graduate Collaboration on the 2016 Little Rock Congregations Study." *Journal of Political Science Education* 17 (2): 234–252. Available at https://doi.org/10.1080/15512169.2019.1629299.

Glazier, Rebecca A., Gerald Driskill, and Dominika Hanson. 2022. "Race and Faith: The Role of Congregations in Racial Justice." APSA preprint. Available at https://doi.org/10.33774/apsa-2022-2cq20.

Glazier, Rebecca A., Gerald Driskill, and Kirk Leach. 2020. "Connecting with Community and Facilitating Learning through the Little Rock Congregations Study." *Metropolitan Universities* 31 (3): 22–43. Available at https://doi.org/10.18060/23990.

Glazier, Rebecca A., and Emilie Street. 2020. "When Spiritual and Material Meet: Explaining Congregational Engagement in the Local Community." *Interdisciplinary Journal of Research on Religion* 16 (6): 2–35.

Glazier, Rebecca A., and Morgan Paige Topping. 2021. "Using Social Media to Advance Community-Based Research." *PS: Political Science and Politics* 54 (2): 254–258. Available at https://doi.org/10.1017/S1049096520001705.

Goertz, Gary. 2016. "Multimethod Research." *Security Studies* 25 (1): 3–24. Available at https://doi.org/10.1080/09636412.2016.1134016.

Goldberg-Freeman, Clara, Nancy Kass, Andrea Gielen, Patricia Tracey, Barbara Bates-Hopkins, and Mark Farfel. 2010. "Faculty Beliefs, Perceptions, and Level of Community Involvement in Their Research: A Survey at One Urban Academic Institution." *Journal of Empirical Research on Human Research Ethics* 5 (4): 65–76.

Goldzwig, Steve, and George Cheney. 1984. "The U. S. Catholic Bishops on Nuclear Arms: Corporate Advocacy, Role Redefinition, and Rhetorical Adaptation." *Central States Speech Journal* 35 (1): 8–23. Available at https://doi.org/10.1080/10510978409368156.

Gonzalez, Michelle. 2012. "Faith Matters: Religion in the 2012 Presidential Election." *Political Theology* 13 (5): 529–535. Available at https://doi.org/10.1558/poth.v13i5.529.

Gorski, Paul C. 2019. "Racial Battle Fatigue and Activist Burnout in Racial Justice Activists of Color at Predominately White Colleges and Universities." *Race Ethnicity and Education* 22 (1): 1–20. Available at https://doi.org/10.1080/13613324.2018.1497966.

Gray, Barbara. 1989. *Collaborating: Finding Common Ground for Multiparty Problems.* San Francisco, CA: Jossey-Bass.

Greenberg, Anna. 2000. "The Church and the Revitalization of Politics and Community." *Political Science Quarterly* 115 (3): 377–394. Available at https://doi.org/10.2307/265 8124.

Greenberg, Michael, Gwendolyn Greenberg, and Lauren Mazza. 2010. "Food Pantries, Poverty, and Social Justice." *American Journal of Public Health* 100 (11): 2021–2022.

Greene, Jennifer C., Valerie J. Caracelli, and Wendy F. Graham. 1989. "Toward a Conceptual Framework for Mixed-Method Evaluation Designs." *Educational Evaluation and Policy Analysis* 11 (3): 255–274. Available at https://doi.org/10.3102/0162373701100 3255.

Guth, James L., John C. Green, Corwin E. Smidt, and Lyman A. Kellstedt. 1997. *The Bully Pulpit: The Politics of Protestant Clergy.* Lawrence: University Press of Kansas.

Hadden, Jeffrey K. 1969. "Some Broader Implications of Ideological Conflict between Clergy and Laity." *Social Science Quarterly* 49 (4): 923–925.

———. 1970. "Clergy Involvement in Civil Rights." *The Annals of the American Academy of Political and Social Science* 387 (1): 118–127. Available at https://doi.org/10.1177/000 271627038700114.

Halvorsen, Kathleen E. 2003. "Assessing the Effects of Public Participation." *Public Administration Review* 63 (5): 535–543. Available at https://doi.org/https://doi.org/10.11 11/1540-6210.00317.

Hammond, Cathie. 2005. "The Wider Benefits of Adult Learning: An Illustration of the Advantages of Multi-method Research." *International Journal of Social Research Methodology* 8 (3): 239–255. Available at https://doi.org/10.1080/13645570500155037.

Hampton, Anthony. 2022. "Saint Andrews and Western Hills 'Together.'" CityChurch Network. September 13, 2022. Available at https://citychurchar.org/saint-andrews-and -western-hills-together/.

Harris, Adam. 2019. "An Attempt to Resegregate Little Rock, of All Places." *The Atlantic,* October 22, 2019.

Harris, Christopher Eugene. 2020. "The Impact of Sunday School Participation on Spiritual Formation in African American Baptist Churches in North Carolina." Ed.D. diss., Liberty University (28264905 Ed.D.).

Harris, Fredrick C. 1994. "Something Within: Religion as a Mobilizer of African-American Political Activism." *Journal of Politics* 56 (1): 42–68.

———. 1999. *Something Within: Religion in African-American Political Activism.* Oxford: Oxford University Press.

Harris, Margaret. 1998. *Organizing God's Work: Challenges for Churches and Synagogues.* London: Palgrave Macmillan.

Harris, Richard A. 2016. "Farewell to the Urban Growth Machine: Community Development Regimes in Smaller, Distressed Cities." In *Urban Citizenship and American Democracy: The Historical and Institutional Roots of Local Politics and Policy,* edited by A. Bridges and M. Fortner, 125–159. Albany: State University of New York Press.

Hartford Institute for Religion Research. 2021. "Congregational Response to the Pandemic: Extraordinary Social Outreach in a Time of Crisis." In *Exploring the Pandemic Impact on Congregations.* Hartford, CT: Hartford International University for Religion and Peace. Available at https://www.covidreligionresearch.org/wp-content/up

loads/2021/12/Congregational-Response-to-the-Pandemic_Extraordinary-Social-Out reach-in-a-Time-of-Crisis_Dec-2021.pdf.

Harvard Kennedy School Institute of Politics. 2022. *Harvard Youth Poll: Top Findings and Takeaways.* Cambridge, MA: Harvard Kennedy School. Accessed January 23, 2023. Available at https://iop.harvard.edu/youth-poll/44th-edition-fall-2022.

Harvey, Jennifer. 2020. *Dear White Christians: For Those Still Longing for Racial Recon-ciliation.* Grand Rapids, MI: Wm. B. Eerdmans Publishing.

Herring, Cedric. 2009. "Does Diversity Pay?: Race, Gender, and the Business Case for Diversity." *American Sociological Review* 74 (2): 208–224.

Hollar, Brian. 2020. "Will COVID-19 Cause a Religious Recession?" *Religion and Diplomacy* (blog). Transatlantic Policy Network on Religion and Diplomacy. April 8, 2020. Available at http://religionanddiplomacy.org/2020/04/08/will-covid-19-cause-a-reli gious-recession/.

Hollenbach, David. 2020. "Welcoming Refugees and Migrants: Catholic Narratives and the Challenge of Inclusion." *Annals of the American Academy of Political and Social Science* 690 (1): 153–167. Available at https://doi.org/10.1177/0002716220936608.

Holt-Lunstad, Julianne, Timothy B. Smith, Mark Baker, Tyler Harris, and David Stephen-son. 2015. "Loneliness and Social Isolation as Risk Factors for Mortality: A Meta-Ana-lytic Review." *Perspectives on Psychological Science* 10 (2): 227–237. Available at https://doi.org/10.1177/1745691614568352.

Hotze, Timothy. 2011. "Identifying the Challenges in Community-Based Participatory Research Collaboration." *AMA Journal of Ethics* 13 (2): 105–108.

Hougland, James G., Jr., and James A. Christenson. 1983. "Religion and Politics: The Rela-tionship of Religious Participation to Political Efficacy and Involvement." *Sociology and Social Research* 67 (4): 405–420.

Hsu, Becky, Conrad Hackett, and Leslie Hinkson. 2014. "The Importance of Race and Religion in Social Service Providers." *Social Science Quarterly* 95 (2): 393–410. Avail-able at https://doi.org/10.1111/ssqu.12050.

Huang, Francis L. 2016. "Alternatives to Multilevel Modeling for the Analysis of Clus-tered Data." *Journal of Experimental Education* 84 (1): 175–196. Available at https://doi.org/10.1080/00220973.2014.952397.

Huckfeldt, R. Robert, and John Sprague. 1995. *Citizens, Politics and Social Communica-tion: Information and Influence in an Election Campaign.* New York: Cambridge Uni-versity Press.

Huq, Aziz Z. 2022. "The Supreme Court and the Dynamics of Democratic Backsliding." *Annals of the American Academy of Political and Social Science* 699 (1): 50–65. Avail-able at https://doi.org/10.1177/00027162211061124.

Hussey, Ian. 2020. "Investigating High Levels of Small Group Participation in Churches: Case Study Research from Australia." *Practical Theology* 13 (4): 372–384. Available at https://doi.org/10.1080/1756073X.2019.1636478.

Iannaccone, Laurence R. 1988. "A Formal Model of Church and Sect." *American Journal of Sociology* 94:S241–S268.

Idler, Ellen L. 2014. *Religion as a Social Determinant of Public Health.* Oxford, United King-dom: Oxford University Press.

Inglehart, Ronald F. 2021. *Religion's Sudden Decline: What's Causing It, and What Comes Next?* Oxford, United Kingdom: Oxford University Press.

Inzlicht, Michael, Alexa M. Tullett, and Marie Good. 2011. "The Need to Believe: A Neu-roscience Account of Religion as a Motivated Process." *Religion, Brain and Behavior* 1 (3): 192–212. Available at https://doi.org/10.1080/2153599X.2011.647849.

Iqbal, Muhammad, Kerry S. O'Brien, and Ana-Maria Bliuc. 2022. "The Relationship between Existential Anxiety, Political Efficacy, Extrinsic Religiosity and Support for Violent Extremism in Indonesia." *Studies in Conflict and Terrorism*. Published online February 20, 2022. Available at https://doi.org/10.1080/1057610X.2022.203 4221.

Israel, Barbara A., Amy J. Schulz, Edith A. Parker, and Adam B. Becker. 1998. "Review of Community-Based Research: Assessing Partnership Approaches to Improve Public Health." *Annual Review of Public Health* 19 (1): 173–202.

Jamal, Amaney. 2005. "The Political Participation and Engagement of Muslim Americans: Mosque Involvement and Group Consciousness." *American Politics Research* 33 (4): 521–544. Available at https://doi.org/10.1177/1532673x04271385.

Janzen, Rich, Alethea Stobbe, Mark Chapman, and James Watson. 2016. "Canadian Christian Churches as Partners in Immigrant Settlement and Integration." *Journal of Immigrant and Refugee Studies* 14 (4): 390–410. Available at https://doi.org/10.1080/15562 948.2015.1123792.

Jaradat, Mya. 2020. "Gen Z's Looking for Religion. You'd Be Surprised Where They Find It." *Deseret News*, September 13, 2020. Available at https://www.deseret.com/indepth /2020/9/13/21428404/gen-z-religion-spirituality-social-justice-black-lives-matter-par ents-family-pandemic.

Jeynes, William H. 2015. "A Meta-Analysis on the Factors That Best Reduce the Achievement Gap." *Education and Urban Society* 47 (5): 523–554. Available at https://doi.org /10.1177/0013124514529155.

Johnson, Ben F. 2019. *Arkansas in Modern America since 1930*. Fayetteville: University of Arkansas Press.

Johnson, Kathryn A., Adam B. Cohen, and Morris A. Okun. 2013. "Intrinsic Religiosity and Volunteering during Emerging Adulthood: A Comparison of Mormons with Catholics and Non-Catholic Christians." *Journal for the Scientific Study of Religion* 52 (4): 842–851. Available at https://doi.org/10.1111/jssr.12068.

Jones, Jeffrey M. 2021. "U.S. Church Membership Falls below Majority for First Time." Gallup. March 29, 2021. Available at https://news.gallup.com/poll/341963/church-mem bership-falls-below-majority-first-time.aspx.

Jones-Correa, Michael A., and David L. Leal. 2001. "Political Participation: Does Religion Matter?" *Political Research Quarterly* 54 (4): 751–770. Available at https://doi.org /10.1177/106591290105400404.

Kaur Luthra, Sangeeta. 2021. "Remembering Guru Nanak: Articulations of Faith and Ethics by Sikh Activists in Post 9/11 America." *Religions* 12 (2): 113.

Kennedy, Caitlin, Amanda Vogel, Clara Goldberg-Freeman, Nancy Kass, and Mark Farfel. 2009. "Faculty Perspectives on Community-Based Research: 'I See This Still as a Journey.'" *Journal of Empirical Research on Human Research Ethics* 4 (2): 3–16.

Kennedy, Courtney, and Hannah Hartig. 2019. "Response Rates in Telephone Surveys Have Resumed Their Decline." Pew Research Center. February 27, 2019. Available at https://www.pewresearch.org/fact-tank/2019/02/27/response-rates-in-telephone-sur veys-have-resumed-their-decline/.

Kenworthy, Lane. 1997. "Civic Engagement, Social Capital, and Economic Cooperation." *American Behavioral Scientist* 40 (5): 645–656.

Kerley, Kent R., John P. Bartkowski, Todd L. Matthews, and Tracy L. Emond. 2010. "From the Sanctuary to the Slammer: Exploring the Narratives of Evangelical Prison Ministry Workers." *Sociological Spectrum* 30 (5): 504–525. Available at https://doi.org/10.1080 /02732173.2010.495938.

Kessler, Ronald C., Matthias Angermeyer, James C. Anthony, Ron De Graaf, Koen De-myttenaere, Isabelle Gasquet, Giovanni De Girolamo, Semyon Gluzman, Oye Gure-je, and Josep Maria Haro. 2007. "Lifetime Prevalence and Age-of-Onset Distributions of Mental Disorders in the World Health Organization's World Mental Health Survey Initiative." *World Psychiatry* 6 (3): 168–176.

Kohut, Andrew, John C. Green, Scott Keeter, and Robert C. Toth. 2000. *The Diminishing Divide: Religion's Changing Role in American Politics.* Washington, DC: Brookings Institution Press.

Konow, James, and Joseph Earley. 2008. "The Hedonistic Paradox: Is *Homo economicus* Happier?" *Journal of Public Economics* 92 (1): 1–33. Available at https://doi.org/10.1016/j.jpubeco.2007.04.006.

Krasner, Jonathan. 2013. "The Place of Tikkun Olam in American Jewish Life." *Jewish Political Studies Review* 25 (3/4): 59–98.

Krosnick, Jon A. 1989. "Attitude Importance and Attitude Accessibility." *Personality and Social Psychology Bulletin* 15 (3): 297–308.

Krosnick, Jon A., David S. Boninger, Yao C. Chuang, Matthew K. Berent, and Catherine G. Carnot. 1993. "Attitude Strength: One Construct or Many Related Constructs?" *Journal of Personality and Social Psychology* 65 (6): 1132–1151.

La Due Lake, Ronald, and Robert Huckfeldt. 1998. "Social Capital, Social Networks, and Political Participation." *Political Psychology* 19 (3): 567–584.

Leach, Kirk A. 2016. "Repertoires of Collaboration: The Impact of Local Institutional Ar-rangements on Cross Sector Community Partnerships." Ph.D. diss., The State University of New Jersey.

Leege, David C. 1985. *The Findings of the Notre Dame Study of Catholic Parish Life.* Mah-wah, NJ: New Catholic World.

Leege, David C., and Lyman A. Kellstedt, eds. 1993. *Rediscovering the Religious Factor in American Politics.* Armonk, NY: M. E. Sharpe.

Lenora, Josie. 2023. "School Choice Detractors, Advocates Come to Head over Arkansas Education Bill." KUAR: Public Radio from Little Rock. February 27, 2023. Available at https://www.ualrpublicradio.org/local-regional-news/2023-02-27/school-choice-detractors-advocates-come-to-head-over-arkansas-education-bill.

Levin, Jeff. 2014. "Faith-Based Partnerships for Population Health: Challenges, Initia-tives, and Prospects." *Public Health Reports* 129 (2): 127–131.

Lewis, Charles, and Harold Trulear. 2008. "Rethinking the Role of African American Churches as Social Service Providers." *Black Theology* 6 (3): 343–365. Available at https://doi.org/10.1558/blth2008v6i3.343.

Lewis, Valerie A., Carol Ann MacGregor, and Robert D. Putnam. 2013. "Religion, Net-works, and Neighborliness: The Impact of Religious Social Networks on Civic Engage-ment." *Social Science Research* 42 (2): 331–346.

Ley, David. 2008. "The Immigrant Church as an Urban Service Hub." *Urban Studies* 45 (10): 2057–2074.

Li, Shanshan, Olivia I. Okereke, Shun-Chiao Chang, Ichiro Kawachi, and Tyler J. Vander-Weele. 2016. "Religious Service Attendance and Lower Depression among Women—A Prospective Cohort Study." *Annals of Behavioral Medicine* 50 (6): 876–884.

Liang, Belle, and Sharon Galgay Ketcham. 2017. "Emerging Adults' Perceptions of Their Faith-Related Purpose." *Psychology of Religion and Spirituality* 9 (Suppl. 1): S22–S31. Available at https://doi.org/10.1037/rel0000116.

Lieberman, Gretchen Hughes. 2004. "Caring For Creation: Investigating Faith-Based En-vironmentalism In Four Congregations." Master's thesis, University of Oregon.

Lim, Chaeyoon, and Robert D. Putnam. 2010. "Religion, Social Networks, and Life Satisfaction." *American Sociological Review* 75 (6): 914–933.

Lincoln, C. Eric, and Lawrence H. Mamiya. 1990. *The Black Church in the African American Experience*. Durham, NC: Duke University Press.

Little Rock Police Department. 2023. *Preliminary Yearly Crime Stats, 2022*. Little Rock, AR: Little Rock Police Department.

Liu, Baodong, Sharon D. Wright Austin, and Byron D'Andrá Orey. 2009. "Church Attendance, Social Capital, and Black Voting Participation." *Social Science Quarterly* 90 (3): 576–592. Available at https://doi.org/10.1111/j.1540-6237.2009.00632.x.

Livezey, Lowell W. 2000. *Public Religion and Urban Transformation: Faith in the City*. New York: New York University Press.

Losen, Daniel J., and Russell J. Skiba. 2010. *Suspended Education: Urban Middle Schools in Crisis*. UCLA: The Civil Rights Project / Proyecto Derechos Civiles.

Love, Harold M., Jr. 2017. "African-American Clergy Engagement in Politics and Public Policy: Liberation Theology as a Civic Engagement Motivator." Ph.D. diss., Tennessee State University Graduate and Professional Studies.

Loveland, Matthew, Keely Jones Stater, and Jerry Z. Park. 2008. "Religion and the Logic of the Civic Sphere: Religious Tradition, Religious Practice, and Voluntary Association." *Interdisciplinary Journal of Research on Religion* 4:1–26.

Lucero, Julie E., Blake Boursaw, Milton "Mickey" Eder, Ella Greene-Moton, Nina Wallerstein, and John G. Oetzel. 2020. "Engage for Equity: The Role of Trust and Synergy in Community-Based Participatory Research." *Health Education and Behavior* 47 (3): 372–379. Available at https://doi.org/10.1177/1090198120918838.

Lupia, Arthur, and Mathew D. McCubbins. 1998. *The Democratic Dilemma: Can Citizens Learn What They Need to Know?* Cambridge: Cambridge University Press.

Lupton, Robert D., and Patrick Girard Lawlor. 2011. *Toxic Charity: How the Church Hurts Those They Help and How to Reverse It*. New York: HarperCollins.

Macaluso, Theodore F., and John Wanat. 1979. "Voting Turnout and Religiosity." *Polity* 12 (1): 158–169. Available at https://doi.org/10.2307/3234388.

Mangum, Maruice. 2008. "Examining the Association between Church and the Party Identification of Black Americans." *Politics and Religion* 1 (2): 200–215.

Marcus, Marianne, Thomas Walker, J. Michael Swint, Brenda Page Smith, Cleon Brown, Nancy Busen, Thelissa Edwards, et al. 2004. "Community-based Participatory Research to Prevent Substance Abuse and HIV/AIDS in African-American Adolescents." *Journal of Interprofessional Care* 18 (4): 347–359. Available at https://doi.org/10.1080/1356 1820400011776.

Mark, Melvin M., and R. Shotland. 1987. *Multiple Methods in Program Evaluation*. San Francisco: Jossey-Bass.

Marsden, Lee. 2012. "Religion and Conflict Resolution: An Introduction." In *The Ashgate Research Companion to Religion and Conflict Resolution*, edited by Lee Marsden, 1–14. Burlington, VT: Ashgate.

McAdams, Kimberly K., Richard E. Lucas, and M. Brent Donnellan. 2012. "The Role of Domain Satisfaction in Explaining the Paradoxical Association between Life Satisfaction and Age." *Social Indicators Research* 109 (2): 295–303. Available at https://doi .org/10.1007/s11205-011-9903-9.

McClendon, Gwyneth, and Rachel Beatty Riedl. 2015. "Religion as a Stimulant of Political Participation: Experimental Evidence from Nairobi, Kenya." *Journal of Politics* 77 (4): 1045–1057. Available at https://doi.org/10.1086/682717.

McClure, Jennifer M. 2014. "Religious Tradition and Involvement in Congregational Activities That Focus on the Community." *Interdisciplinary Journal of Research on Religion* 10:1–25.

———. 2015. "The Cost of Being Lost in the Crowd: How Congregational Size and Social Networks Shape Attenders' Involvement in Community Organizations." *Review of Religious Research* 57 (2): 269–286. Available at https://doi.org/10.1007/s13644-014 -0201-2.

———. 2017. "'Go and Do Likewise': Investigating Whether Involvement in Congregationally Sponsored Community Service Activities Predicts Prosocial Behavior." *Review of Religious Research* 59 (3): 341–366. Available at https://doi.org/10.1007/s13644 -017-0290-9.

McGuire, Michael. 2006. "Collaborative Public Management: Assessing What We Know and How We Know It." *Public Administration Review* 66 (s1): 33–43.

McKinney, Stephen J., Robert J. Hill, and Honor Hania. 2015. "Welcoming the Stranger: New Testament and Catholic Social Teaching Perspectives on Migrants and Refugees." *Pastoral Review* 11 (6): 50–55.

McRoberts, Omar M. 2003. "Worldly or Otherworldly?" In *Handbook of the Sociology of Religion*, edited by Michele Dillon, 412–422. Cambridge: Cambridge University Press.

———. 2005. *Streets of Glory: Church and Community in a Black Urban Neighborhood.* Chicago: University of Chicago Press.

Mekouar, Dora. 2022. "Are Americans Purposely Moving Next to People Who Share Their Politics?" *Voice of America News*, May 18, 2022. Available at https://www.voanews .com/a/are-americans-purposely-moving-next-to-people-who-share-their-politics -/6577320.html.

Mendez, Linda M. Raffaele, and Howard M. Knoff. 2003. "Who Gets Suspended from School and Why: A Demographic Analysis of Schools and Disciplinary Infractions in a Large School District." *Education and Treatment of Children* 26 (1): 30–51.

Mettler, Suzanne, and Trevor Brown. 2022. "The Growing Rural-Urban Political Divide and Democratic Vulnerability." *Annals of the American Academy of Political and Social Science* 699 (1): 130–142.

Mettler, Suzanne, and Robert C. Lieberman. 2020. "The Fragile Republic: American Democracy Has Never Faced So Many Threats All at Once." *Foreign Affairs* 99:182–195.

Meyer, Holly. 2019. "What New LifeWay Research Survey Says about Why Young Adults Are Dropping Out of Church." *The Tennessean*, January 15, 2019. Available at https:// www.tennessean.com/story/news/religion/2019/01/15/lifeway-research-survey-says -young-adults-dropping-out-church/2550997002/.

Michels, Ank, and Laurens De Graaf. 2010. "Examining Citizen Participation: Local Participatory Policy Making and Democracy." *Local Government Studies* 36 (4): 477–491. Available at https://doi.org/10.1080/03003930.2010.494101.

Miller, Lindsey. 2019. "A Faith Leader Weighs In on State's Plan for LRSD: 'Neither Fair, Just nor Equitable.'" *Arkansas Times*, October 9, 2019. Available at https://arktimes .com/arkansas-blog/2019/10/09/a-faith-leader-weighs-in-on-states-plan-for-lrsd-nei ther-fair-just-nor-equitable.

Min, Pyong Gap. 1992. "The Structure and Social Functions of Korean Immigrant Churches in the United States." *International Migration Review* 26 (4): 1370–1394. Available at https://doi.org/10.1177/019791839202600413.

Moon, Penelope Adams. 2003. "'Peace on Earth—Peace in Vietnam': The Catholic Peace Fellowship and Antiwar Witness, 1964–1976." *Journal of Social History* 36 (4): 1033–1057.

Mulder, Mark T. 2015. *Shades of White Flight: Evangelical Congregations and Urban Departure.* New Brunswick, NJ: Rutgers University Press.

Mulder, Mark T., and Amy Jonason. 2017. "White Evangelical Congregations in Cities and Suburbs: Social Engagement, Geography, Diffusion, and Disembeddedness." *City and Society* 29 (1): 104–126.

Mulroy, Elizabeth A., and Sharon Shay. 1997. "Nonprofit Organizations and Innovation: A Model of Neighborhood-Based Collaboration to Prevent Child Maltreatment." *Social Work* 42 (5): 515–524. Available at https://doi.org/10.1093/sw/42.5.515.

Munro, Geoffrey D., Peter H. Ditto, Lisa K. Lockhart, Angela Fagerlin, Mitchell Gready, and Elizabeth Peterson. 2002. "Biased Assimilation of Sociopolitical Arguments: Evaluating the 1996 US Presidential Debate." *Basic and Applied Social Psychology* 24 (1): 15–26.

Musca, Serban C., Rodolphe Kamiejski, Armelle Nugier, Alain Méot, Abdelatif Er-Rafiy, and Markus Brauer. 2011. "Data with Hierarchical Structure: Impact of Intraclass Correlation and Sample Size on Type-I Error." *Frontiers in Psychology* 2:74 (April). Available at https://doi.org/10.3389/fpsyg.2011.00074.

Nalbandian, John. 1999. "Facilitating Community, Enabling Democracy: New Roles for Local Government Managers." *Public Administration Review* 59 (3): 187–197. Available at https://doi.org/10.2307/3109948.

Narayan, Deepa, and Michael F. Cassidy. 2001. "A Dimensional Approach to Measuring Social Capital: Development and Validation of a Social Capital Inventory." *Current Sociology* 49 (2): 59–102.

National Institutes of Health. 2023. "Drug Overdose Death Rates." National Institute on Drug Abuse. Last modified February 9, 2023. Available at https://nida.nih.gov/research-topics/trends-statistics/overdose-death-rates.

Neiheisel, Jacob R., Paul A. Djupe, and Anand E. Sokhey. 2009. "Veni, Vidi, Disseri: Churches and the Promise of Democratic Deliberation." *American Politics Research* 37 (4): 614–643.

Netting, F. Ellen, Mary Katherine O'Connor, M. Lori Thomas, and Gaynor Yancey. 2005. "Mixing and Phasing of Roles among Volunteers, Staff, and Participants in Faith-Based Programs." *Nonprofit and Voluntary Sector Quarterly* 34 (2): 179–205. Available at https://doi.org/10.1177/0899764005275204.

Newmark, Adam J., and Anthony J. Nownes. 2019. "Lobbying Conflict, Competition, and Working in Coalitions." *Social Science Quarterly* 100 (4): 1284–1296. Available at https://doi.org/10.1111/ssqu.12644.

Norris, Pippa. 2013. "Does Praying Together Mean Staying Together? Religion and Civic Engagement in Europe and the United States." In *Religion and Civil Society in Europe*, edited by Joep de Hart, Paul Dekker, and Loek Halman, 285–305. Dordrecht: Springer Netherlands.

Nortey, Justin. 2022. "More Houses of Worship Are Returning to Normal Operations, but In-Person Attendance Is Unchanged since Fall." Pew Research Center. March 22, 2022. Available at https://www.pewresearch.org/fact-tank/2022/03/22/more-houses-of-worship-are-returning-to-normal-operations-but-in-person-attendance-is-unchanged-since-fall.

Nortey, Justin, and Michael Lipka. 2021. "Most Americans Who Go to Religious Services Say They Would Trust Their Clergy's Advice on COVID-19 Vaccines." Pew Research Center. October 15, 2021. Available at https://www.pewresearch.org/religion/2021/10/15/most-americans-who-go-to-religious-services-say-they-would-trust-their-clergys

-advice-on-covid-19-vaccines/#most-americans-say-churches-and-other-religious-organizations-should-keep-out-of-politics.

Olson, Laura R. 2009. "Clergy and American Politics." In *The Oxford Handbook of Religion and American Politics*, edited by Corwin E. Smidt, Lyman A. Kellstedt, and James L. Guth, 371–393. Oxford, United Kingdom: Oxford Handbooks Online.

Onyx, Jenny, and Jeni Warburton. 2003. "Volunteering and Health among Older People: A Review." *Australasian Journal on Ageing* 22 (2): 65–69. Available at https://doi.org/10.1111/j.1741-6612.2003.tb00468.x.

Outka, Gene H. 1972. *Agape: An Ethical Analysis*. New Haven, CT: Yale University Press.

Owens, Jayanti, and Sara S. McLanahan. 2019. "Unpacking the Drivers of Racial Disparities in School Suspension and Expulsion." *Social Forces* 98 (4): 1548–1577. Available at https://doi.org/10.1093/sf/soz095.

Owens, Michael Leo. 2008. *God and Government in the Ghetto: The Politics of Church-State Collaboration in Black America*. Chicago: University of Chicago Press.

Packard, Josh. 2016. "The Emerging Church: Intentionally Marginalised Community." In *Handbook of Global Contemporary Christianity: Movements, Institutions, and Allegiance*, edited by Stephen J. Hunt, 317–335. Leiden, Netherlands: Brill.

Parent, Michael, Christine A. Vandebeek, and Andrew C. Gemino. 2005. "Building Citizen Trust through e-Government." *Government Information Quarterly* 22 (4): 720–736.

Park, Crystal L. 2005. "Religion as a Meaning-Making Framework in Coping with Life Stress." *Journal of Social Issues* 61:707–729. Available at https://doi.org/10.1111/j.1540-4560.2005.00428.x.

Park, Crystal L., Donald Edmondson, and Amy Hale-Smith. 2013. "Why Religion? Meaning as Motivation." In *APA Handbook of Psychology, Religion, and Spirituality: Context, Theory, and Research*, 157–171. Washington, DC: American Psychological Association.

Patterson, Sarah E., Sarah E. Madsen, and Nathan F. Alleman. 2022. "Exploring Ideologically Diverse Friend Groups among College Students at a Christian University." *Christian Higher Education*. November 10, 2022. Available at https://doi.org/10.1080/15363759.2022.2127430.

Pattillo-McCoy, Mary. 1998. "Church Culture as a Strategy of Action in the Black Community." *American Sociological Review* 63 (6): 767–784. Available at https://doi.org/10.2307/2657500.

Pearce, Lisa D., and Claire Chipman Gilliland. 2020. *Religion in America*. Berkeley: University of California Press.

Pew Forum on Religion & Public Life. 2009. *Faith in Flux: Changes in Religious Affiliation in the U.S.* Washington, DC: Pew Research Center.

Pew Research Center. 2019a. *In U.S., Decline of Christianity Continues at Rapid Pace: An Update on America's Changing Religious Landscape*. Washington, DC: Pew Research Center.

———. 2019b. *Religion's Relationship to Happiness, Civic Engagement and Health around the World: In the U.S. and Other Countries, Participation in a Congregation Is a Key Factor*. Washington, DC: Pew Research Center.

———. 2020. *In Changing U.S. Electorate, Race and Education Remain Stark Dividing Lines*. Washington, DC: Pew Research Center.

———. 2022a. *As Partisan Hostility Grows, Signs of Frustration with the Two-Party System*. Washington, DC: Pew Research Center.

———. 2022b. *Public Trust in Government 1958–2022*. Washington, DC: Pew Research Center.

Polson, Edward C. 2016. "Putting Civic Participation in Context: Examining the Effects of Congregational Structure and Culture." *Review of Religious Research* 58 (1): 75–100. Available at https://doi.org/10.1007/s13644-015-0223-4.

Pope, Liston. 1942. *Millhands and Preachers: A Study of Gastonia*. New Haven, CT: Yale University Press.

Portes, Alejandro. 1998. "Social Capital: Its Origins and Applications in Modern Sociology." *Annual Review of Sociology* 24 (1): 1–24.

Primo, David M., Matthew L. Jacobsmeier, and Jeffrey Milyo. 2007. "Estimating the Impact of State Policies and Institutions with Mixed-Level Data." *State Politics and Policy Quarterly* 7 (4): 446–459.

Prothero, Arianna. 2017. "'Precious Little Evidence' That Vouchers Improve Achievement, Recent Research Finds." *Education Week*, November 17, 2017. Available at https://www.edweek.org/leadership/precious-little-evidence-that-vouchers-improve-achievement-recent-research-finds/2017/11.

Putnam, Robert D. 1993. "The Prosperous Community: Social Capital and Public Life." In *Cross Currents: Cultures, Communities, Technologies*, edited by Kris Blair, Robin M. Murphy, and Jen Almjeld, 35–42. Boston, MA: Cengage Learning.

———. 2000. *Bowling Alone: The Collapse and Revival of American Community*. New York: Simon & Schuster.

Putnam, Robert D., and David E. Campbell. 2012. *American Grace: How Religion Divides and Unites Us*. New York: Simon & Schuster.

Putnam, Robert D., Robert Leonardi, and Raffaella Y. Nanetti. 1994. *Making Democracy Work: Civic Traditions in Modern Italy*. Princeton, NJ: Princeton University Press.

Quinley, Harold E. 1974. *The Prophetic Clergy: Social Activism among Protestant Ministers*. New York: Wiley.

Reeves, Samuel Broomfield. 2004. *Congregation-to-Congregation Relationship: A Case Study of the Partnership between a Liberian Church and a North American Church*. Dallas: University Press of America.

Religion News Service. 2021. "One Year after George Floyd's Murder, Faith Leaders Continue the Call for Racial Reckoning." Religion News Service. May 25, 2021. Available at https://religionnews.com/2021/05/25/one-year-after-george-floyds-murder-faith-leaders-continue-the-call-for-racial-reckoning/.

———. 2022. "Declining Church Giving Facts and Solution: Empty Tomb's Latest The State of Church Giving Edition." Religion News Service, August 30, 2022. Available at https://religionnews.com/2022/08/30/declining-church-giving-facts-solution-empty-tombs-latest-the-state-of-church-giving-edition/.

Rich, Michael J., Micheal W. Giles, and Emily Stern. 2001. "Collaborating to Reduce Poverty: Views from City Halls and Community-based Organizations." *Urban Affairs Review* 37 (2): 184–204.

Rickenbacker, Harold, Fred Brown, and Melissa Bilec. 2019. "Creating Environmental Consciousness in Underserved Communities: Implementation and Outcomes of Community-Based Environmental Justice and Air Pollution Research." *Sustainable Cities and Society* 47:101473. Available at https://doi.org/10.1016/j.scs.2019.101473.

Riffin, Catherine, Cara Kenien, Angela Ghesquiere, Ashley Dorime, Carolina Villanueva, Daniel Gardner, Jean Callahan, Elizabeth Capezuti, and M Carrington Reid. 2016. "Community-Based Participatory Research: Understanding a Promising Approach to Addressing Knowledge Gaps in Palliative Care." *Annals of Palliative Medicine* 5 (3): 218–224.

Roher, Acadia. 2019. "Segregated Neighborhoods, Segregated Schools." University of Arkansas at Little Rock. September 2, 2019. Available at https://ualrexhibits.org/map pingblog/2019/09/02/segregated-neighborhoods-segregated-schools/.

Rosenstone, Steven, and John M. Hansen. 1993. *Mobilization, Participation and Democracy in America*. New York: MacMillan.

Rothberg, Donald. 1998. "Responding to the Cries of the World: Socially Engaged Buddhism in North America." In *The Faces of Buddhism in America*, edited by Charles S. Prebish and Kenneth T. Tanaka, 266–286. Berkeley: University of California Press.

Russett, Bruce M. 2015. "Ethical Dilemmas of Nuclear Deterrence." In *Bruce M. Russett: Pioneer in the Scientific and Normative Study of War, Peace, and Policy*, edited by H. Starr, 153–168. New York: Springer.

Sapp, Christy Lohr. 2011. "Obama's Interfaith Service Challenge: A Call for a New Theology of Service in American Higher Education." *Dialog* 50 (3): 280–288. Available at https://doi.org/10.1111/j.1540-6385.2011.00623.x.

Sarkissian, Ani. 2012. "Religious Regulation and the Muslim Democracy Gap." *Politics and Religion* 5 (3): 501–527. Available at https://doi.org/10.1017/S1755048312000284.

Satyavrata, Ivan. 2016. "Power to the Poor: Towards a Pentecostal Theology of Social Engagement." *Asian Journal of Pentecostal Studies* 19 (1): 45–57.

Sax, Linda. 1997. "The Benefits of Service: Evidence from Undergraduates." *Higher Education*, Summer/Fall 1997, 25–32. Available at https://digitalcommons.unomaha.edu /slcehighered/38.

Scanlon, Leslie. 2022. "PC(USA) Releases 2021 Statistical Report, Showing a Denomination of Small Churches and Aging Membership." *Presbyterian Outlook*, last modified May 19, 2022. Available at https://pres-outlook.org/2022/04/pcusa-releases-2021 -statistical-report-showing-a-denomination-of-small-churches-and-aging-member ship/.

Schwadel, Philip. 2005. "Individual, Congregational, and Denominational Effects on Church Members' Civic Participation." *Journal for the Scientific Study of Religion* 44 (2): 159–171. Available at https://doi.org/10.1111/j.1468-5906.2005.00273.x.

Schwadel, Philip, Jacob E. Cheadle, Sarah E. Malone, and Michael Stout. 2016. "Social Networks and Civic Participation and Efficacy in Two Evangelical Protestant Churches." *Review of Religious Research* 58 (2): 305–317.

Semuels, Alana. 2016. "How Segregation Has Persisted in Little Rock." *The Atlantic*, April 27, 2016.

Sharp, David. 2021. "Millions Skipped Church during Pandemic. Will They Return?" Associated Press, June 29, 2021. Available at https://apnews.com/article/coronavirus -pandemic-pandemics-lifestyle-health-religion-cd5fbac2318cb58e1d5ec4a5d1c00ecc.

Sheppard, Donald Lee. 2018. "The Dividends of Diversity: The Win-Win-Win Model Is Taking Over Business and It Necessitates Diversity." *Strategic HR Review* 17 (3): 126–130. Available at https://doi.org/10.1108/SHR-03-2018-0017.

Shi, Feng, Misha Teplitskiy, Eamon Duede, and James A. Evans. 2019. "The Wisdom of Polarized Crowds." *Nature Human Behaviour* 3 (4): 329–336. Available at https://doi .org/10.1038/s41562-019-0541-6.

Shimron, Yonat. 2021. "Study: More Churches Closing than Opening." Religion News Service, May 26, 2021. Available at https://religionnews.com/2021/05/26/study-more -churches-closing-than-opening/.

Sinha, Jill Witmer, Itay Greenspan, and Femida Handy. 2011. "Volunteering and Civic Participation among Immigrant Members of Ethnic Congregations: Complementary NOT Competitive." *Journal of Civil Society* 7 (1): 23–40. Available at https://doi.org/10.1080/17448689.2011.553409.

Smidt, Corwin E. 2003. "Clergy in American Politics: An Introduction." *Journal for the Scientific Study of Religion* 42 (4): 495–499.

———. 2004. *Pulpit and Politics: Clergy in American Politics at the Advent of the Millennium.* Waco, TX: Baylor University Press.

Smith, Christian, and Hilary Davidson. 2014. *The Paradox of Generosity: Giving We Receive, Grasping We Lose.* Oxford, United Kingdom: Oxford University Press.

Smith, Gregory A., Claire Gecewicz, Anna Schiller, and Haley Nolan. 2019. *Americans Have Positive Views about Religion's Role in Society, but Want It Out of Politics.* Washington, DC: Pew Research Center.

Snijders, Tom A. B., and Roel J. Bosker. 1999. *Multilevel Analysis: An Introduction to Basic and Advanced Multilevel Modeling.* London: Sage.

Snyder, Josh. 2023. "Aid Groups in Arkansas Adapted to Tornado Survivors' Urgent Needs; Now, They Are Preparing for 'Long Haul.'" *Arkansas Democrat Gazette*, April 15, 2023. Available at https://www.arkansasonline.com/news/2023/apr/15/aid-groups-in-arkansas-adapted-to-tornado/.

Social Security Administration. n.d. "Popular Names in 1960." Accessed October 1, 2022. https://www.ssa.gov/cgi-bin/popularnames.cgi.

Speiser, Matthew. 2015. "The US Cities with the Most Religious Venues per Capita Aren't Quite What You'd Expect." *Business Insider*, June 3, 2015.

Steensland, Brian, and Philip Goff, eds. 2013. *The New Evangelical Social Engagement.* Oxford: Oxford University Press.

Strawbridge, William J., Sarah J. Shema, Richard D. Cohen, and George A. Kaplan. 2001. "Religious Attendance Increases Survival by Improving and Maintaining Good Health Behaviors, Mental Health, and Social Relationships." *Annals of Behavioral Medicine* 23 (1): 68–74.

Stroope, Samuel. 2011. "How Culture Shapes Community: Bible Belief, Theological Unity, and a Sense of Belonging in Religious Congregations." *Sociological Quarterly* 52 (4): 568–592. Available at https://doi.org/10.1111/j.1533-8525.2011.01220.x.

Stroope, Samuel, and Joseph O. Baker. 2014. "Structural and Cultural Sources of Community in American Congregations." *Social Science Research* 45:1–17. Available at https://doi.org/10.1016/j.ssresearch.2013.12.010.

Tam Cho, Wendy K., James G. Gimpel, and Iris S. Hui. 2013. "Voter Migration and the Geographic Sorting of the American Electorate." *Annals of the Association of American Geographers* 103 (4): 856–870.

Tanenbaum Center for Interreligious Understanding. n.d. "The Golden Rule." Accessed October 1. Available at https://tanenbaum.org/wp-content/uploads/2021/06/The-Golden-Rule.pdf.

Taylor, Robert Joseph, Dawne M. Mouzon, Ann W. Nguyen, and Linda M. Chatters. 2016. "Reciprocal Family, Friendship and Church Support Networks of African Americans: Findings from the National Survey of American Life." *Race and Social Problems* 8 (4): 326–339. Available at https://doi.org/10.1007/s12552-016-9186-5.

Teufel-Shone, Nicolette I., Anna L. Schwartz, Lisa J. Hardy, Hendrik D. De Heer, Heather J. Williamson, Dorothy J. Dunn, Kellen Polingyumptewa, and Carmenlita Chief. 2019. "Supporting New Community-Based Participatory Research Partnerships." *International Journal of Environmental Research and Public Health* 16 (1): 44.

Tevington, Patricia. 2022. "Covid, Churches and Community Service." Hartford Institute for Religion Research. March 16, 2022. Available at https://www.covidreligion research.org/covid-churches-and-community-service/.

Thomas, Charles B. 1985. "Clergy in Racial Controversy: A Replication of the Campbell and Pettigrew Study." *Review of Religious Research* 26 (4): 379–390. Available at https://doi.org/10.2307/3511051.

Thomas, Scott L., and Ronald H. Heck. 2001. "Analysis of Large-Scale Secondary Data in Higher Education Research: Potential Perils Associated with Complex Sampling Designs." *Research in Higher Education* 42 (5): 517–540.

Thomas, Scott L., Ronald H. Heck, and Karen W. Bauer. 2005. "Weighting and Adjusting for Design Effects in Secondary Data Analyses." *New Directions for Institutional Research* 2005 (127): 51–72.

Thumma, Scott. 2021. *Twenty Years of Congregational Change: The 2020 Faith Communities Today Overview*. Hartford, CT: Hartford Institute for Religion Research.

Tisby, Jemar. 2019. *The Color of Compromise: The Truth about the American Church's Complicity in Racism*. Grand Rapids, MI: Zondervan.

———. 2021. *How to Fight Racism: Courageous Christianity and the Journey toward Racial Justice*. Grand Rapids, MI: Zondervan.

Tripses, Jenny, and Lori Scroggs. 2009. "Spirituality and Respect: Study of a Model School-Church-Community Collaboration." *School Community Journal* 19 (1): 77–98.

Twombly, Eric C. 2002. "Religious Versus Secular Human Service Organizations: Implications for Public Policy." *Social Science Quarterly* 83 (4): 947–961. Available at https://doi.org/10.1111/1540-6237.00125.

Ukanwa, Kalinda, Aziza C. Jones, and Broderick L. Turner Jr. 2022. "School Choice Increases Racial Segregation Even When Parents Do Not Care about Race." *Proceedings of the National Academy of Sciences* 119 (35): e2117979119.

Unruh, Heidi Rolland, and Ronald J. Sider. 2005. *Saving Souls, Serving Society: Understanding the Faith Factor in Church-Based Social Ministry*. New York: Oxford University Press.

U.S. Census Bureau. 2017. *ACS Demographic and Housing Estimates, 2013–2017, American Community Survey 5-Year Estimates*. Washington, DC: United States Census Bureau.

———. 2021. *City and Town Population Totals: 2020–2021*. Washington, DC: United States Census Bureau.

Uslaner, Eric M. 2002. "Religion and Civic Engagement in Canada and the United States." *Journal for the Scientific Study of Religion* 41 (2): 239–254.

VanderWeele, Tyler J., Shanshan Li, Alexander C. Tsai, and Ichiro Kawachi. 2016. "Association between Religious Service Attendance and Lower Suicide Rates among US Women." *JAMA Psychiatry* 73 (8): 845–851.

Verba, Sidney, and Norman H. Nie. 1987. *Participation in America: Political Democracy and Social Equality*. Chicago: University of Chicago Press.

Verba, Sidney, Kay Lehman Schlozman, and Henry E. Brady. 1995. *Voice and Equality: Civic Voluntarism in American Politics*. Vol. 4. Cambridge, MA: Harvard University Press.

Vergani, Matteo, Amelia Johns, Michele Lobo, and Fethi Mansouri. 2017. "Examining Islamic Religiosity and Civic Engagement in Melbourne." *Journal of Sociology* 53 (1): 63–78. Available at https://doi.org/10.1177/1440783315621167.

Voas, David. 2009. "The Rise and Fall of Fuzzy Fidelity in Europe." *European Sociological Review* 25 (2): 155–168.

Voorintholt, Lieke. 2023. "Substitutes or Complements: A Budget-based Analysis of the Relationship Between Donating and Volunteering." *Oxford Economic Papers* 75 (4): 1033–1052.

Vraga, Emily K., and Leticia Bode. 2017. "Leveraging Institutions, Educators, and Networks to Correct Misinformation: A Commentary on Lewandosky, Ecker, and Cook." *Journal of Applied Research in Memory and Cognition* 6 (4): 382–388.

Wald, Kenneth D., and Allison Calhoun-Brown. 2010. *Religion and Politics in the United States*. 6th ed. Lanham, MD: Rowman & Littlefield.

Wald, Kenneth D., Dennis E. Owen, and Samuel S. Hill. 1988. "Churches as Political Communities." *American Political Science Review* 82 (2): 531–548.

Wallsten, Kevin, and Tatishe M. Nteta. 2016. "For You Were Strangers in the Land of Egypt: Clergy, Religiosity, and Public Opinion toward Immigration Reform in the United States." *Politics and Religion* 9 (3): 566–604. Available at https://doi.org/10.1017/S175 5048316000444.

Wang, Wendy. 2022. "The Decline in Church Attendance in COVID America." Institute for Family Studies. January 20, 2022. Available at https://ifstudies.org/blog/the-decline -in-church-attendance-in-covid-america.

Warburg, Margit. 2018. *Citizens of the World: A History and Sociology of the Baha'is from a Globalisation Perspective*. Leiden, Netherlands: Brill.

Warren, Emily J., Melody K. Waring, and Daniel R. Meyer. 2019. "Are US Congregations Patching the Social Safety Net: Trends from 1998 to 2012." *Journal of Sociology and Social Welfare* 46 (3): 39–62.

Wattles, Jeffrey. 1996. *The Golden Rule*. Oxford: Oxford University Press.

Webb Hooper, Monica, Charlene Mitchell, Vanessa J. Marshall, Chesley Cheatham, Kristina Austin, Kimberly Sanders, Smitha Krishnamurthi, and Lena L. Grafton. 2019. "Understanding Multilevel Factors Related to Urban Community Trust in Healthcare and Research." *International Journal of Environmental Research and Public Health* 16 (18): 3280. Available at https://doi.org/10.3390/ijerph16183280.

Welch, Michael R., David Sikkink, and Matthew T. Loveland. 2007. "The Radius of Trust: Religion, Social Embeddedness and Trust in Strangers." *Social Forces* 86 (1): 23–46. Available at https://doi.org/10.1353/sof.2007.0116.

Wielhouwer, Peter W. 2004. "The Impact of Church Activities and Socialization on African-American Religious Commitment." *Social Science Quarterly* 85 (3): 767–792. Available at https://doi.org/10.1111/j.0038-4941.2004.00244.x.

Williams, Christopher J., and Martijn Schoonvelde. 2018. "It Takes Three: How Mass Media Coverage Conditions Public Responsiveness to Policy Outputs in the United States." *Social Science Quarterly* 99 (5): 1627–1636.

Wilson, John. 2000. "Volunteering." *Annual Review of Sociology* 26:215–240.

Winer, Mark L. 2008. "Tikkun Olam: A Jewish Theology of 'Repairing the World.'" *Theology* 111 (864): 433–441.

Wingfield, Mark. 2021. "Houston Pastor Voted off Local School Board by Angry Parents Who Called Him a Black Liberal Racist." Baptist News Global, December 14, 2021. Available at https://baptistnews.com/article/houston-pastor-voted-off-local-school -board-by-angry-parents-who-called-him-a-black-liberal-racist/.

Winters, Mary Francis. 2020. *Black Fatigue: How Racism Erodes the Mind, Body, and Spirit*. Oakland, CA: Berrett-Koehler Publishers.

Wojcieszak, Magdalena, and Benjamin R. Warner. 2020. "Can Interparty Contact Reduce Affective Polarization? A Systematic Test of Different Forms of Intergroup Contact." *Political Communication* 37 (6): 789–811. Available at https://doi.org/10.1080/10 584609.2020.1760406.

Wood, Richard L. 2002. *Faith in Action: Religion, Race, and Democratic Organizing in America*. Chicago: University of Chicago Press.

Wright, Jemall. 2022. "Little Rock School District: A Community Report." August 16, 2022.

Wuthnow, Robert. 1988. *The Restructuring of American Religion: Society and Faith since World War II*. Princeton, NJ: Princeton University Press.

———. 2002. "Religious Involvement and Status-Bridging Social Capital." *Journal for the Scientific Study of Religion* 41 (4): 669–684.

Yukich, Grace. 2017. "Progressive Activism among Buddhists, Hindus, and Muslims in the US." In *Religion and Progressive Activism: New Stories about Faith and Politics*, edited by Ruth Braunstein, Todd Nicholas Fuist, and Rhys H. Williams, 225–245. New York: New York University Press.

Zhang, Hansong, Joshua N. Hook, Jennifer E. Farrell, David K. Mosher, Daryl R. Van Tongeren, and Don E. Davis. 2018. "The Effect of Religious Diversity on Religious Belonging and Meaning: The Role of Intellectual Humility." *Psychology of Religion and Spirituality* 10:72–78. Available at https://doi.org/10.1037/rel0000108.

Ziegler, Brett. 2022. "Education Rankings." *US News & World Report*. Accessed January 9, 2023. Available at https://www.usnews.com/news/best-states/rankings/education.

Index

References to figures and tables are indicated by "f" and "t" following page numbers.

Rebecca A. Glazier is a Professor in the School of Public Affairs at the University of Arkansas at Little Rock. She is the Director of the Little Rock Congregations Study and the author of *Connecting in the Online Classroom: Building Rapport between Teachers and Students.*